Philosophical Perspectives on Democracy in the 21st Century

AMINTAPHIL
The Philosophical Foundations of Law and Justice

For further volumes:
http://www.springer.com/series/7372

Ann E. Cudd • Sally J. Scholz
Editors

Philosophical Perspectives on Democracy in the 21st Century

Springer

Editors
Ann E. Cudd
Department of Philosophy
University of Kansas
Lawrence, KS, USA

Sally J. Scholz
Department of Philosophy
Villanova University
Villanova, PA, USA

ISSN 1873-877X ISSN 2351-9851 (electronic)
ISBN 978-3-319-34518-5 ISBN 978-3-319-02312-0 (eBook)
DOI 10.1007/978-3-319-02312-0
Springer Cham Heidelberg New York Dordrecht London

Softcover reprint of the hardcover 1st edition 2014

Printed on acid-free paper

Springer is part of Springer Science+Business Media (www.springer.com)

Acknowledgement

We would like to acknowledge the support and assistance of several institutions and individuals who made our work on this volume possible, efficient, and enjoyable. Ann thanks the University of Kansas College of Liberal Arts and Sciences for financial support of her research and travel to the 2012 AMINTAPHIL conference. Sally thanks Villanova University Department of Philosophy for research support. Mortimer Sellers and the University of Baltimore School of Law hosted the 2012 conference and we are grateful for their hospitality. Bruce Landesman has been the Executive Director of AMINTAPHIL for many years and we thank him for his dedication to an organization that has treated us so well over the years.

Ashley Acosta-Fox, Ph.D. student at the University of Kansas, assisted us with the copyediting and formatting of the manuscript. We thank her for good sense and attention to detail. Thanks also go to all the participants in the conference. The essays published here reflect your lively conversations and constructive criticism. Finally, we thank the contributors to this volume, who withstood numerous requests for revisions, responded to queries about copyediting and other details, and did so with efficiency and good humor.

Ann would like to dedicate this volume to Richard DeGeorge and Rex Martin, her colleagues in political philosophy at the University of Kansas for over 25 years, who introduced her to the AMINTAPHIL Society, and Sally would like to dedicate this volume to Bill McBride and Joe Betz, who value and encourage philosophical engagement with the real world.

Contents

Chapter 1
Philosophical Perspectives on Democracy in the Twenty-First Century: Introduction

Ann E. Cudd and Sally J. Scholz

Abstract Recent global movements, including the Arab Spring, the Occupy Movement, as well as polarizing events in the US, such as the *Citizens United* ruling, invite a rethinking of the meaning, desirability, and feasibility of democracy in the twenty-first century. Technological changes have increased democratic participation, but have yet to improve democratic deliberation. Ideological differences have engendered incivility and unwillingness to compromise. Philosophical reflection offers opportunities not only to scrutinize the implications of these changes for democracy but also to reevaluate the nature and meaning of the core concepts of political theory. This chapter interprets the contemporary context of democracy in light of recent developments, and offers an overview of the issues considered in the chapters of this book.

Recent global movements invite a rethinking of the meaning, desirability, and feasibility of democracy in the twenty-first century, especially in light of economic or corporate globalization. While the Arab Spring demonstrates the sacrifices individuals are willing to make in the struggle for democracy, the Occupy Movement raises the question of who has a voice and access to power in a democracy. All over the world, we see individuals and collectives exerting renewed democratic political power through social media and transnational protest, but simultaneously the power of multinational corporations in domestic politics challenges the very ideal of democratic equality and who counts as a rights holder. Philosophical discussions

A.E. Cudd (✉)
Department of Philosophy, University of Kansas,
1445 Jayhawk Blvd Rm 3090, 66045 Lawrence, KS, USA
e-mail: acudd@ku.edu

S.J. Scholz
Department of Philosophy, Villanova University, 800 Lancaster Ave,
19085-1478 Villanova, PA, USA
e-mail: sally.scholz@villanova.edu

A.E. Cudd and S.J. Scholz (eds.), *Philosophical Perspectives on Democracy in the 21st Century*, AMINTAPHIL: The Philosophical Foundations of Law and Justice 5,
DOI 10.1007/978-3-319-02312-0_1,

of the rapidly changing landscape in the twenty-first century offer an opportunity not only to scrutinize the implications of these changes for democracy but also to reevaluate the nature and meaning of the core concepts of political theory.

This volume explores the meaning of democracy today, the causes and effects of polarization in U.S. politics, the influence of big money and capitalism on democracy, and the role of information and the media in democratic elections. Authors of essays are established scholars in philosophy, political science, and law, and fall along the full range of the political spectrum from libertarian to welfare state democrat to socialist democrat. The combination of essays allows readers to consider opposing views concerning property rights, economic inequality, free speech rights, and the role of information. Of course, debating opposing viewpoints is a hallmark of the practice of democracy. It might be argued, however, that the debate itself has come to replace the political end or goal. What is the state of a democracy where "compromise" is a bad word and civility no longer governs behavior?

American politics, widely characterized as hyperpolarized between the neoconservatives and the progressive liberals, demonstrates the challenge of ideological differences in political discussions domestically and internationally. A central point of contention in the United States concerns individual freedom versus government responsibility. The U.S. Congress is perhaps the most frequent focal point for this ideological polarization, but a growing chasm divides the electorate as well. Concrete issues like gun control, health care, and welfare benefits get cast in terms of governmental intervention in or impingement on individual liberties, or alternatively as the government's responsibility for the well-being of each citizen. The diversity of views could be a valuable source for insight in a dynamic democracy, but the ideological opponents tend, instead, to see differing viewpoints as obstructions to their own conceptions of justice.

In addition to ideological differences, contemporary democratic politics is often characterized by a loss of civility. Politicians in Congress model this incivility by shouting down their opponents or refusing to listen to supporting arguments. Senator Joe Wilson, a Republican from South Carolina, famously interrupted President Obama's speech to a joint session of Congress by shouting "You lie." Wilson opposed Obama's proposal to health care reform, but his decision to voice his opposition in this manner is one illustration of the erosion of respect that makes democratic deliberation all but impossible.

Of course the practice of democracy has always been more complicated than the theory of democracy discloses. Consider, for instance, the problem of majoritarian results that are intolerable (rightly or wrongly) to at least some citizens. Such an outcome may be partly what is at work when politicians opt for a route of incivility rather than respectful debate. Perhaps the ideological divide is so stark that the prospect of adopting policies supported by one's opponents is simply intolerable. This problem challenges the theory as well as the practice of democracy insofar as it raises the question of whether democracy itself is possible. What do we mean by democracy and how are we to understand the peoples' views when the people disagree so fundamentally? Further, is it possible that embracing democracy could yield results that threaten the legitimacy of the government?

Although democracy is widely recognized as an effective means of ensuring the protection of human rights—and indeed the United Nations identifies democracy as one of its core values—these questions about the theory and practice of democracy do highlight additional concerns for global democracy movements. President George W. Bush famously stated in his second inaugural address that "It is the policy of the United States to seek and support the growth of democratic movements and institutions in every nation and culture, with the ultimate goal of ending tyranny in our world" (Bush Pledges 2005). Bush's commitment to spread democracy was hailed by many as a defense of liberty and a stance against oppression. Others, however, saw an imperialist use of his claim to "spread democracy," especially in the invasion and occupation of Iraq. Serious fundamental differences in the conception and practices of democracy mark these varying interpretations of Bush's speech and actions.

As philosophers, how, then, can we think about problems of ideological differences, incivility, and uncertain motivations behind claims of democracy while we seek conceptual clarification of the nature and practice of contemporary democracy? Do these issues of polarization spell the end of democracy or are there creative or constructive avenues past this apparent impasse?

Ideal democratic polities with more or less homogenous ideological viewpoints and more or less equitable distributions of wealth and resources do not exist. Every major theorist of democracy, however, includes some discussion of equality as a central element to democracy. The nature of equality and the allowable inequality (especially socio-economic inequality) is one of the chief elements that divide democracy theorists. The ideal of equality is central to Jean-Jacques Rousseau's political theory, but also appears in a prominent principle of the liberal democratic theories of John Locke and John Rawls. Of course, Rousseau included relative socio-economic equality in his account, whereas Locke emphasizes political equality. Rawls, it might be argued, tries to walk the fine line between the two so that socio-economic equality never compromises political equality. This debate regarding the proper role of socio-economic equality in liberal political theory generally and the ability to participate in democratic politics specifically emerges with renewed vigor as the gap between the wealthy and the poor continues to grow exponentially.

Aristotle identified oligarchy as the opposite of democracy and argued that the poor would be more powerful than the rich in a democracy simply because they were the majority. Unchecked campaign spending, however, defies Aristotle's careful reasoning. Modern practices of democracy, especially those in the United States, tempt a rethinking of the opposition between oligarchy and democracy and force the question of whether democracy can be preserved in conditions of great disparities of wealth. Socioeconomic inequality among the citizenry and corporate involvement in politics through political campaign contributions, in different ways, invite philosophical scrutiny of the effects of economic inequality on the theory and practice of democracy.

John Rawls identified economic inequality as a threat to the ability to exercise freedom of speech as well as the ability to obtain the information necessary for participation in democratic debate. As he says,

> The liberties protected by the principle of participation lose much of their value whenever those who have greater private means are permitted to use their advantages to control the course of public debate. For eventually these inequalities will enable those better situated to exercise a larger influence over the development of legislation. In due time, they are likely to acquire a preponderant weight in settling social questions, at least in regard to those matters upon which they normally agree, which is to say in regard to those things that support their favored circumstances (1999, 198).

The core values of democracy, according to Rawls, are threatened when the power of political decision-making revert to the "better situated."

The impact of economic inequality on democracy and the effects of capitalism on political speech gained attention in the United States in the 2010 case *Citizens United v. Federal Election Commission* in which the United States Supreme Court upheld the rights of corporations and associations to spend unlimited resources on political issues. The case was decided on the basis of the First Amendment and brought new light to the nature of free speech in a democracy. Some critics argued that the decision posed a serious threat to democracy itself insofar as corporations could wield unrestricted influence in political campaigns. The voices of individual people, even individuals joined in a collectivity, could easily be drowned out with the massive influx of money from corporations—including foreign corporations seeking to influence U.S. politics. Moreover, critics also wonder about the legitimacy of thinking of corporations as rights holders. On the other hand, supporters of the *Citizens United* decision argued that it was a bold defense of the freedom of speech and a necessary check on the power of incumbents. The decision would encourage more speech, not less, and the corporations would not be noticeably more dominant. Not surprisingly, these differing interpretations of the possible effects of *Citizens United* parallel many of the ideological and economic issues contributing to the polarization in politics mentioned previously.

Citizens United also touched off a variety of activist responses as individual citizens sought to maintain their hold on democratic ideals. Indeed, many scholars and activists argued that the rise of social media will negate the effects of *Citizens United.* Social media allows not only a platform for discussing issues but also a rapid, coordinated response to events. Facebook and Twitter were instrumental in calling out and organizing the protesters during the Arab Spring; the Occupy Movement continues its campaign virtually with over 3.5 million participants on Facebook. Social and activist networks, often with the clever use of social media, have also globalized and the effects are truly revolutionary.

Democracy is also challenged by corporate globalization. Multinational corporations increasingly shape state policies to facilitate better trade deals. Given this economic and political climate, it is worth wondering whether this is the same conception of democracy that inspired the protests that sparked the Arab Spring and the Occupy Movement. Clearly the nature of democracy is undergoing radical changes in quite divergent directions. Some theorists and activists argue that the spread of capitalism is contrary to democracy, while others argue that the intersections of capitalism and democracy provide a fruitful means of advancing individual and collective interests globally. So while wealth certainly reshapes liberal democracy domestically and internationally, the ever new technological innovations ignite expansive networks committed to a people's democracy gaining increasing importance and power.

Given all the real and potential uses for social media, however, might it be worth asking whether social media could be used by anti-democratic governments and entrenched powers to thwart democracy? The implications of imperialist uses of social media are not confined to anti-democratic governments, however; so-called democratic regimes have also used social media in surveillance monitoring their own citizens. The loss of privacy counters the ease of mobilization through social media.

Globalized communication networks further facilitate more formal interaction across borders and global media enhance access to information around the world. The theory and practice of democracy is greatly affected by recent changes in information sources. Democratic participation relies on citizens having enough of the right information to contribute meaningfully to debate and make informed decisions. The question of legitimacy is not merely a question of turning important matters over to the people; as the essays in this collection demonstrate, there are also questions about the access to information, the quality of information, the obligations to attain epistemic competence among the electorate, and the power of money.

Newspapers, television news, and the internet have long been considered not only viable as sources of information but also probable purveyors of political bias. Media that is controlled by private companies are not always motivated by a moral imperative to disseminate information but by a profit imperative to gain greater market share. Jürgen Habermas raised a similar concern, calling it "colonization of the public sphere." He further connects private ownership of the media to the increased polarization discussed earlier:

> Under the pressure of shareholders who thirst for higher revenues, it is the intrusion of the functional imperatives of the market economy into the "internal logic" of the production and presentation of messages that leads to the covert displacement of one category of communication by another: Issues of political discourse become assimilated into and absorbed by the modes and contents of entertainment. Besides personalization, the dramatization of events, the simplification of complex matters, and the vivid polarization of conflicts promote civic privatism and a mood of antipolitics (Habermas 2006, 411–426).

Of course, faulty or incomplete information is not solely the responsibility of the media. Individual citizens often consume media in such a way as to insulate themselves from opposing ideas. Twenty-first century democracy, then, faces an appalling paradox: a media saturated environment in which the electorate nevertheless make democratic decisions based on a dismaying lack of information.

As is clear from this brief excursion into the ever-changing social landscape, the theory and practice of democracy face enormous challenges. The essays in this volume contribute evocative philosophical analysis to our collective understanding of these challenges as well as some concrete proposals for how we might overcome them. In the rest of this introduction, we offer brief summaries of the articles and debates they address.

The concept of democracy is inextricably context specific. At times it means a system of rule by the people in their own interest. At other times, democracy means something closer to a state sponsored redistribution of resources in the interest of the good of the community. Political theorists have distinguished aggregate democracy, deliberative democracy, dialogic democracy, republican democracy, and representative democracy, as well as the libertarian, liberal, and socialist democracy distinctions mentioned earlier. The rapid transformations of the political landscape in the twenty-first century require a reexamination of these variations in the concept in order to uncover whether "democracy" is still meaningful across ideological, socio-economic, and national divides. The contributors to the first section of this book explore the some of the fundamental principles associated with claims to democracy as well as the social myths that unite communities for democratic decision-making.

Emily R. Gill's "Democracy: A Paradox of Rights" (Chap. 2) offers a unique perspective on the government's role in promoting core democratic values of freedom and equality. A liberal democracy like the United States, according to Gill, must balance the preservation of freedom and equality while encouraging a flourishing pluralism. Gill uses three cases to illustrate local, state, and national governmental actions that show that the state does not always act to promote the core values of free and equal citizenship. At times, the state itself fails to support free and equal citizenship. Liberal democracies ought also to avoid granting too much power to the state to determine whether, for instance, tax exemptions ought to be withheld from a group on the basis of the group's intolerant beliefs or values. Gill argues that "the true threat to free and equal citizenship lies not in the beliefs that we fail to transform, but in the practices that individuals and groups may attempt to impose not only on others but also potentially on the larger community." She suggests that shifting our gaze to what organizations *do* rather than what they believe better accords with the principles of freedom and equality in a democracy.

In "Rights and the American Constitution: The Issue of Judicial Review and Its Compatibility With Democracy" (Chap. 3), Rex Martin examines the concept of democracy by asking whether it is compatible with the Fourteenth Amendment to the US Constitution as interpreted, and with the practice of judicial review by the US Supreme Court. The Fourteenth Amendment redefined citizenship to include freed Black slaves and guarantees due process and equal protection of the laws for all citizens. Martin argues that this amendment transformed the Bill of Rights, first by extending citizenship and its protections, and second through its incorporation into the state laws by means of Supreme Court decisions that overturn laws that conflict with its provisions. In these ways the Fourteenth Amendment extends political values that were becoming more democratic through the nineteenth and twentieth centuries in America, and thus is compatible with democracy. The compatibility of the institution of judicial review with democracy is more complicated. Although judicial review may serve to identify and implement laws that serve the interests of a majority, that only holds if judges uphold the basic rights and well being of the citizens. Since majoritarian rule sometimes makes laws that impair civil rights as well, however, the existence of a countervailing power serves democratic principles. Martin points out that many countries have nonetheless decided that an unelected judiciary is undemocratic, and that those countries, other than the US, which have judicial review place greater restrictions on the power of judges. Lifetime appointment, for example, is unique to the US system. Martin argues that encouraging early (i.e., at age 70) retirement of judges would help to make US judicial review more democratic.

Richard DeGeorge offers a skeptical view of "democracy" in his essay "Democracy as Social Myth" (Chap. 4). He points to the many countries that call themselves "democratic", such as the German Democratic Republic, and offers an analysis of the rhetoric of democracy in terms of Levi-Strauss's concept of a social myth. A social myth is an overarching narrative in terms of which a society understands relations among its people, institutions, and norms. De George describes four strands of the social myth of democracy: the global strand, which consists of the many national narratives of democracy, the popular strand, which is the story of democracy in social life, the political strand, which refers to the particular democratic form of government in a society, and the academic strand, which is the way that scholars discuss and critique the other strands. This analysis offers a way to explain why American politics is so polarized, because of the clashing of different strands, and why so many different societies can consider themselves to be democratic without cynicism. One consequence of this view of democracy is that any particular instantiation is not to be objected to as not democratic, but rather its social myths to be deconstructed.

The second section scrutinizes various forms of polarization within democratic systems. Stephen Nathanson's essay, "Political Polarization and the Markets vs. Government Debate" (Chap. 5), discusses political polarization as a result of oversimplified conceptual disagreements about the proper roles of and relation between government and the free market economic system. He suggests we abandon the one-dimensional binary between capitalism and socialism, and acknowledge that there have long been nuanced distinctions that allow for a variety of forms of welfare statism as well as distinctions within capitalist and socialist systems. Nathanson describes four types of capitalist systems (anarcho-capitalism, minimal state capitalism, umpire state capitalism, and pragmatic capitalism) and three types of welfare state (emergency relief, opportunity, and decent level). His brief discussion of each highlights the essential points of commonality as well as difference; while he does not discuss the varieties of socialism given his focus on U.S. politics, it is clear that he would similarly suggest a more nuanced conceptualization of socialism that invites distinctions. Nathanson's aim is to provide a richer vocabulary that challenges the rhetoric used especially by politicians to polarize the citizenry and threaten the democratic process.

Polarization of a different sort appears in Richard Parker's "Two Visions of Democracy: Why the American Government is Paralyzed and What Can be Done About It" (Chap. 6). Parker focuses on polarized conceptions of democracy itself. He offers two major visions of democracy and democratic citizenship. One vision is democracy based on individual freedom and political equality. The other is founded on the economic and social equality of individuals in a community. Parker offers a reading of the history of the United States to show why the first type of democracy appears to be so prevalent here, whereas the rest of the world favors the second type of democracy. His provocative interpretation traces numerous political threads to explain the current political polarization in American politics. Parker concludes with a reflection on issues in which he speculates both types of democrats might find common ground. In contrast to the polarization discussed in Nathanson's essay, Parker sees some possible common ground around public goods; however, he notes that both types of democrats will have to sacrifice rhetoric and strong positions against such things as taxes to support public goods.

Richard Nunan's "Proportional Representation, the Single Transferable Vote, and Electoral Pragmatism" (Chap. 7) offers an alternative explanation of and solution to the polarization of the American political system. He points out that the system of single-member district plurality voting (also called "first past the post") can lead to voter frustration and apathy, as well as poor representation of minorities. Single transferable voting, however, where voters ordinally rank candidates for multi-member district seats, leads to greater minority representation and therefore, less apathy. Nunan then compares John Stuart Mill's vision of participatory democracy, for which Mill also prescribed STV, with Richard Posner's and Joseph Schumpeter's cynical, pragmatic view of democratic elections as merely an orderly process of succession and a check on quality of representatives. Nunan argues that moving to STV in election of the US House would transform the US democracy to a more participatory and fair system of representation.

In his contribution, "The Problem of Democracy in the Context of Polarization" (Chap. 8), Imer Flores asks whether polarization is in fact problematic for democracy. He first distinguishes two familiar conceptions of democracy: majoritarian, which is simply the outcome of majority rule in a context of universal suffrage, and partnership, in which each citizen is a full partner in the collective political enterprise, and requires that the status and interests of each are protected. Flores then offers four conceptions of polarization, including two that are incompatible with any form of democracy, one that is compatible only with majoritarian democracy, and one that is not only compatible with, but also conducive to a robust partnership conception of democracy. The compatibility of polarization and democracy on this view, he argues, requires conditions of robust debate, including an educated citizenry.

Nathanson raised the issue of economic discrepancies causing political polarization. The third part of this collection confronts the rather dramatic increase in economic inequality as it affects political participation and speech.

Steven P Lee's "Is Justice Possible under Welfare State Capitalism?" (Chap. 9) challenges John Rawls' critique of welfare state capitalism (WSC). Lee disagrees with Rawls' conclusion that justice cannot be realized under WSC. Rawls argues that welfare state capitalism did not provide the adequate equality of the social basis of self-respect. Lee counters that there are other bases of self-respect for the non-wealthy, contrary to what Rawls argues, such as trade unionism. If Lee is correct that the social bases of self-respect might be independent of economic distribution, then welfare state capitalism could serve as a reasonable system of justice that ensured the fair value of political liberties, fair equality of opportunity. Rawls also argues that property owning democracy (POD) is a better system for realizing justice. The second main point of Lee's chapter calls that into question as well. Lee argues that property owning democracy might not be either coherent or plausible. Rawls' "commitment to economic egalitarianism," according to Lee, "may not be strong enough to overcome the conflicting element of the cultural commitment to a foundational notion of desert and individual responsibility." Welfare state capitalism is more direct, reliable, and coherent as a path to justice than property owning democracy according to Lee.

Mark Navin's essay, "Social Segregation, Complacency, & Democracy" (Chap. 10), offers an interpretation of Rawls's accounts of envy and resentment and their relation to social segregation. On Rawls's view, envy is a vicious emotion, while resentment is a non-vicious feeling of hostility over unjust inequality. Navin argues that while it is a good thing in ideal theory that social segregation tends to decrease envy, in non-ideal theory, where unjust inequality is present, social segregation will also tend to dampen resentment. Furthermore, the same inequalities that cause the disadvantaged to voluntarily segregate from civic association with more advantaged citizens will also lead to a lack of political participation. Thus, inequality decreases the political participation of the less advantaged, and makes it less likely that the unjust inequalities that constitute their disadvantage will be addressed. This analysis suggests that the political polarization we observe in the US is either less than it would be with greater equality, or else that the polarization is not caused by inequality.

The next two essays examine the recent Supreme Court Case *Citizens United v. FEC* (2010). Patrick Hubbard and Jonathan Schonsheck offer decidedly different understandings of the implications of the case for freedom of speech and democracy. In "Mass Democracy in a Postfactual Market Society: *Citizens United* and the Role of Corporate Political Speech" (Chap. 11), Patrick Hubbard argues that the Court acted in accordance with significant precedence when it ruled the way it did. He further notes that the impact of corporate speech is relatively small for a variety of reasons. Most business corporations, for instance, seek to avoid political controversy because it is bad for business. Further, he suggests that the very scale of a candidate's campaign expenditures diminishes the impact of independent entities. Hubbard concludes by saying that the decision in *Citizens United* is not necessarily incorrect; rather than criticizing the court, perhaps we ought to turn our attention to Congress, "which has not adopted strong restrictions on campaign speech that would be constitutional" even while we notice "that wealth inequality among citizens makes the right to free speech very unequal in practice."

In contrast, Jonathan Schonsheck argues that the entire line of Supreme Court cases leading up to the *Citizens United* decision fails to protect freedom of speech. Schonsheck suggests that the impact of wealth is contrary to freedom of speech and freedom more generally. Wealthy individuals and corporations exercise an influence on politics through contributions that amounts to bribery that manipulates the democratic system to their own advantage. "A Tsunami of Filthy

Lucre: How SCOTUS Threatens to Obliterate American Democracy" (Chap. 12) explores the jurisprudence that grounds the Court's decisions leading up to *Citizens United* and argues that the consistent use of the metaphor of a "marketplace of ideas" is wrongheaded. Schonsheck concludes with an appeal to Rawls' conception of justice for a democratic polity.

The final article in this section, "Democracy & Economic Inequality" (Chap. 13), by Alistair Macleod, catalogues a number of ways that the economic elite exercise disproportionate power and hence threaten democratic ideals. Macleod discusses strategies that restrict the franchise, strategies that manipulate the electoral processes, strategies that undermine the background conditions for true democracy. This framework provides a useful way to understand the intersections between economic inequality and political inequality. Democratic theory ought not to single-mindedly focus on alleviating the latter, according to Macleod, because it is inextricably tied up with economic inequality. Macleod also offers a useful analysis of "first-past-the-post" voting systems, arguing that they violate political equality and preserve economic inequality. His argument calls for "institutions and procedures that give practical effect to the political equality of all the members of a society."

The final section of the book centrally addresses a theme that has been running through many of the essays in this collection: the electorate's access to information necessary for informed decision-making in the democratic process. As philosophers, many of the contributors draw on the tools of epistemology to understand the problems of lack of information and the shaping of information in a polity.

Jason Brennan, in his essay, "Epistocracy within Public Reason" (Chap. 14), asks whether epistocracy, a political system in which political power is assigned to experts on policy matters, is compatible with public reason. Objecting to David Estlund's argument against epistocracy, Brennan argues that the only bar to the legitimacy of epistocracy is the pragmatic difficulty of finding agreement on who is competent to make policy decisions. If an umpire can be found who will apply a fair and reliable decision procedure, then Estlund's argument against epistocracy fails. Brennan then turns to the task of describing such an umpire. He tentatively concludes that democracy may be fair and reliable when deciding what counts as political competence. Thus democracy may legitimately authorize epistocracy, provided the demos maintains control over judgments of political competence.

Russell Waltz turns attention to the media and its power to shape or influence public perception. In "Journalists as Purveyors of Partial Truths: How Media Bias Inhibits Democratic Citizens from Becoming Informed and Motivated" (Chap. 15), Waltz suggests that journalism ought to enable the effective equality of citizens to vote and voice their displeasure with the government, but in order to do this, the presentation of material must be both appropriately broad and narrow. The narrow context indicates a presentation of subjective experience which allows for consumers of media to make a personal connection to a story. The broad context ensures that sufficient social information or contextualization accompanies the personal context for a richer, more nuanced understanding of a situation. Journalists ought to "avoid presenting news in ways that are liable to cause false inferences from the inevitably partial presentation of information." While it is not possible to obviate the need for journalists to frame the issues they present, Waltz argues that they ought to avoid episodic framing because it relies on a bias that invites selective attention and inattention. One possible outcome of Waltz's approach is that citizens must claim the responsibility to obtain information from a variety of news outlets. In a way, then, one could see the political polarization of Section II as a function of both a politicized media and a citizenry that fails to live up to its responsibility to obtain information from a multiplicity sources from different ideological perspectives.

Ken Henley is skeptical of our ability to reason impartially about political matters, even if we have access to evidence and engage in public dialogue. In his "Motivated Reasoning, Group Identification, and Representative Democracy" (Chap. 16), Henley distinguishes between explanatory reason, which uses relevant evidence to discover the best supported conclusion, and motivated reason, which is biased in favor of the view held prior to the examination of evidence. Social cognitive psychology shows that we are overwhelmingly prone to motivated reasoning. This and our tendency to promote the interests or beliefs of our group largely explain political polarization beyond all (explanatory) reason. Contrary to the ideals of representation and public reason offered by Burke, Rawls, or Habermas, our politicians are equally susceptible to motivated reason and groupishness. Henley offers a plan for reducing this effect in our elected representatives, which includes (among others) renewed solemnity on an oath of office that requires them to swear to represent the whole people, rather than only their own partisan supporters.

Wade Robison, like Waltz, suggests that new technologies have altered the relation between citizens and their states, and can improve the ability of people to overthrow authoritarian regimes. In "Republics, Passions, & Protections" (Chap. 17), he points out that Hume's and Madison's reasons for preferring a that a republic have large territory to a small one, namely in order to reduce the growth of factions, is otiose now with the advent of the cellphone. He describes how the Moldovan citizens successfully protested the rigged parliamentary elections of April 2009 using Facebook and Twitter, and how Iranian protesters after their June 2009 election used Twitter to avoid government crackdowns. Although these did not lead to successful revolutions, Robison argues against Malcolm Gladwell's view that such tools can never lead to the discipline and hierarchy needed for revolution. In Robison's view, the use of such new media can lead to cooperative enterprises that can form, like Hume's rowers, without a single leader or clear lines of authority.

This collection includes essays on freedom and equality—fundamental principles of democracy—as well as the philosophical explorations of contemporary problems like the current polarization within American democracy, the effects of money or the market on democracy, and the access to information for democratic decision-making, provokes further reexamination of the ideal of democracy. The theory and practice of democracy has undergone quite radical transformation in the last 10 years. We hope that these essays will serve—collectively and individually—as fodder for much more discussion and debate and the meaning and challenge of democracy in the twenty-first century.

References

Bush pledges to spread democracy. 2005. CNN.com. Thursday, January 20. http://www.cnn.com/2005/ALLPOLITICS/01/20/bush.speech/. Accessed 2 June 2013.

Habermas, Jurgen. 2006. Political communication in media society: Does democracy still enjoy an epistemic dimension? The impact of normative theory on empirical research. *Communication Theory* 16(4): 411–426.

Rawls, J. 1999. *A theory of justice: Revised edition*. Cambridge, MA: Harvard University Press.

Part I
The Meaning of Democracy

Chapter 2
Democracy: A Paradox of Rights?

Emily R. Gill

Abstract Theorist Corey Brettschneider argues that in a "paradox of rights," liberal democracies are expected to allow freedom of association, expression, and conscience, but viewpoint neutrality dictates that they cannot themselves express the values of free and equal citizenship that undergird these rights. According to what he terms value democracy, the state should abrogate viewpoint neutrality and instead speak in ways that would transform recalcitrant citizens' views to support these core values. Although I support the values of free and equal citizenship, I question some of the means Brettschneider would use to promote these values. First, we cannot always count on the state itself to support the values of free and equal citizenship. Second, although he would withdraw tax exemptions from groups that oppose these values, making this determination accords too much power to public authority, and voluntary associations are not always monolithic in their values. Finally, the true threat to free and equal citizenship lies not in the beliefs that we fail to transform, but in the practices that individuals and groups may attempt to impose not only on others but also potentially on the larger community.

2.1 Introduction

What makes a democracy a democracy? A liberal democracy that is also diverse faces a recurring question. How much agreement on the core values of free and equal citizenship is necessary to preserve a balance between the encouragement of a flourishing pluralism, on the one hand, and the maintenance of these core values, on the other? Although a plurality of voluntary associations has historically been viewed as a check on the tyranny of majoritarian values and a hallmark of personal

E.R. Gill (✉)
Political Science Department, Bradley University, 61625 Peoria, IL, USA
e-mail: gill@bradley.edu

A.E. Cudd and S.J. Scholz (eds.), *Philosophical Perspectives on Democracy in the 21st Century*, AMINTAPHIL: The Philosophical Foundations of Law and Justice 5, DOI 10.1007/978-3-319-02312-0_2,

liberty, today "civil society is seen as a school of virtue where men and women develop the dispositions essential to liberal democracy" (Rosenblum 1998). According to what Nancy Rosenblum terms the logic of congruence, this premise "rests on the assumption that dispositions and practices shaped in one association spill over to other contexts" (1998). Therefore, many advocates of congruence would enforce by law the norms and practices of public institutions on the internal life of voluntary associations.

For Rosenblum, on the other hand, membership in voluntary associations is a source of self-respect, both through individuals' active contributions to associational life and through support by others for conceptions of the good life that may not be affirmed by the larger society. We do not always know what dispositions associational membership may promote. Although legal limitations must exist on exploitative or violent behavior, "deviance is as much a part of social life as the reproduction of norms… Surely it is important that groups provide relatively benign outlets for ineradicable viciousness, intolerance, or narrow self-interest, and that antidemocratic dispositions are contained even if they cannot be corrected" (Rosenblum 1998).

Political theorist and constitutional scholar Corey Brettschneider, however, believes that antidemocratic dispositions may indeed be corrected. In what he terms a paradox of rights, "liberal rights recognize the status of citizens as free and equal, yet the protection of rights to free association, expression, and conscience provides cover for groups and individuals who attack the equality of citizens" (Brettschneider 2012). On the one hand, "Citizens must be free from coercive threat as they develop their own notion of justice and the good. Otherwise, they would not be able to affirm and choose their own ideas about the most fundamental matters of politics (the just) and what constitutes, in their view, a valuable life (the good)" (Brettschneider 2012). On the other hand, on his view the government's viewpoint neutrality towards citizens' right to expression should not extend to neutrality in its own expression. "While liberal rights should be neutral in the sense that they protect all citizens regardless of the viewpoints they hold and express, the public values that underlie these rights cannot be neutral" (Brettschneider 2012).

According to what Brettschneider calls value democracy, the state should engage in democratic persuasion by expressing the values of freedom and equality that underlie the right to freedom of association, expression, and conscience in the first place. Specifically, he supports deliberate state efforts to change or transform beliefs that would undermine these core values. Value democracy expresses both the liberal element of limitations on the state's coercive power and the democratic element of freedom and equality for all. "A state is not fully democratic if it formally guarantees rights and democratic procedures, while failing to endorse the underlying values of self-government in its broader culture" (Brettschneider 2010b). Therefore, when the state protects expression that counteracts these values, "it is essential that it also use *its* expressive capacities to clarify that it is not expressing support for the viewpoints themselves, but instead is guaranteeing an entitlement that stems from the need to respect all citizens as free and equal" (Brettschneider 2010b).

When the Supreme Court, for example, struck down the Florida city of Hialeah's ordinance against animal sacrifice, Brettschneider argues that it was not only protecting the free exercise of Santeria, but was also sending a message that the councilmen's views that it was their Christian moral duty to ban such sacrifices "have no place in a free society's deliberations about coercion" (2010a). The council had agreed to single out and ban animal sacrifice, an occasional but central practice of the Santeria religion, on the grounds that such a practice conflicted with the Bible and was morally repugnant—although it did not ban other animal killings. To the Supreme Court, this kind of animus was an illegitimate basis for the coercion involved in curtailing a practice. The councilmen's beliefs themselves deserve both a rebuke and a transformation by the state, although Brettschneider would rely on persuasion rather than coercion and would limit his efforts to beliefs that are inconsistent with the values of equal citizenship (2010a). Although at some times religious arguments will reinforce our commitment to free and equal citizenship, at other times they will undermine this commitment. "In such cases, existing religious beliefs are rightly targeted by the state for transformation" (Brettschneider 2010a). According to what he calls the *Lukumi* principle, the state must protect religious belief and practice, but it also "should explain why the democratic values underlying religious freedom are incompatible with religious beliefs that contradict the values of free and equal citizenship" (Brettschneider 2010b, 2012).

In addition to the dissemination of court decisions as a means of transformation, Brettschneider also supports the selective withdrawal of tax exemptions, upheld by the Supreme Court in 1983 when the Internal Revenue Service began withholding this status from groups that engaged in racial discrimination. Bob Jones University formerly prohibited not only interracial dating, an arguably internal matter at a private institution, but also public support for interracial marriage and membership in the NAACP. Although the IRS's revocation of tax-free, nonprofit status was "quasi-coercive" as well as persuasive, the University still had the right to resist or ignore this transformative pressure. When the University changed its policy against interracial dating 17 years later despite its earlier rhetoric about the religious grounding of its policies, on Brettschneider's view it is not therefore a less religious institution than before. Despite the widespread idea that religion is supposed to be insulated from the surrounding culture, "The static nature of such an insular account of religion ignores the reality that religions have survived for centuries precisely because they are able to evolve—not only to fit various cultural contexts but also to incorporate fundamental values" such as those of free and equal citizenship (Brettschneider 2010a).

Although I support the values of free and equal citizenship, in this chapter I raise questions about Brettschneider's means of promoting these values. First, we cannot always count on public authority itself to support the values of free and equal citizenship. Second, although I oppose direct funding to organizations that discriminate in ways counter to public values, determining which organizations espouse values that comprehensively oppose free and equal citizenship for purposes of withholding tax exemptions itself accords too much power to public authority. Many voluntary associations are not monolithic in their values, moreover, and many evolve over time. Finally, the true threat to free and equal citizenship lies not in voluntary associations the *beliefs* of which we fail to transform, but in *practices* they may seek to impose not only on individuals but also sometimes on the larger community.

2.2 Congruence and Transformation

I agree with Brettschneider that allowing the imposition of some people's religious views on the religious freedom of others contradicts the justification itself for religious freedom, which is the idea that individuals should be accorded freedom of belief and, absent harm to others, of practice. It is one thing, however, for the state to prevent the imposition, whether through law or social pressure, of some people's religious beliefs on others, and another matter entirely to want the state to transform their beliefs to prevent this imposition. Brettschneider argues, however, that "individuals have an obligation to endorse and internalize a commitment to public values through a process of reflective revision" (2012). He appeals to a principle of public relevance, which "claims that personal beliefs and actions should be in accordance with public values to the extent that private life affects the ability of citizens to function in society and to see others as free and equal citizens" (2012). To the objection that citizens' beliefs are not matters of public concern, he responds that democratic legitimacy requires not only the state's protection of democratic rights, but also "democratic congruence," or "democratic endorsement or citizens' agreement with the values that justify rights." That is, citizens must support the freedom and equality on which a legitimate democracy is grounded. Otherwise, "strict deference to popular opinion would mean the enactment of policies that potentially undermine the very values that undergird the right to participate in democracy in the first place" (Brettschneider 2012). Over time, moreover, a widespread rejection of the values of free and equal citizenship might undermine formal and/or informal respect for these values (Brettschneider 2010b).

To avoid an overweening state influence, Brettschneider does impose two limitations on the state's efforts at transformation (2010a, b). The means-based limit stipulates that the state use its expressive rather than its coercive capacities in this effort. It cannot "pursue the transformation of citizens' views through any method that violates fundamental rights such as freedom of expression, conscience, or association," even if a group such as the Ku Klux Klan rejects the reasons for these rights. The substance-based limit distinguishes beliefs and actions that threaten free and equal citizenship from those that do not. Only those that pose true threats should be subject to transformation. But for those that challenge the core values of freedom and equality, Brettschneider is correct in stating, "The right to hold and express a belief at odds with the ideal of equal citizenship does not entail a right to hold it unchallenged" (2010a, 2012).

I strongly support citizens' collective commitment to public purposes and to the values they represent, and I agree that through laws and their enforcement, the government can be an appropriate spokesperson for these purposes. My underlying disagreement with Brettschneider, however, is that he places greater trust in state speech than I do. Frequently, the system works as Brettschneider desires. Just as the Santeria case not only preserved religious freedom but also on Brettschneider's interpretation condemned the illiberal beliefs behind the Hialeah ordinance, the 1996 Supreme Court case of *Romer v. Evans* could be seen not only as striking down Colorado's Amendment 2, which prohibited political subdivisions from passing antidiscrimination laws protecting sexual orientation, but also as condemning the illiberal intentions of the people of Colorado. According to Justice Anthony Kennedy, the Amendment imposed a broad disability on one particular group for reasons that seem "inexplicable by anything but animus toward the class it affects," therefore failing to meet even the test of a rational relationship to legitimate state interests, and constituting "a denial of equal protection of the laws in the most literal sense" (*Romer v. Evans* 1996). Additionally, "Amendment 2 classifies homosexuals not to further a proper legislative end but to make them unequal to everyone else. This Colorado cannot do. A State cannot so deem a class of persons a stranger to its laws" (*Romer v. Evans* 1996). This forthright condemnation might or might not, however, effect a transformation in the views of Coloradans about the conflict between Amendment 2 and the values of free and equal citizenship. It did, however, prevent them from enforcing an unjust constitutional amendment that threatened the core values of free and equal citizenship, and that is what matters.

In other cases, however, the state may speak in ways that do not support the core values of free and equal citizenship. I believe that in these cases, we as citizens need to speak and to vote in ways that may transform *the state's* viewpoint. In 1991 in *Rust v. Sullivan*, for example, the Supreme Court upheld public funding for a family planning program that was contingent on private social service providers' silence about abortion as an option, ruling that "the government can, without violating the Constitution, selectively fund a program to encourage certain activities it believes to be in the public interest, without at the same time funding an alternative program which seeks to deal with the problem in another way" (1991). Although I disagree vehemently with what is sometimes called "the gag rule," the point stands. Public authority may with democratic input determine the scope of our public purposes and may render public funding contingent upon recipients conducting their programs in accord with these purposes. Because the state used its own money to support birth control clinics, it was entitled to express its own values and viewpoint.

Brettschneider agrees with the legitimacy of the state's expressive interest in *Rust*, but argues that with respect to the gag rule, "the state expressed itself in a way inconsistent with the most basic values of a legitimate society, violating the substance-based limit. The authors of the rule sought to deny information to citizens, not only about their medical options but also about their legal rights." Withholding this information denies the core values of free and equal citizenship, implying that citizens cannot or should not make their own decisions about how to use their rights. The state should promote values in its expressive capacity, but here, Brettschneider argues, it promoted the wrong values. "The substance-based limit on democratic persuasion establishes that the content of the state's expression—the reason it gives for rights—should focus on the promotion of the ideal of free and equal citizenship… *Rust* serves as an example of state expression that is illegitimate" (2010b). Although the state need not be viewpoint-neutral in its utterances, limits exist. "I argue that these limits should be based on what is substantively illegitimate for the state to say. When the state speaks, it does not have the entitlement to say anything it wishes" (2012).

I agree with Brettschneider that in its expressive capacity, the state *should* focus on promoting the core values of free and equal citizenship. It will not always do so, however, as the Hialeah City Council, Colorado's Amendment 2, and *Rust* illustrate at the local, state, and national levels respectively. Congress may pass and the Supreme Court may uphold laws that in the eyes of some violate rather than uphold the values of free and equal citizenship. Therefore, we should be more cautious than Brettschneider in our desires that the state, at whatever level, seek to change people's beliefs. The value of dissent lies in its potential to influence and perhaps to change the beliefs of the dominant culture. Sometimes state speech counteracts the larger society's disrespect for free and equal citizenship. At other times, however, the state itself is the source of disrespect. The larger society or elements within it must then act against this disrespect to transform state speech. Additionally, it may be more difficult than Brettschneider indicates to determine which illiberal beliefs are hostile to the values of free and equal citizenship. It is to this issue that I now turn.

2.3 Public Funding, Tax Exemptions, and Public Power

Brettschneider's second limitation, the substance-based limit, stipulates that the state should not challenge all inegalitarian beliefs, but "only those that challenge the ideal of free and equal citizenship." This ideal is a political one, and it does not require the logic of congruence, or equality in all spheres of life. It does require, however, efforts at transformation of "those views which are openly hostile to the ideal of equal citizenship, or implausibly compatible with it" (Brettschneider 2010b). Importantly, he includes here religious views "that would seek to impose by law religious beliefs at odds with this ideal" (2010a) which is well exemplified by the Hialeah case and by *Romer*. Not all cases, however, are so clear cut.

As mentioned above, Brettschneider also supports the selective withdrawal of tax exemptions as a means of transformation, arguing that the change or transformation of religious identity need not mean the complete replacement of one kind of identity with another. Although unlike the city of Hialeah, Bob Jones University is a private institution, its former policy was tantamount to public advocacy of beliefs and practices at odds with free and equal citizenship. Its prohibition not only against interracial dating, but also against membership in organizations supporting interracial marriage and in the NAACP, violated both freedom of expression and of association. The resulting denial of nonprofit status was justifiable, argues Brettschneider, despite its quasi-coercive character. Although nonprofit institutions need not actively promote public values, "nonprofit status is a tax advantage that should be linked at minimum to an institution's willingness not to undermine the ideal of free and equal citizenship" (2010a).

After the school desegregation decisions of the 1950's and 1960's, the IRS ruled in 1971 that tax exemptions were not necessarily available to all charitable, religious, and public interest organizations and their donors, but only to organizations whose purposes were neither illegal nor contrary to public policy. Although most abhorred the University's stance, for Jonathan Turley a larger principle is involved. "Once neutrality was abandoned, the government was free to determine whether some forms of preferential treatment or exclusion are good or bad forms of discrimination" (Turley 2008). At the root of the new regulation, Turley explains, is the mistaken conviction that a tax exemption is equivalent to a direct subsidy and that facilitating the expression of views is a justification for regulating them. The Supreme Court has held, however, that unlike the positive action of granting revenue to an organization, a tax exemption means *refraining* from action. Although discriminatory views and policies are detrimental to society, "there is no way to foster the pluralistic ideals of our society if we cross the constitutional rubicon of content-based discrimination on the part of the government" (Turley 2008). The law may still bar the direct funding of discriminatory organizations. Moreover, although it is legitimate to penalize discrimination by public accommodations, a tax exemption is not a tool to force… [private] organizations to conform to majoritarian views" (Turley 2008). Douglas Kmiec agrees that tax exemptions, which should be viewpoint-neutral, cannot be equated with subsidies, where "it should not be surprising that the government gets to decide how to spend its own resources" (Kmiec 2008), and may therefore stipulate conditions for their receipt.

For Brettschneider, however, discrimination concerning tax exemptions is still noncoercive. Organizations, after all, may legitimately resist transformation. In 2006, when Catholic Charities of Boston chose to shut down its adoption services in order to avoid a state law prohibiting adoption agencies from discriminating against families headed by gays or lesbians, the law was not coercive because Catholic Charities could continue to operate under its chosen policies; it simply would not receive its customary state funding (2010a), just as Bob Jones University continued to operate for 17 years without its tax exemption.

The result of Brettschneider's test, suggests Jeff Spinner-Halev, is the possibility that the tax exemptions of many organizations could be withdrawn, including those of the Roman Catholic Church, Southern Baptists, and many Orthodox Jewish and Islamic organizations that treat women differently than men. Like Rosenblum, he believes that nonprofit status "can encourage and support a rich associational life, and one that can shift with people's views and preferences." For Spinner-Halev, the key difference between tax exemptions and subsidies is that the government awards subsidies to accomplish specific ends, such as encouraging scientific research or facilitating adoptions. "When this occurs, the agency is acting for the government. It is doing the government's bidding and performing a specific public service. In these cases, it is usually appropriate that strings come with the government's funding," unlike exemptions for voluntary organizations that do not perform a direct service (Spinner-Halev 2011). Unless we want to limit tax-exempt status to just a few organizations, he suggests, the use of nonprofit status should be scrutinized mainly for fraud or abuse.

Spinner-Halev offers several reasons for skepticism about Brettschneider's proposal. Even when they violate the tenets of equal citizenship, religious organizations contribute in valuable ways to the public good through the provision of education and social services. Moreover, issues of equal citizenship are often matters of discussion within religious organizations themselves. "Debate and discussion are virtues of citizenship that should not be blithely dismissed because these groups do not already embrace the liberal ideal of equality" (Spinner-Halev 2011). In fact, religious organizations themselves may be influenced by the egalitarian ideals of the larger society to rethink some of their own policies. Some organizations that are reluctant to do so, such as the Boy Scouts with reference to their exclusion of gays, gradually become more particularistic and marginalized (Gill 2010). The transformation that Brettschneider desires may be better accomplished by indirect methods. Children whose religious parents remove them from uncooperative public schools will receive less exposure than otherwise to the values of equal citizenship if they are sent to religious schools or home-schooled. Finally, gender inequality within religious organizations is not always paralleled by gender inequality in the home. Spinner-Halev recommends that organizations only forfeit tax-exempt status if they practice *invidious discrimination*, or "systematic discrimination within a group that is part of a larger, unambiguous institutional effort to undermine the basic idea of the equality of citizens" (Spinner-Halev 2011). *Bob Jones* is covered by this standard, he explains, both because of the context of attempts to maintain de facto segregation and also because the discrimination represented a systematic institutional policy. Otherwise, he asks, "Do we want the IRS determining the meaning of equality?" This activity would be "under the direction of a political appointee" and subject "to the vagaries of democratic politics" (Spinner-Halev 2011).

Brettschneider responds by arguing that a tax exemption *is* actually a form of subsidy. By not collecting taxes on donations to nonprofits, the government is indirectly subsidizing these organizations. By denying tax-exempt status to Bob Jones University, the government was basically refusing to subsidize an organization opposing free and equal citizenship. Brettschneider would address the issue of political decision-making about tax exemptions by codifying the conditions for this status in the law; organizations that oppose free and equal citizenship do not provide the public benefit that nonprofits are expected to offer. He believes that his conditions for tax exemption do not threaten the diversity of civil society, because freedom of association, expression, and religion are in no way suppressed. Religious organizations need not display a public purpose to receive tax exemptions anyway. Brettschneider argues, nevertheless, that when a church or religious organization unambiguously opposes the ideal of free and equal citizenship, it should be denied a tax exemption (Brettschneider 2011).

Brettschneider's Exhibit A is the Westboro Baptist Church of Topeka, Kansas, known for picketing military funerals with the message that dead soldiers reflect God's disapproval of a nation tolerant of homosexuality. Its website's central message is that "God hates fags," and it supports the idea that gay citizens deserve to die. Although the Supreme Court ruled that these protests at military funerals merited free speech protection, "it is equally important to express criticism of its message. By not granting tax exemption, the state would send a clear signal that its protection of the Westboro's rights to free speech and religion should not be confused with approval of the Church's hateful viewpoint" (Brettschneider 2011). Although the Court did condemn Westboro's viewpoint, the state would make even clearer that it can protect free speech and religion yet criticize this viewpoint by removing the tax exemption. The Roman Catholic Church, by contrast, bars neither women nor gays from membership, it does not suggest that women or gays are not equal citizens, and its stances on women in the priesthood and on homosexuality may be regarded as theologically based rather than as a judgment on qualifications for citizenship in the liberal democratic polity.

Despite Brettschneider's advocacy of codifying in the law lack of opposition to free and equal citizenship as a criterion for tax-exempt status, I agree with Spinner-Halev. The difficulty of reaching a consensus on what kinds of beliefs and practices constitute a denial of the core values of free and equal citizenship is in my opinion insurmountable. First, although like most individuals, I abhor the viewpoint of Westboro Baptist Church, why might it not be argued that *its* viewpoint is a theological one? Although tax exemptions may function as indirect subsidies, the relationship is attenuated. The government could decide to eliminate tax exemptions altogether for nonprofit organizations, but short of doing this, the proposal is too difficult to implement. More generally, Brettschneider takes too narrow a view of what constitutes a public benefit, a clear condition for which is that "the organization does not seek to oppose or undermine the values of free and equal citizenship" (2011). On my view, organizations that provide public benefits may do so simply by contributing to the broad spectrum of viewpoints that make up civil society, even if aspects of each group's viewpoint are not supportive of liberal democratic values. Individuals and groups develop and hone their convictions through exposure to ideas that may conflict with their own. Although on occasion this interchange may push some in an illiberal direction, in other circumstances it can refine and strengthen liberal democratic values by inducing individuals to think about and defend them.

Second, although the state need not offer tax exemptions to any organization, the viewpoint-based withholding of exemptions could be regarded as coercive. On Brettschneider's view, coercion is involved when the state aims to prohibit an action, expression, or the holding of a belief by threatening an individual or group with a sanction or punishment (2011). If, as he argues, a tax exemption is an indirect form of subsidy, however, withholding subsidies from voluntary organizations based on their viewpoints would be a form of sanction. The implication would be that if they changed their viewpoints, they could resume their status as tax-exempt organizations. According to F.A. Hayek, "Coercion implies both the threat of inflicting harm and the intention thereby to bring about certain conduct" (Hayek 1960). Many nonprofit organizations would feel threatened by the loss of their tax exemptions and harmed by a subsequent loss of contributions from donors whose incentive is a tax deduction for their donations. They could resist transformation, of course, but at the cost of the loss of their former status.

Brettschneider maintains, however, that the state's use of its spending power as a means of democratic persuasion would only be coercive if there were no other sources of funding available to support an organization's expression. "State coercion is employed in an attempt to deny the ability to make a choice… By contrast, offering financial inducements, like pure persuasion, is clearly an attempt to convince citizens to make a particular choice, but it does not deny the citizen the right to reject that choice" (2012). The presence of coercion, however, is not always absolute; it may be relative and tied to the perceptions of the agent. Nonprofit organizations losing their tax exemptions might feel coerced to change their views, at least for public consumption, especially given the fact that such organizations are often in competition for scarce dollars. This motivation could be operative regardless of the availability of other, private funding.

Third, a bright line does not always exist between organizations that oppose the ideals of free and equal citizenship and those that do not. Unlike the Roman Catholic Church, the Boy Scouts has historically excluded gays and has done so without any clear explanation of its identity-based discrimination. Says Andrew Koppelman, "The BSA does not appear to care much whether it is implying that gays are intrinsically inferior. This insouciance conveys its own message" (Koppelman and Wolff 2009). There is no evidence, however, that the Scout policy towards gays has met Spinner-Halev's definition of invidious discrimination, or "systematic discrimination within a group that is part of a larger, institutional effort to undermine the basic idea of the equality of citizens" (2011). Furthermore, the Scouts itself has been internally divided about the role of gays in the organization. In early 2013, the Scouts said that it might drop the total ban on gay Scouts, eventually deciding that it would allow gay Scouts but not gay leaders (Eckholm 2013). Predictably, some have accused the Scouts of selling out, while others believe the organization has not gone far enough. Regardless of the reaction, the Scouts provides a good example of ways in which voluntary organizations may change without heavy-handed pressures by the government.

2.4 Imposing Beliefs by Law

Brettschneider himself mentions something, however, that I believe is the beginning of a clearer criterion for checking voluntary organizations that oppose the core values of free and equal citizenship. In introducing the substance-based limit, he suggests that only views that conflict with the ideals of free and equal citizenship need be transformed, "including those views that would seek to impose by law religious beliefs at odds with this ideal" (2010a). I agree that religious beliefs and practices are not and should not be immune from criticism. The key point, however, relates to "views that would seek to impose by law… beliefs at odds with this ideal," whether these beliefs are religiously or secularly based. If, for example, Westboro Baptist Church were seeking to punish same-sex intimacy, whether by trying to revive laws against it that became unenforceable in 2003 or by passing laws threatening gay citizens with imprisonment or death, I would vehemently oppose these efforts. But it is the *activity* that I would be opposing, not the belief that "God hates fags." Similarly, the difficulty with Colorado's Amendment 2 was not that a majority of Coloradans did not *believe* that laws should protect sexual orientation, but that they *acted* to disempower political subdivisions from passing antidiscrimination legislation covering sexual orientation. The problem with both Westboro members and Colorado citizens revolves around public policies they might or did seek to enact into law, not what their beliefs are or whether these beliefs are religiously or secularly motivated.

In an interesting reexamination of the politics of multiculturalism, Sarah Song argues that many scholars concerned about women's subordination in minority cultures characterize these cultures as "well-integrated, clearly bounded, and self-generated entities," and as "largely unified and distinct wholes." Because they regard these cultures as monolithic, they tend to criticize entire cultures, rather than the specific practices of which they disapprove. "Such an account overlooks the polyvocal nature of all cultures and the ways in which gender practices in both minority and majority cultures have evolved through cross-cultural interactions" (Song 2007). Sometimes the gender norms of the majority culture indirectly support patriarchal practices in minority cultures in what she terms the congruence effect; at other times the minority culture influences the norms of the majority culture. The majority's condemnation of minority cultural practices, moreover, may exert a diversionary effect on attention to its own inequitable hierarchies. Greater awareness of this interactive dynamic, suggests Song, "shifts the focus of debate from asking what cultures *are* to what cultural affiliations *do*" we can recognize inequalities, albeit in different forms, that transcend cultural boundaries, we need not choose between cultural accommodation that can leave internal minorities vulnerable, on the one hand, and forced assimilation to majority norms, on the other. "On this reformulation, then, 'culture' is not the problem; oppressive practices are" (Song 2007).

Brettschneider seems to look at charitable organizations as the "largely unified and distinct wholes" that Song thinks mischaracterize cultures. His support for the withdrawal of tax exemptions from organizations deemed to act against the core values of free and equal citizenship bolsters my interpretation. He is willing to consider nuances, as in the case of the Roman Catholic Church, in deciding whether a religious organization deserves to retain its status. Once this determination is made, however, it draws a bright line between those who do and those who do not have a right to this status. This view is somewhat at odds with his criticism of those who adhere to static conceptions of religious freedom. Although he thinks they want to preserve religious beliefs and practices as they are, rendering them immune to alteration or transformation from outside, he underestimates "cross-cultural interactions" between religious or charitable organizations and the larger society. Brettschneider's proposal appears not to recognize the permeable character of religious groups, just as critics of illiberal cultural practices can fail to recognize this feature of those groups.

The historically heterosexist norms of the Scouts reflected norms that have historically characterized the majority culture. Over time the "minority culture" of the Scouts is more likely to come to reflect the majority's more egalitarian norms than the reverse. The logic of congruence that Rosenblum criticizes mandates that organizations reflect the values of liberal democracy. Song's congruence effect, however, demonstrates that that the values promoted by liberal democracy may not themselves always promote free and equal citizenship. In accordance with Song's diversionary effect, moreover, efforts to bring faulty organizations into line distract us from the ongoing failings of the larger culture. The focus should not then be on particular religious or charitable organizations as such, but instead on specific practices that are oppressive, whether perpetrated within these organizations or by the larger society.

Following this logic, we can perhaps shift our gaze, in Song's terms, from what these organizations *are*, or what its members think or believe, to what they *do*. When organizations seek to *impose by law* beliefs at odds with the ideals of free and equal citizenship, whether these are religious or not, those who support free and equal citizenship should oppose these efforts with all the tools at their disposal. On this point, Brettschneider and I are in full agreement.

References

Brettschneider, C. 2010a. A transformative theory of religious freedom: Promoting the reasons for rights. *Political Theory* 18(2): 187–213.

Brettschneider, C. 2010b. When the state speaks, what should it say? The dilemmas of free expression and democratic persuasion. *Perspectives on Politics* 8(4): 1005–1019.

Brettschneider, C. 2011. Reply to Spinner-Halev. *Political Theory* 39(6): 785–792.

Brettschneider, C. 2012. *When the state speaks, what should it say? How democracies can protect expression and promote equality*. Princeton: Princeton University Press.

Eckholm, E. 2013. Boy Scouts end longtime ban on gay youth. *New York Times*, A1, A16.

Gill, Emily R. 2010. When free speech meets free association: The case of the Boy Scouts. In *Freedom of expression in a diverse world*, ed. Deirdre Golash, 147–161. Dordrecht: Springer.

Hayek, F.A. 1960. *The constitution of liberty*. Chicago: University of Chicago Press.

Kmiec, D.W. 2008. Same-sex marriage and the coming antidiscrimination campaigns against religion. In *Same-sex marriage: Emerging conflicts*, ed. Douglas Laycock, Anthony R. Picarello Jr., and Robin Fretwell Wilson. Lanham: The Becket Fund for Religious Liberty/Rowman & Littlefield.

Koppelman, A., and Tobias Barrington Wolff. 2009. *A right to discriminate? How the case of Boy Scouts of America v. James Dale warped the law of free association*. New Haven/London: Yale University Press.

Romer v. Evans.1996. 517 U.S. 620, at 632, 633.

Rosenblum, N. 1998. *Membership and morals: The personal uses of pluralism in America*. Princeton: Princeton University Press.

Rust v. Sullivan. 1991. 500 U.S. 173, at 193.
Song, S. 2007. *Justice, gender, and the politics of multiculturalism*. New York: Cambridge University Press.
Spinner-Halev, J. 2011. A restrained view of transformation. *Political Theory* 39(6): 777–784.
Turley, J. 2008. An unholy union: Same-sex marriage and the use of government programs to penalize religious groups with unpopular practices. In *Same-sex marriage: Emerging conflicts*, ed. Douglas Laycock, Anthony R. Picarello Jr., and Robin Fretwell Wilson. Lanham: The Becket Fund for Religious Liberty/Rowman & Littlefield.

Chapter 3
Rights and the American Constitution: The Issue of Judicial Review and Its Compatibility with Democracy

Rex Martin

Abstract This chapter deals with American judicial interpretation of two key constitutional ideas—the idea of 'due process' and the idea that the Fourteenth Amendment selectively brings in or 'incorporates' many of the rights of the Bill of Rights and applies these rights as a standard for assessing the laws not only of the federal union but also of the various states in the USA. This sketch provides both a rationale for one line of development of American law in the twentieth and twenty-first centuries (to date) and a template for examining the role courts (in a number of countries as well as the EU) have taken, or might take, in identifying and protecting, through judicial review, important basic constitutional rights. The chapter turns (in its final section) to a discussion of judicial review and attempts to provide a principled resolution of the problematic that judicial review poses within a democratic system of rights.

3.1 The Original Constitution and the Bill of Rights

The animating principles of the original constitutional government of the United States were distinctive: separation of powers, checks and balances, federalism, a written constitution and bill of rights, republicanism.[1] But, interestingly, two important institutional features characteristic of American government today were missing from that initial constitution.

[1] For an interesting account, and interpretation, of American constitutional thinking in the revolutionary period (around 1776) up through the time the Constitution was written and then ratified (1787–1789), see Shapiro (2011), *Legality*, ch. 11; also pp. 366–368.

R. Martin (✉)
Department of Philosophy, University of Kansas, Lawrence, KS, 66045, USA
e-mail: rexm@ku.edu

A.E. Cudd and S.J. Scholz (eds.), *Philosophical Perspectives on Democracy in the 21st Century*, AMINTAPHIL: The Philosophical Foundations of Law and Justice 5,
DOI 10.1007/978-3-319-02312-0_3,

(i) The government contemplated there was not democratic, nor did it claim to be. By our contemporary standards, the original constitutional government failed to be democratic in two main particulars: there was no commitment to universal franchise (on a one person, one vote basis) and the principle of majority rule was not taken to be fundamental. And (ii) there was no notion of judicial review expressly stated in the Constitution (though it had been advocated in the *Federalist Papers*, a series of essays published in 1787–1788 in New York newspapers arguing in favor of ratification of the Constitution; see here essay 78). This particular institution (which involves the power of courts to declare laws passed by Congress—or by a state—to be unconstitutional and therefore void) was added by a Supreme Court ruling in 1803 (in *Marbury v. Madison*, 1 Cranch 137).

I'll return to these two novel principles and institutions, democratic rule and judicial review, as the discussion progresses. And in Sect. 3.5 of the present chapter I will take up the issue of their compatibility.

3.2 The Bill of Rights and Basic Rights

The principal American constitutional rights are the right of habeas corpus (found in the body of the Constitution), the rights of the Bill of Rights in Amendments 1–10 (ratified 1791), and the right to vote (as secured in Article I and modified by subsequent amendments). These rights cannot be regarded as constitutional (or basic) simply because they are part of the written Constitution (for some of the rights mentioned there are not regarded as basic today). In short, we cannot say that the rights of the Bill of Rights, for example, are basic *because* they are incorporated in the written Constitution; instead, we should say that they ought to be and have been incorporated because of the inherent importance they have. They cannot have *this* importance, the requisite importance, simply by being incorporated into the written Constitution. To put the same point differently, one might believe as an act of constitutional piety that the rights of the Bill of Rights have importance simply in virtue of their being *in* the Constitution; but one could not explain or justify their being there in the first place, for that reason.

What I have in mind with basic rights, sometimes called fundamental civil or constitutional rights, then, is something like this. They are, paradigmatically, those civil rights (such as freedom of political speech or liberty of conscience) that have passed the double test of being enacted by legislative majorities and of being affirmed and, then, supported over the years by the checking devices (such as judicial review). And they are rights that have survived the scrutiny of time and experience and public discussion; they have been winnowed by the self-correcting character of the democratic process, and now continue to enjoy a very high level of social consensus.

Nonetheless, *most* of the basic rights I referred to earlier—the right of habeas corpus, the rights in the Bill of Rights, the right to vote—would count as basic constitutional rights, given the crucial tests of constitutional basicness just outlined. But others probably would as well (for example, the right to an education).

The Bill of Rights is one of the great rights documents of the eighteenth century. It is, indeed, one of the two most important public and authoritative manifestos of rights produced by Americans in that century, the other being the famous prefatory paragraphs (followed by the catalogue of grievances) in the Declaration of Independence. But the historical importance of the Bill of Rights is not confined to its century of origin or to the incidental fact of its present great age. Rather, two other significant historical events (one in the nineteenth century and one in the twentieth) have helped change the status of the Bill of Rights and radically transformed its character.

3.3 The Fourteenth Amendment

Let me describe these two transforming events briefly. In a very early decision (in *Barron v. Baltimore* 1833, 32 U.S. [7 Pet.] 243) the Supreme Court had ruled that the Bill of Rights amendments did not bind the *states* but only the federal government. However, the Court in the century following that began to 'incorporate' certain of the Bill of Rights protections into the Fourteenth Amendment (1868), as holding against the states too.

The Fourteenth Amendment, then, is the first of the two transforming events I spoke of earlier. It is the one that belongs to the nineteenth century; it came *after* the decision of 1833 and substantially changed the picture. And the 'incorporation' of parts of the Bill of Rights into the Fourteenth Amendment as a standard governing *state* laws, an event of the twentieth century (and continuing in our own), is the second of the important transforming events.

Let us look at these two events in greater detail, starting with the Fourteenth Amendment. That amendment is one of three passed by Congress and ratified by the states in the period during or immediately after the American Civil War (1861–1865). These three amendments radically changed the American constitution, so much so that the period after the war—the so-called period of Reconstruction—is sometimes called the Second American Revolution.

The first of these amendments, the Thirteenth (1865), abolished slavery, an institution that had been recognized and protected in the original Constitution of 1787 and that had led to continual sectional strife from that time on, culminating in the bloody Civil War itself. The Fourteenth (1868) was complex; it had several sections. The first and most important section, I will describe in detail in just a moment. Finally, the Fifteenth Amendment (1870) enfranchised the freed blacks by saying that states could not disallow people from voting on such grounds as their "race, color, or previous condition of servitude."

The various provisions of section one of the Fourteenth Amendment lie at the heart of the matter. The section begins with a definition of citizenship (both state and U. S. citizenship) and says, next, that no *state* shall by law "abridge the privileges or immunities of citizens of the United States." Following that came two other important clauses (as these are often called): the 'due process' clause and the 'equal protection of the laws' clause.

There is much debate about what these clauses meant ('privileges and immunities,' etc.), but three things do seem reasonably clear here. The authors of the Amendment are trying to state long-standing American (indeed, human) political values, values that can be traced back in U.S. history at least to the Declaration. The authors are trying to address the problem of the civil status of the freed blacks by making them citizens on a par with other citizens. And, finally, the authors were consciously laying the groundwork for certain *national* standards, standards that would hold throughout the country and that would shape or help shape state as well as federal laws.[2]

3.4 The Fourteenth Amendment: The Incorporation Thesis

We move now to the twentieth century and to the second main transforming event in the history of the Bill of Rights: to the incorporation thesis. This story can be told quickly enough, in its main details.

In a number of twentieth-century cases, most notably in Justice Hugo Black's dissent in the *Adamson* decision, a dissent joined by Justice William Douglas, various 'incorporationist' theses were advanced. But at no time did the Court say *explicitly* and officially (in a majority opinion) that *all* of the rights in the Bill of Rights (specifically those in amendments 1 through 8) have been incorporated into the Fourteenth Amendment as holding against the states. Nor has the Court ever agreed with Black that it was the intent of the original authors of the fourteenth amendment to effect such a wholesale incorporation.[3]

Rather, the Court's incorporation has been piecemeal, selective. Clearly, the rights of amendments 1, 2, 4, 5 (except for the grand jury provision there), 6, and 8 have all been incorporated at present. It is not clear, however, whether those rights in amendments 3 and 7 are to be considered incorporated. To this date they have not been. Piecemeal, then, the Bill of Rights came to apply to the content of state laws—not all the Bill of Rights, but most of it. This is the first step in the story of the historical transformation of the Bill of Rights mainly in the century previous to our own.

---

[2] In a brief summary at the end of his article, "Does the Fourteenth Amendment Incorporate the Bill of Rights?" Charles Fairman (1949) says, "[Congress] undoubtedly purposed [in the various clauses of the amendment's first section] to establish a federal standard below which state action must not fall."

[3] See the dissent of Justice Hugo Black in *Adamson v. California* (1947). The historical accuracy of Black's contentions has been widely challenged. The account of incorporation developed in the present chapter emphasizes, contrary to Black, the idea of selective or piecemeal incorporation and does not require the claim that the authors of the Fourteenth Amendment intended incorporation but, rather, only the weaker claim that they contemplated *some* incorporation as within the scope of section 1 of that Amendment.

Then, second, there has been interpretation of the Bill of Rights itself. One such interpretation led to establishing privacy as a fundamental constitutional right. In the *Griswold* decision (1965, 381 U.S. 479) Justice William Douglas (delivering the decision of the Court) said that privacy, while not an express feature of the Bill of Rights, comes along, inevitably, as part of the Bill of Rights package. He reasoned as follows: the right of association, while not mentioned by name in the First Amendment, has been recognized by the Court as a right guaranteed under that amendment (for, without it, the express rights mentioned there would be incompletely specified or inadequately supported). Likewise and by analogy, the right of privacy lies alongside the rights of *several* Bill of Rights Amendments (not merely the First but also the Fourth and Fifth and perhaps others as well, as selectively incorporated). It is a sort of background right that holds if the explicit rights, recognized in the Bill of Rights, themselves hold. Or, to use Douglas' metaphors, the right of privacy is in the 'penumbra' of the Bill of Rights; it is an 'emanation' from the Bill of Rights.

Not all the judges agreed with Douglas' reasoning, but a majority of them did think there was a constitutional right of privacy and that it governed the case they were considering. Moreover, since Douglas was writing the Court's opinion (the majority opinion) we can say that a majority concurred in this particular use of the incorporation thesis.

Clearly, we have only a partially specified right at this point (given the details of Douglas' opinion): we know merely what the right of privacy means, what it covers, in the precise sort of case the Court had in mind in *Griswold*. We know that, but not much else. It is through further specification of details, and elaboration of reasons, in subsequent cases that we come to know the specific content of the constitutional right of privacy—as regards such matters as its conditions of possession and its content and scope and its competitive weight in relation to other constitutional rights.

One very controversial decision, and perhaps the most important to date in the elaboration of the privacy doctrine, is *Roe v. Wade* (1973, 410 U.S. 113). Here the right of privacy is extended to cover the right of a woman (whether married or unmarried) to make the decision to terminate her pregnancy (a decision that was incontestably hers to make, in consultation with her doctor, in the first trimester). Thus, the right of privacy here determined a right of abortion on the part of the pregnant woman; the right of abortion, as a specification of the constitutional right of privacy, itself becomes, then, a constitutional right, a right against which no state interest in fact arises (at least in the first trimester).

Justice Harry Blackmun, who wrote the decision for the Court in *Roe*, did not rely on the idea of an intimate union or of a peculiarly private place (as had Douglas in *Griswold*). Rather, his stress was on the intimacy of the decision to abort and on the personal autonomy of a woman to make such a decision (in a medical context). The essentially personal or self-regarding character of the woman's decision was emphasized in subsequent Court cases, where it was made clear that the consent of the woman's husband or of the biological father was not required, under the privacy doctrine, for abortions.

In sum, three things happened in the twentieth century that, together, radically transformed the constitutional status and character of the Bill of Rights. First, there was a piecemeal, selective incorporation into the Fourteenth Amendment of certain rights of the Bill of Rights as themselves, then, holding as protections for individual persons against *state* as well as against federal laws. Second, there was an ongoing interpretation of the incorporated rights of the Bill of Rights. This has on occasion meant the generation of new, often unspecified rights, out of these incorporated rights; thus, we encounter here novel rights not mentioned in the Bill of Rights explicitly—such as the rights of association, expression, conscience (from the First Amendment) and privacy (from the First and Fourth and other amendments as well). Then, finally, there has been the judicial shaping of these relatively unspecified or only partially specified rights into various determinate specifications—as, for example, the right of privacy has been specified to include or cover not only a right to abortion but also, to cite another well-known example, a right to remove a life support system (as in the *Quinlan*, 1976, and *Cruzan*, 1990, cases).

What happened, in short, in this tying together of the Bill of Rights with the Fourteenth Amendment is that the constitutional status of the Bill of Rights has changed. For these rights, as selectively linked with—incorporated into—the Fourteenth Amendment, now govern state as well as federal law. And the list of rights, along with the content of individual rights, has itself changed in the process. Thus, the Bill of Rights was radically transformed in character by the court decisions of the twentieth century.

This is, clearly, an important historical development. But it is not the only important one worth noting. The famous rights of the U. S. Bill of Rights (and the same is true of the right to vote enunciated in effect in Article I) were at the time of their adoption merely a 'form' of civil rights; they were not civil rights pure and simple. I say this because, though they were nominally rights of all citizens/of all persons, they were not really universal within the body politic. Consider here the permanent exclusion, from the right to vote, of women (and of slaves) at that time. And the rights of the Bill of Rights in the original understanding of the Constitution (before 1868), though universal in description, are rights of all persons (excepting slaves) *only under federal law*. Thus, they are, given those qualifications, not legal or civil rights of literally all persons, in all cases.

The really significant transformation of the Bill of Rights (through its linkage with the Fourteenth Amendment) has been the making of these rights into true civil rights (that is, into established ways of acting or of being treated that hold across the board for literally all citizens—or literally all persons—within the American body politic). This is the significant change that the previous century has effected in the ongoing history of the Bill of Rights. And it is *this* transformation that has chiefly made the Bill of Rights into something of more than merely historical significance.

One other change (suggested in Sect. 3.1) is worth mentioning here: the increasing democratization, beginning late in the nineteenth and continuing over into the early twentieth century, of American political institutions. And, along with that, the emergence of a democratic ideology emphasizing majority rule and the significance of a broad-based electorate with important voting powers. This ideology has virtually supplanted the republicanism of the founders. I would argue that this trend toward democracy is fully compatible with and, indeed, has proven instrumental to the developments I have sketched in the present section (developments culminating in the constitutional embodiment and working out of the incorporation thesis and the transforming effect this has had on the Bill of Rights).

The U.S. today seems committed to two political values beyond all others: to basic constitutional rights, understood as both truly national and politically universal, and to democratic institutions, including majority rule. And, beyond that, there has been a growing commitment simply to the idea of democracy itself.

3.5 The Issue of Judicial Review

3.5.1 Two Questions

Two main questions have been raised, historically, about the two 'novel' institutions in the American constitutional picture, as sketched in Sect. 3.1. I mean (a) the institutions or main practices of political democracy (universal franchise on a one person/one vote basis, regular and contested voting on a continuing basis at both the electoral and the legislative level, and majority rule) and (b) the institution of judicial review.

The first question is whether majoritarian democracy is compatible with the notion of basic constitutional rights. Besides the simple fact that these rights are *in* the Constitution on a majoritarian basis in the first place (and are rendered basic by, among other things, that fact and the fact of a continuing high level of consensual support), one could construct philosophical arguments favoring their compatibility.

One could argue, for example, that democratically derived policies can be expected to be beneficial to a whole lot of people, ranging from everybody to a substantial number. More precisely, one could argue that the decision procedures associated with democratic practices are a stable and reliable way of identifying, and then implementing, laws and policies that serve interests common to the voters or to a large number of them, presumably at least a majority.

On reflection, though, we see that this answer is deeply ambiguous. In order to remove this ambiguity, one might attempt to identify certain standard cases and to assign priorities among these cases. I think a reasonable list of priorities among such cases might be established by starting from the most widespread set of benefits and then moving from there to cases that afforded less general benefits. Such a list might take the following form. (i) We begin by identifying a standard case in which democratic policies were in the interests of each and all, and thus were policies that benefited everyone (and here would be included policies that are characteristically found in basic civil and constitutional rights).[4] Next we go to (ii) a standard case where policies and laws are concerned with things that are in the corporate or collective interests of the group of which each is a member (though not necessarily in the interests of each person there); in this case such matters as national defense or the growth of gross domestic product (GDP) would be found. Finally, we'd go a third and very common standard case, to (iii) those policies and laws that are in the interests of indeterminately many (presumably a majority) though not in the interests of some others (presumably a minority).

We would not want to eliminate any of these options from the list altogether. But to stick with all of them in a completely unstructured way, taking them pell mell, would prove unworkable and inconsistent. Consider. Policies under the third option might violate basic rights or, alternatively, might actually harm the corporate or collective interests of the group of which each is a member. This would run counter to the priorities already established. So we add a proviso (call it iiia) that the policies therein specified did not violate basic rights or harm the wellbeing of the corporate whole.

So conceived the third option is now compatible with serving interests under the first two categories, compatible, that is, with (i) the interest of each and all and with (ii) the good of the corporate or collective interests of the group of which each is a member. It follows too, on this account, that some policies—(iiib) policies that help or hurt interests in a way that is incompatible with the priorities outlined in the first two options—would be ranked last and ruled out as impermissible.[5]

Justified majority rule then would include this particular profile of priorities. Thus, the idea of the priority of basic rights belongs (or so I have argued) to the very justification for having and relying on democratic institutions in the first place.[6]

The second main question is whether majoritarian democracy is compatible with judicial review. This question, a long-standing one, dominated the jurisprudential literature of much of the twentieth century (and is still a live topic today). On the one hand, the British long ago decided that judicial review (in the American sense)

---

[4] The Fifteenth Amendment (1870), as has already been noted, requires in effect that adult black male citizens have the right to vote on the same basis as those citizens already entitled to vote. The Nineteenth Amendment (1920) in effect requires that adult female citizens have the same right to vote as do all other adult citizens. The net effect of these amendments, taken together, is for all adult citizens to have, without discrimination, the same right to vote. In this respect these amendments, though they explicitly single out distinct groups, contribute to the universalizing character or tendency that I have attributed to civil and constitutional rights, when such rights are understood as in some significant sense the rights in law of each and all citizens (or persons).

[5] On this new understanding (as given in iiia), the third option could allow for legislative coalitions involving diverse interests and thus allow for logrolling and so-called pork barrel politics, so long as the result of so allowing did not devolve into iiib. For further discussion, see my book *System of Rights* (1993a), pp. 163–164.

[6] In *A System of Rights*, I develop the idea of a democratic system of rights. For the main argument on the point at issue, see chs. 5–7 (as summarized at pp. 127–128 and 166–169) and ch. 12. And, for a convenient summary of the main argument I was making in this book, see the short paper (1993b) "Basic Rights," *Rechtstheorie* Beiheft,191–201—and see sect. 2 of that paper for the particular point under discussion here.

was not compatible; it permitted democratically based legislation to be set aside and nullified by a non-elected, unrepresentative body. American-style judicial review could not align with the idea (with the supposed fact) that Parliament had a democratic electoral basis; judicial review (so conceived) did not allow for and could not fully support the very thing which underlies the authority and validity of parliamentary legislation and serves to legitimize the sovereignty of Parliament to begin with.[7] On the other hand, countries that call themselves democratic have continued to retain judicial review (as has the U.S.) or to have added it as a permanent (e.g., Canada) or at least as a sometime institution (e.g., Australia) in their constitutional apparatus. And, again, one could construct philosophical arguments favoring the fundamental compatibility of judicial review and majoritarian democracy (on a universal franchise, one person/one vote basis).[8]

3.5.2 Institutional and Philosophical Issues

The analysis sketched out in Sect. 3.5.1 suggests that, in the view of many, there is no *necessary* tension between democracy and civil/constitutional rights or between democracy and judicial review. This preliminary conclusion, however, does not mean that there is nothing at stake in the debate over the justification of judicial review. Rather, I'd suggest that there is more than one aspect to the debate.

---

[7] A number of writers with British or Commonwealth backgrounds have addressed the issue of judicial review with respect to its compatibility with the sovereignty of Parliament (and with democratic institutions). Probably the most prominent critic of American-style judicial review, in this regard, is Jeremy Waldron (1999) in *Law and Disagreement.* See as well Tom Campbell (2006), *Rights: A Critical Introduction*, ch. 5, also ch. 11.

In 1998, the British Parliament passed the Human Rights Act which incorporated, in whole or part, most of the rights of the European Convention on Human Rights (of 1950) into British domestic law. The British people now had an up-to-date written list of important rights as part of British law. The basic ground rule was that the courts could issue statements of incompatibility between a given parliamentary statute and the rights of the Human Rights Act; Parliament is not required to respond to these statements and the courts cannot unilaterally annul the offending statute. So, the British do *not* have American-style judicial review but they do have a canonical list of fundamental rights. In short, they've entered a gray area (an area that requires management and negotiation) as regards the compatibility issues raised in the present chapter. For discussion, see Raymond Plant (2005), "Social Justice, Rights and Social Democracy," and Tom Campbell (2001), "Incorporation through Interpretation," pp. 79–101 in *Sceptical Essays on Human Rights.* This volume, edited by Tom Campbell, et al., includes a number of essays on the 1998 U.K. Human Rights Act, as well as a set of essays (by various authors) on judicial review in Europe and throughout the world.

[8] For a deft summary of the central argument here, respecting the compatibility of judicial review with majoritarian democracy, see Stephen M. Griffin (2002), "Judicial Supremacy and Equal Protection in a Democracy of Rights," pp. 296–301. Additional arguments in favor of the basic compatibility of judicial review with democracy are made by Samuel Freeman (1990/1991, 1992) in several of his papers—for example, in "Constitutional Democracy and the Legitimacy of Judicial Review," and in "Original Meaning, Democratic Interpretation, and the Constitution."

(i) If the question is one of *justifying* judicial review in the abstract, such issues are best analyzed through ideal normative theories such as that of a democratic system of rights. Let me spell this point out a bit more fully. If one justifies democratic rule in the way recommended (as developed in the previous subsection, before note 6), one shows and then builds on the fundamental coherence of democratic institutions with civil and constitutional rights. Democratic institutions will *tend* to produce civil rights laws (among other things) and will not supersede or significantly impair civil or constitutional rights. In justifying democratic decision making in this way, one has in effect rejected *unrestricted* majority rule as itself unjustifiable—because allowing sway to such rule could go, at given points, against any of the various priorities already established. And institutions and practices may allowably be installed to prevent unrestricted majority rule and to help keep democratic institutions true to what justifies them. Accordingly, institutional design could plausibly include certain checking devices (such as judicial review or executive veto) among the democratic practices. These checks are not 'external' to democratic ideals or in any way antidemocratic. They are, rather, to be numbered among the fundamental democratic institutions.

(ii) But if the question posed by the exercise of power by the U.S. Supreme Court is one of *practical* political justification, then a more fine-grained, institutional analysis is required. Let us shift our focus, then, to this latter question and concern ourselves with the justification of the specific *institutional embodiment* of the power of judicial review in the U.S. Supreme Court. We might do well to begin here by noting that there are other ways of specifying an institutional embodiment of that power; the American way is only one of them.

Historical experience with judicial review in the U.S., Canada, Europe, India, Australia, and Japan suggests, indeed, the relevance of several important institutional issues. How is the court to be selected? What term of office should the justices hold and how can they be removed from office? Is the court part of a larger national judicial system enabling it to hear ordinary cases of law, or should it be a special constitutional tribunal? Are the constitutional rights provisions the court is to enforce written broadly or narrowly? How does the court make its decisions known? What is the court's conception of its own role in terms of being relatively active or passive in defense of constitutional rights and other basic standards? The questions raised by these issues are important because in answering them we specify and embody the power of the court relative to other government institutions.

For example, justices of the U.S. Supreme Court have life tenure, sit at the head of a national judicial system that can follow out their decisions; they hear ordinary legal claims as well as constitutional claims, interpret a document that has many ambiguous clauses (for example, as in section one of the Fourteenth Amendment), and have had an active conception of their role in the post-World War Two period. All of these institutional elements, especially life tenure and the sometimes ambiguous language of the U.S. Constitution, serve to increase the power of the Court.

It is noteworthy that the other countries that have established judicial review since World War Two have chosen a different institutional embodiment of that power. First, the American commitment to life tenure for justices has been rejected in favor of nonrenewable terms that vary between 9 and 12 years and of mandatory retirement ages. Second, a feature common to American courts (at the appellate and higher levels) is signed opinions and the issuing, in particular, of dissenting opinions or other separate opinions; but these things are not typically found elsewhere (Greenhouse 2012, A17). Third, in light of the unfortunate American experience in the era of the *Lochner* decision (1905, 198 U.S. 45), use of the phrase "due process of law" and hence the doctrine of substantive due process have been avoided. The drafters of the Constitution of India received advice from Justice Felix Frankfurter on this very point. And, for another example, the definitive lists of rights in post-World War Two democratic constitutions have generally been more lengthy and precise than is true of the American Bill of Rights.

These points suggest that a justification for judicial review, as it exists in the U.S., must go beyond ideal normative theory and must, as well, specifically address and attempt to justify the particular institutional details that create the impressive power (and partisan divisiveness) of the U. S. Supreme Court. Admittedly, it may prove difficult for Americans to accomplish fundamental change at the point of mandatory retirement, given the explicit language of the U.S. Constitution, but incentives for federal judges and U.S. Supreme Court justices to take on inactive status at age 70, say, coupled with a practice of judges actually taking such 'early' retirement may yield something like the effect desired.

But the issues surrounding the ambiguous and highly interpretable language of the U.S. Constitution, as revealed in the light of both American judicial history and the experience of other countries, may call for more heroic measures. Or, to make roughly the same point, the justification of judicial review even in an ideal setting, as afforded by the account of its place in a democratic system of rights referred to earlier, would require of the *practice* of judicial review certain conceptual modifications or institutional limitations that have not hitherto existed in American historical experience or judicial thought. Specifically, judicial review, when justified within a democratic system of rights, should be presumed to serve one or both of two main purposes: (i) to improve the democratic process in accordance with values inherent in the democratic institutions themselves, (ii) to formulate (or reformulate), preserve, and harmonize basic rights. Judicial review may be presumed to serve other aims as well but never at cost to these primary aims.

A number of theorists and judges have responded to the problem of the ambiguous language and the over-generality of the U.S. Constitution by arguing that the Supreme Court should apply highly interpretable phrases (such as the 'equal protection' or 'due process' clauses of the Fourteenth Amendment) only when, by so doing, they would advance basic rights or improve the democratic process. Justice Harlan Stone propounded such a theory of interpretation for the Court in the famous footnote four of *Carolene Products* (1938, 304 U.S. 144, at 152–153 n. 4).[9]

[9] For a more recent expression of a similar view, see John Hart Ely (1980), *Democracy and Distrust: A Theory of Judicial Review*.

Such restrictive theories of judicial review can be seen as a reasonable response to the difficulty of interpreting the Constitution's ambiguous or open-ended provisions (including those in the Fourteenth Amendment). Probably the most practical way to reconcile the sometimes questionable exercise of the power of judicial review by the Supreme Court with the ideal of a democratic system of rights is for U.S. courts to incorporate within that system, as one of their contributions to its institutional details, certain principles of self-limitation on their own adjudicative activity. For instance, an important example of such self-limitation can be found in the period 1937–1941 (beginning with *West Coast Hotel v. Parrish* 1937, 300 U.S. 379), when the Court repudiated use of the due process clause—found in Amendments 5 and 14 of the U. S. Constitution—and other constitutional standards as grounds for judicial decisions striking down state and federal legislation in the 'economic' area. This repudiation was reaffirmed in *Carolene Products* and strongly so in a series of decisions in 1941. The Court has resolutely stayed with this repudiation, with but few exceptions (all of them by justices in the minority), since then. Its view has been that economic regulation is primarily the province of Congress, not the Court.[10]

In this section of the present chapter, and following Stephen Griffin, I have distinguished questions of ideal normative theory from questions of specific institutional embodiment, and suggested that many of the real, live issues concerning judicial review arise at the latter point. Indeed, when analysis is carried out at that point, it becomes apparent that American judicial review is indeed a controversial institution from the standpoint of democratic theory. And institutional reforms (such as all-but-mandatory retirement ages for justices and limitations, including self-limitations, on the Court's practice of judicial review) may be needed in order to bring the Court into line with democratic principles.[11]

---

[10] Consider here another important matter. The passage by Congress of the Civil Rights Act of 1964 was probably the most significant piece of civil rights legislation passed in the twentieth century. Congress has the power under section 5 of the Fourteenth Amendment "to enforce, by appropriate legislation, the provisions of this [Amendment]." But Congress, aware of an earlier nineteenth-century Court exercise of judicial review (concerning the issue of private discrimination limiting access to "public establishments" such as restaurants and hotels) and fearing the hold of precedent on the Court in the matter at hand, passed the public accommodations section of the 1964 Civil Rights Act, not merely under the authority of that amendment but, rather, principally under the Article I plenary power of Congress to regulate interstate commerce. And the 1964 Act was upheld on that basis.

The self-limitation I've been describing appears to be receding. In June 2012 the Supreme Court in *National Federation of Independent Business, et al. v. Sebelius* upheld the constitutionality (as a tax) of the 'individual mandate' in the Affordable Care Act (passed by Congress under President Obama's sponsorship in 2010); but, to all appearances, the Court by a 5–4 vote denied that such a mandate could be upheld under the Commerce Clause.

[11] Section 3.5.2 is drawn, with revisions, from two sections of my paper on "Constitutional Rights and Democracy in the U.S.A.: the Issue of Judicial Review," with Stephen M. Griffin (1995) (co-author). In the writing of the present chapter I have drawn on the *Ratio Juris* paper and as well on two other of my papers (1994, 2003).

References

Adamson v. California. 1947. 322 U.S. 46, at 68–123.

Barron v. Baltimore. 1833. 32 U.S. [7 Pet.] 243.

Campbell, T. 2001. Incorporation through interpretation. In *Sceptical essays on human rights*, ed. Tom Campbell, K.D. Ewing, and Adam Tomkins, 79–101. Oxford: Oxford University Press.

Campbell, T. 2006. *Rights: A critical introduction*. London/New York: Routledge.

Ely, J.H. 1980. *Democracy and distrust: A theory of judicial review*. Cambridge, MA: Harvard University Press.

Fairman, C. 1949. Does the fourteenth amendment incorporate the Bill of Rights? *Stanford Law Review* 2: 5–139.

Freeman, S. 1990/1991. Constitutional democracy and the legitimacy of judicial review. *Law and Philosophy* 9: 327–379.

Freeman, S. 1992. Original meaning, democratic interpretation, and the constitution. *Philosophy and Public Affairs* 21: 3–42.

Greenhouse, L. 2012. Op-ed. *The New York Times*, April 24.

Griffin, S.M. 2002. Judicial supremacy and equal protection in a democracy of rights. *University of Pennsylvania Journal of Constitutional Law* 4(2): 281–313.

Griffin, S.M., and Rex Martin. 1995. Constitutional rights and democracy in the U.S.A.: The issue of judicial review. *Ratio Juris* 8(2): 180–198.

Griswold v. Connecticut. 1965. 381 U.S. 479.

Lochner v. New York. 1905. 198 U.S. 45.

Martin, R. 1993a. *System of rights*. Oxford: Clarendon Press.

Martin, R. 1993b. Basic rights. *Rechtstheorie Beiheft* 15: 191–201.

Martin, R. 1994. Civil rights and the U. S. Constitution. In *The Bill of Rights: A bicentennial assessment*, ed. Gary C. Bryner and A. Don Sorenson. Albany: State University of New York Press.

Martin, R. 2003. Rights and human rights. In *Multiculturalism, identity and rights*, ed. Bruce Haddock and Peter Sutch, 175–194. London: Routledge.

Plant, R. 2005. Social justice, rights and social democracy. In *Social justice: Building a fairer Britain*, ed. Nick Pearce and Will Paxton, 199–218. London: Politicos.

Roe v. Wade. 1973. 410 U.S. 113.

Shapiro, S. 2011. *Legality*. Cambridge, MA: Harvard University Press.

United States v. Carolene Products. 1938. 304 U.S. 144.

Waldron, J. 1999. *Law and disagreement*. Oxford: Oxford University Press.

West Coast Hotel v. Parrish. 1937. 300 U.S. 379.

Chapter 4
Democracy as a Social Myth

Richard T. De George

Abstract Liberal democracy is not the only kind of democracy, and it itself has variations. This chapter attempts to look at the broad variety of uses of 'democracy,' and tries to make sense of the present state of discussion of democracy and the broad range of topics it encompasses. The approach that best captures the variety, that allows a variant to have continuity over time, and that highlights its function in society is Lévi-Strauss's sense of a social myth. The approach as developed herein could help scholarship as well as foreign policy and offset cultural imperialism and artificially closed paradigms.

4.1 Introduction

In 1917, speaking to a joint session of Congress President Wilson gave his famous speech in which he asked Congress to declare war against Germany to make the world "safe for democracy".[1] Two weeks later Congress declared war. The Second World War was similarly seen as a war for democracy. Yet Roosevelt and Churchill[2]

[1] The speech continued and Wilson enlarged his notion of democracy: "...we shall fight for the things which we have always carried nearest our hearts, for democracy, for the right of those who submit to authority to have a voice in their own governments, for the rights and liberties of small nations, for a universal dominion of right by such a concert of free peoples as shall bring peace and safety to all nations and make the world itself at last free." (Wilson 1917).

[2] Churchill said famously (in the House of Commons and in *Churchill by Himself*), referencing some unknown source, "Many forms of Government have been tried, and will be tried in this world of sin and woe. No one pretends that democracy is perfect or all-wise. Indeed it has been said that democracy is the worst form of Government except for all those other forms that have been tried from time to time..." (Langworth 2009).

R.T. De George (✉)
Department of Philosophy, University of Kansas,
1445 Jayhawk Blvd Rm 3090, 66045 Lawrence, KS, USA
e-mail: degeorge@ku.edu

A.E. Cudd and S.J. Scholz (eds.), *Philosophical Perspectives on Democracy in the 21st Century*, AMINTAPHIL: The Philosophical Foundations of Law and Justice 5,
DOI 10.1007/978-3-319-02312-0_4, © Springer International Publishing Switzerland 2014

did not have in mind making the world safe for the likes of the German Democratic Republic (aka East Germany) but for the likes of the Federal Republic of Germany (West Germany). In 1949 China was renamed the People's Republic of China, while Taiwan became the Republic of China. Had the word 'democratic' been hijacked by Stalin and Mao, who were clearly totalitarian? Or are the credentials of their communitarian view of democracy as valid as those of the liberal individualistic view?

Communist regimes trace their views back not to Mill but to Marx. Marx saw democracy as a stepping-stone to human liberation under communism, in which the people actually rule themselves. Marx saw what we call liberal democracy as a sham in which the people are allowed every 4 years to choose their leaders from two parties, both of which represent the interests of the capitalist elite. For him, all government is oppressive. The aim of the true liberation of all goes beyond what he calls "the supposed rights of man" found in French and American constitutions. What is expressed there are the rights of "egoistic man, of man separated from other men and from community…" (Marx 1978)[3] His aim, as is the aim of many who defend democracy, is liberty; but his conception of it is not the standard liberal democratic variety. Marx was also one of the sources of the ideology of the German Social Democrats in the Nineteenth Century, and his influence continues today in many European and other democratic parties. Individualistic liberal democracy is not the only democratic game viable on the international scene.

In today's world even most tyrants claim the mantle of democracy, and the people in countries emerging from dictatorial control are frequently given the right to vote, even if only once, when they choose their new leaders. Tyrants as well as liberal leaders claim to speak and govern for their people. Democracy has come to be a global honorific. Democracy is paid lip service by almost all, although what it means varies greatly.

Although some may wish democracy to be identified with liberal democracy, and act as if that wish reflected reality, they have no control over how the term is used or what its true meaning is, as if that could somehow be authoritatively determined or decided. The essence of democracy is variously described, and in every case the description is remarkably vague and fluid. What are we to do with all these descriptions?

Rather than argue for a particular version of democracy or against some versions of democracy as illegitimate, I will suggest that a broad perspective, which includes all variations of and approaches to democracy, is a useful antidote to parochialism and can help inform public policy. I suggest that we take our cue from the anthropologist Claude Lévi-Strauss (1955). What he found in his pioneering work of cross-cultural comparisons was that all societies have their own historical narratives, in which they express the values of the society, justify its existence, make sense of its practices, and help guide its development toward an ideal. The narratives in ancient societies and in some more primitive contemporary

---

[3] The passage continues, "thus man was not liberated from religion; he received religious liberty. He was not liberated from property; he received the liberty to own property. He was not liberated from the egoism of business; he received the liberty to engage in business."

societies are composed of what we call myths. They are stories with many variations, all of which make up the myth. Within the overarching myth, there are many sub-narratives. Lévi-Strauss argued that contemporary societies similarly have narratives that carry out the same functions. In this sense they can also with justification be called social myths. Contemporary political and social narratives, just as ancient myths, in part reveal reality to those who hold them, and in part cover over portions of reality. To take democracy as a social myth in Lévi-Strauss's sense forces us to put it in historical context. We then can see democracy as part of a narrative stretching back to Ancient Greece, as well as focus on particular parts of its global development, e.g., the narrative of the development of, for instance, democracy in the United States. In a democratic society there is a dominant narrative, which includes a host of variants. It is connected with a subset of concepts, each of which has its own set of narratives, in which and through which it is understood in its social context. Thus, historically, democracy is related to a number of other concepts: freedom, liberty, self-realization, self-determination, majority rule, human and civil (including minority) rights, consent of the governed, the rule of law, and so on. The cluster of concepts a society links to democracy determines in part the kind of democracy it is.

4.2 The Social Myth of Democracy

There are many varieties of democracy: communitarian democracy, individualistic democracy, social democracy, liberal democracy, conservative democracy, direct democracy, and so on. For purposes of analysis I shall identify four interrelated strands of the social myth of democracy. Each is a myth in its own right, and contains a cluster of subordinate myths, which make up the whole.

1. The first strand is the global strand. Both the term democracy and the notion of democracy are widely used as positives and are claimed to provide justification for a regime. The Chinese Government claims to be democratic not only in that it holds elections, but also in that it justifies all its actions as being done for the benefit of the people. Chavez in Venezuela held elections and claimed to be democratic, even though many outsiders saw him as autocratic and some questioned whether the elections were free in the liberal democratic sense. Nonetheless, the Chinese and Chavez and many others use the word democracy and rather than simply dismiss their use as inappropriate, counterfeit or something of the sort, the notion of a social myth asks us to account for its use in different contexts and see how it functions in those contexts. This strand does not consist of a single global social myth for all societies. It includes the great variety of national social myths. On this level we can make comparisons, see similarities and differences, and trace the influence of one society's version of democracy on that of other societies. We can also trace the rise of democracy historically and investigate, for instance, the relation of economic development to democracy in general and to particular types of democracy in particular.

Democracy as found in America (or American democracy) is different from the social democracy dominant in Europe; and the varieties of democracy that are developing or emerging in the Arab world are not the same as American democracy. Each has its own subset of narratives. Yet they all fit into the overarching narrative of the globalization of democracy and democratization, with emphasis on elections and governmental responsiveness to demands of the people.

Since it is a *social* myth, it should not be surprising that there are different variants for different societies. The remaining three strands are the popular, the political, and the academic.

2. The popular strand is the broadest of the three and is that held by the people of a society. It includes the story of democracy in social life—if it is found there—as well as in politics and government as found in the history of the country. The popular strand includes the use of the story and of its values in the popular press and by media pundits. In a democratic country comments that a policy of the government is undemocratic, or that the country is moving away from democracy have this notion of democracy as the accepted baseline that it is assumed needs no explicit justification and is widely held as a given. Such comments rarely mean that the political structures are illegal, but rather that some ideal is not being realized or is being lost. The popular strand includes ideals and hopes and possibilities; it involves and can pervade civil society as a whole, and not just political structures and political party oppositions and disputes. It is of course related to the third strand, which would be ineffective without acceptance of the story on this level.

3. The political strand refers to the particular democratic form of government in a society. It is the particular embodiment of the ideals and norms found in the popular strand expressed in governmental structures, laws, and rules. Embodiment always falls short of the ideal and reflects the local conditions, history, desires, and possibly opposing forces in a particular society. The popular strand makes possible and supplies the government with its legitimacy. The political strand operates within the confines of the established structure, often set by a constitution. Within that structure political parties argue for their views, courts render decisions, and the people hold their government legally accountable.

4. The academic strand includes the articles, books, and studies—both theoretical and empirical—on democracy as found in the other strands, but especially in the third strand, by historians, political scientists, philosophers, and other scholars. This strand is often critical of various elements of the contents of the other strands. It is rife with distinctions and suggestions for making political institutions more democratic or more just—the two often being equated. Some of the academic theorists and scholars of democracy may claim that it is a mistake to describe their work in such a way that it is a strand of the social myth of democracy, and that to do so disparages their work. On the contrary, to omit their work from the narrative would be to be to deny that their work has any influence on either practice or theory, and to imply that it is ineffectual in the development of democracy. Including their work acknowledges their importance, even though many of them would and do describe their work differently.

To say that the four strands are interrelated is to emphasize that they interact and each influences the others. In none of the strands do those who adhere to the content of the strand say they are holding a myth, since the term "myth" in most discourse stands for a falsehood.[4] And of course, taken in that sense they are correct. For as I have been using the term social myth it describes a group of practices, beliefs and/or values expressed in a narrative or story that both reveals and hides parts of reality, and that is compatible with internal contradictions in the story, inconsistencies, and so on. The academic strand takes it as one of its functions to point out these latter and to present arguments for preferred forms of democracy. But for the most part, although uncovering and emphasizing inconsistencies, contradictions, and failures may improve the political process, the results of this activity tend not to undermine the validity of the popular strand of democracy.

4.3 American Democracy as a Social Myth

I shall use American democracy as an example to describe the second, third and fourth strands. Many counterparts of each of them can be found in other societies.

To speak of American democracy is not to add to the list but to describe the democratic narrative found in the United States. Seeing American democracy as a social myth allows us to acknowledge that there is no iconic version of American democracy, and that it includes all its variants, while being part of the first strand. This, I suggest, helps us make better sense of the polarization of American politics than alternative approaches that argue for the correctness of a Democratic or Republican version of democracy or of a liberal or conservative version, which at their extremes brand the other version as "un-American" and "undemocratic." The polarization takes place primarily in the political strand, and while it affects the popular to some degree, the popular strand includes the divisions and debates as part of the larger umbrella of democracy, which its adherents cherish.

One mistake the American story avoids is equating American democracy exclusively with the U.S. form of government. The popular strand is arguably more basic and forms the foundation of the political strand.

In the popular sense of democracy that we find in the American narrative, Americans tend to think of their society on the whole as democratic. Although its ideals were stated in the *Declaration of Independence* and include the notion of independence from British rule, of self-determination, and of equality before the law, democracy was also about the openness and self-reliance required by the

[4] There are a few exceptions. For instance, Eric Black (1988), while contrasting historical accuracy with commonly held beliefs, sees the importance of the popular beliefs and consensus as giving the Constitution "the power to bind us" (p. xiii); and Jacob Needleman (2002), who, although he does not take the path of Lévi-Strauss, develops what he refers to as the "myth and meaning of America," which pays attention to the importance of symbols, meanings, feelings and ideals embodied in "the myth of America" (pp. 12–13).

frontier, about the end of aristocratic titles, and about the values associated with the possibility of social mobility, of limitless opportunities, of improving one's lot in life, and of providing a better future for one's children. Americans find democracy in the idea of offices open to all, as they do in the way they run their meetings, the way they organize civil society, the way they utilize voting and majority rule in many aspects of life. The democracy found in civil society provides the foundation for political democracy. American democracy in its popular strand flourished and continues to flourish on the level of civil society as a value that forms a whole with a cluster of other values, as well as an ideal and a work in progress. The American experience lends support to the more general belief that one cannot simply export a democratic form of government and expect it to flourish without the soil prepared by the popular strand.

The *Declaration of Independence* provided the justification for the American Revolution. It boldly declared that all men are created equal and are endowed with inalienable rights. They should therefore have the right to govern themselves or move from the status of a British colony to an independent state. The narrative was not seen the same way in Britain or Canada, where the colonists were simply rebels. Even that document, we know, was a compromise. Unmentioned and hidden behind the brave democratic language was the fact that in the Southern (and some Northern) colonies, slavery was legal and flourished. Slaves were not equal nor did they have inalienable rights. Nor were the rights of women equal to the rights of men. By today's standards, a country in which slavery was legal and women were denied equal rights would hardly be considered a democratic, much less a liberal democratic, society.

The first political instantiation of the ideals of the *Declaration of Independence* was in the individual states. The U.S. Constitution was the result of the political compromise necessary to form the states into a federation. The resulting structure reflects its historical origins. In modern times democracy on the political level is usually characterized by the election of the leaders of a country by popular vote in free elections, together with regular elections and certain guaranteed rights of all citizens. There is no list of agreed-upon necessary ingredients to make a government democratic,[5] and people often refer to a country as being "on the road to

[5] The Democracy Index (produced by the Economist Intelligence Unit) attempts to provide information on 165 countries to indicate how democratic the society is, measuring 60 indicators grouped in "five categories: electoral process and pluralism; civil liberties; the functioning of government; political participation; and political culture." Of 25 "full democracies", the UK ranks 18 and the U.S. 19, below Austria (13), Germany (14), Canada (8) and Norway (1). France (29), Italy (31), Greece (32), and Israel (36) are listed among 53 "flawed democracies." Then come 37 "hybrid regimes", and 52 "authoritarian regimes," which include Russia (117) and China (141) (Economist 2011). Yet the Index acknowledges that there is no consensus on how to define or measure democracy. Freedom House uses a somewhat different set of criteria and comes out with somewhat different ratings and rankings (Freedomhouse 2013). Both lists define and measure democracy according to liberal democratic criteria, although these are not the only standards that can be used or that are used. Neither list makes any claim that what they measure is either necessary or sufficient for democracy. They measure degrees of freedom in various areas, implying that democracy is equivalent to various kinds of free activity in a society.

democracy" when its people have toppled an authoritarian regime but have not yet established a stable alternative. When democracy has arrived is a rather vague notion.

Despite the vagaries of the instantiation of the political stand of democracy, Americans still cherish the *Declaration of Independence* as the cornerstone of American democracy together with the U.S. Constitution, which established a federalist type government. The Constitution sets the parameters in which the third strand developed and continues to develop. The Constitution reflects the fact that the United States is a union of states. To that extent it is very different from democratically formed governments that are not unions of states. The story of democracy in America typically ignores (but does not deny) that the Constitution explicitly counted slaves as three-fifths of a person for purposes of determining representation in Congress. This was changed only through the passage of the Thirteenth Amendment (1865), followed by the Fourteenth Amendment (1868, civil rights) and the Fifteenth Amendment (1870, which prohibits racial restrictions on voting). Despite these Amendments, women got the right to vote only gradually and it was not secured until 1920 by the Nineteenth Amendment. Civil rights for blacks and women were not made equal to those of white men until the Civil Right Act of 1964 and subsequent legislation.

How much freedom and how much equality of rights are necessary for a country to be democratic? The story of American democracy is silent on those questions, although underlying the notion is some ideal in terms of which changes and progress are made. The story both contains that and hides (or tends to ignore) the reality of the extent to which it falls short. Any full account of American democracy should be able to make sense of these facts. An historical perspective that includes all the variants can do that. Taking American democracy as a social myth allows one to explain the felt continuity of American democracy from its founding period until today, even though by today's criteria America's early period might not reach the level of freedom required to justify the use of the term to describe it. American democracy in the twenty-first century is different from what it was in the eighteenth century. The times are different. But as a story, there is continuity. We are not forced to say that the democracy in America in 1792 was not democracy because it is not so by our standards today. America was seen as a democracy not only in America but also in many other countries, and American democracy cherishes is roots in the *Declaration of Independence*, the Constitution,[6] and the Bill of Rights. Academic niceties, for example, about the political structure being that of a federal republic rather than of a democracy, have a legitimate place, but do not change the basic American popular democratic narrative.

To indicate the historical development of the narrative of American democracy is not to criticize it. The narrative is what it is; but it is complex and it has served and continues to serve an important function in America's perception of itself and in providing justification for American institutions.

---

[6] Concerning the Constitution, the popular strand emphasizes the Preamble, which asserts "We, the People of the United States…" as the founders of the government.

As a social myth the story of democracy is intertwined with the stories of a host of other concepts, as I mentioned earlier. The myth of self-determination is closely linked to that of democracy (De George 1991b). A people have the right to determine their own futures and their own form of government. It is linked with the myth of consent of the governed (De George 1991a). All three have a role to play in the American understanding and justification of the American Revolution and the framing of the U.S. Constitution. But the complex myth covers over, for instance, the story of Southern Secession, which is reframed. The Southern States were as American as the Northern. But the people of the South had different interests from those in the North, and finding life in the Union intolerable expressed their right of self-determination, democratic vote, and consent of the governed to form their own independent nation. The American story chronicles the War Between the States, in which the North, to preserve the Union, defeats the South. The story as told by the South differs. The story today finesses the difference. The American myth of democracy ignores the historical claims of the American South and selectively focuses abroad on the concepts of self-determination of the governed, for example, in the breakup of Yugoslavia into Slovenia, Croatia, Serbia, Bosnia, Montenegro, and Kosovo[7]; in the freeing of people from colonial rule, even though the national borders are a colonial imposition; and so on, but not in other cases.

Some people worry that contemporary historians' accounts of and emphasis on the blemishes in American history with respect to indigenous peoples, blacks, women, minority groups and so on is undercutting the traditional narrative and overshadowing its ideals and goals and its hope for constant improvement. So far that does not seem to have been the case, and the popular social myth seems resilient enough to absorb the negative emphasis. Yet a debate continues about how much of the core narrative should be taught in schools as opposed to emphasizing the past failures and by omission leaving the core untold, and how long the popular strand will continue without the story and its ideals being transmitted from generation to generation in the schools.

4.4 The Social Myth Approach to Democracy as a Useful Heuristic Device

Approaching democracy as a social myth suggests that one way of championing a specific version of democracy, for example, a certain account of liberal democracy, is to show that other accounts have less explanatory force in a given society, that they capture less of that society's reality, that they hide too much of what would negatively affect those who hold that view. Yet in doing so one must be aware that what is considered a negative for some people may be considered by them as something with which they can live, and it may possibly even be considered a positive for

[7] Kosovo has been recognized by over 90 nations, but Serbia still claims it is part of Serbia (BBC News 2012).

and/or by others. There may also be disagreements about what the social reality actually is, how one captures the will of the people, and so on, as the communist view of democracy as opposed to the liberal view shows. The strength of the mythic approach is that it allows enough free space for internal argument, development, scholarly research, and pundits' comments without casting opposing stories out of the overarching story. Narratives are continuing stories, and discussion, analysis, argument, and so on can produce change. A revolution, whether violent or peaceful, is a break in one narrative and the start of a new one in terms of which the revolution is justified. The impetus for the new narrative may well come from the example of other societies, from the writings of political theoreticians who describe and justify parts of the existing social reality previously unarticulated in the society, or from leaders who give voice to emerging ideals.

Another benefit is that a mythic analysis reminds us that democracy as instantiated does not exist, is not understood, and is not defended in isolation. The approach also reminds us that no set of concepts (or of concepts, rights and principles) has been shown to be the only viable, correct, best view, however those terms are understood. Historically we have seen the rise and fall of a large variety of mixes, and the enduring power of a number of them. The notion of faith in a system is a product of motivation and values, often irrespective of countervailing facts. This is not irrational. Adherence to a social myth helps guide the actions of those holding it, and is used in turn to justify those actions or the policies proposed and adopted. The notion of social myth captures this.

Considering the first or global strand of the social myth of democracy can inform the way one thinks about the Arab spring. If the analysis I have given is useful, then the United States should not simply foster democracy, no matter what kind. Nor will it do to export American democracy, as if either that is unambiguous or that it will fit all nations. Rather the U.S. would do well to decide what package of concepts, principles and rights it is championing in supporting and exporting democracy and realize it is attempting to replace one set of social myths with another. Whether free enterprise is part of the package is an open question. Are religious tolerance, the protection of the rights of the minority within the state, or periodic free elections necessary components of the package the U.S. wants to foster, despite the vagueness and ambiguity of these concepts? If so, part of the job of promoting those values and ideals is to see how they fit in with the already held values and ideals of the people in question. Can they be fit into the currently accepted or currently challenged myth, and can they succeed in replacing the current social myth by making sense of what perhaps has been too excessively covered over by the existing social myth? In its championing of democracy in other countries the U.S. is unclear about what it means by democracy or what it is really championing. Unless its approach shows appreciation of the social context it might appear that what it wants is not what is best for the people undergoing change but what is best for the interests of the United States, and the two often are not the same.

The device of seeing various strands to the story of democracy helps makes sense of speaking of an emergent democracy, of a developing democracy, and of democracy as an ideal towards which a society moves. Some societies clearly cannot be fit into the picture. But since democracy is not an all-or-nothing phenomenon, what is important is what other components, what rights and freedoms, what political structures, what other social myths are included in the nation's own story. Using the term democracy may actually stand in the way of championing the rights and freedoms American seeks to promote.

The aspect of democracy being seized on by some in Arab nations is the possibility of being heard by their governments and expecting governments to respond to their grievances. This is not new. If King George II and his ministers had listened and responded to the protests and concerns of the American colonies, there would have been no American revolution. The same is true in some of the Arab nations. The people do not necessarily or even clearly want democracy in its American sense (however described), since democracy is not the only form of government that can respond to their desires.

Historically what most people call democracies tend to succeed when they incorporate into their structures procedures for people to express their approval or disapproval of the actions of their government, usually through periodic elections. This is the way consent of the governed is expressed, according to the social myth, despite frequent low voter turnout and the small number of the population in some countries that end up voting for an elected official. Small voter turnout, however, can be interpreted as implicit acceptance, as apathy, as indifference, as a protest against all the candidates, and in other ways.[8] Even though an official may be elected with only 20 or 30 % of the votes of the population eligible to vote, the basic question is whether the results are accepted by the candidates who lost and by at least the vast majority of the people. And the only way to know whether the results are freely accepted is if there exists the possibility for the people in general, or for particular parts of it, to express their discontent and dissent. That is the foundation for at least internal legitimacy. This is a small but important part of what is meant by the rule of law and national self-determination—two components of the American and many other versions of the complex story that makes up those versions of democracy. But a nation may be democratic (in its sense) without those latter concepts or doctrines fully developed or articulated.

If what is taking place under the general label of the Arab Spring is indeed a demand for people's voices to be heard and for their governments to respond appropriately, and if their leaders won't or don't respond, recent history indicates that they will probably not last long. We cannot say what will replace them, or if the new regimes will be to the liking of the U.S. or other nations. But once the people of a country have learned that they can make their voices heard and topple non-responsive governments, it will be difficult for leaders to govern autocratically. Yet this does not preclude a tyranny of the majority or any guarantee of respect or even recognition of minority rights. Although the package of social doctrines adopted may be

[8] In the United States in presidential election years from 1960 to 2010 the turnout of the voting age population ranged from 63.1 % (1969) to 49.1 % (1996) (Infoplease.com). If a close election is within 1 % point, as it frequently is, then at best scarcely more than 30 % of those eligible to vote express their approval of the victor. People tend to translate this into a claim that the majority won.

very different from the liberal democratic package, the government may accurately claim internal legitimacy and acceptance by the people.

In Islamic societies where religion and social and political structures are intertwined, their religion fulfills the function of explanation and justification. Can that survive democratization? In this regard it is worth noting that the *Declaration of Independence* refers to "the Laws of Nature and of Nature's God" and that all men "are endowed by their Creator with certain unalienable Rights." Many of the colonists came to the United States in search of religious freedom, and that heritage is expressed not only in the *Declaration of Independence* but also in the First Amendment to the Constitution. Religion is not incompatible with democracy; but what fit the American popular outlook and what fits the popular Arab outlook (if there is such a view rather than many national views) will likely be different. If the American Government wishes to promote democracy in the Arab countries where it is beginning to emerge, it might be most successful if it considered how democracy fits with the religious beliefs of the revolutionaries.

Being conscious of all this, one may be more careful in supporting or promoting democracy as if it were a clear concept which included the rule of law, protection of minority rights, free and periodic elections, the right to voice dissent, and the rest of the package Americans assume in speaking of democracy.

I have indicated that the philosophical tasks of analysis, of searching for internal inconsistency, and of evaluating arguments or presuppositions all have a place in the literature of democracy as a social myth. But these findings, though important, may from the point of view of the socially held myth, ultimately be part of the truth that the myth continues to cover over rather than the part on which it chooses to focus (De George 1968). This helps explain why the scholarly literature on democracy, the arguments and analyses, often seem to have little effect on the notion of democracy commonly held. It may also suggest a different approach to some research. Much of the research relates primarily to the political strand of democracy, and often it is addressed simply to other academics and takes place within a framework that accepts a particular notion of liberal democracy. If one's aim is to change political structures or to change the content of the popular strand of democracy, then one should consider who the intended audience is, the role that the various strands play in the overall picture one wishes to change, and how the proposed changes mesh with the history of and the beliefs contained in the currently held social myth embraced by their audience.

In the American story the social myth of democracy continues to play an important role in justifying and explaining American institutions. The story and many of its parts are shared by other societies, each in its own way. And the story seems to have some attraction for some in non-democratic societies that will adapt and use it in forming their own explanations and justifications for the governments they develop. We should not expect all democracies to be like American democracy, nor expect that it can be justified in an ultimate rather than a presumptive sense. We should not expect more of it than any social myth is able to supply. If this is correct, it may make champions of and analysts of democracy both more cautious and more humble in their claims, their aims, and their use of the term democracy.

References

BBC News. Europe, 10 September 2012. Kosovo declared 'fully independent. http://www.bbc.co.uk/news/world-europe-19550809. Accessed 12 May 2013.

Black, Eric. 1988. *Our constitution: The myth that binds us*. Boulder/London: Westview Press.

De George, Richard T. 1968. Philosophy, ideology and 'logical myths'. *Proceedings of the XIVth International Congress of Philosophy* I: 463–467.

De George, Richard T. 1991a. Consent and obedience. *Archiv fuer Rechts-und Sozialphilosophie/Archives for Philosophy of Law and Social Philosophy* (Beiheft #12): 49–61.

De George, Richard T. 1991b. The myth of the right of collective self-determination. In *Issues of self-determination*, ed. William Twining, 1–7. Aberdeen: Aberdeen University Press.

Economist. 2011. The intelligence unit. The democracy index 2011. http//www.eiu.com/public/topical-report.aspx?campaignid=Democracy index2011. Accessed 3 Nov 2013.

Freedomhouse. 2013. Freedom in the World 2013. http://www.freedomhouse.org/. Accessed 3 Nov 2013.

Infoplease.com. National voter turnout in federal elections: 1960–2010. http://www.infoplease.com/ipa/A0781453.html. Accessed 12 May 2013.

Langworth, Richard. 2009. Democracy is the worst form of government. http://richardlangworth.com/worst-form-of-government. Accessed 3 Nov 2013.

Lévi-Strauss, Claude. 1955. The structural study of myth. *Journal of American Folklore* (Oct–Dec), 270: 426–444 (also available in *The Structuralists from Marx to Lévi-Strauss*, eds. Richard and Fernande De George. Garden City: Anchor Books, 1973).

Marx, Karl. 1978. On the Jewish question. In *The Marx-Engels reader*, 2nd ed, ed. Robert C. Tucker, 42–45. New York: W.W. Norton & Company.

Needleman, Jacob. 2002. *The American soul*. New York: Jeremy P. Tarcher/Putnam.

Wilson, Woodrow. 1917. Woodrow Wilson proposes declaration of war to Congress. http://wadsworth.com/history_d/special_features/ilrn_legacy/wawc2c01c/content/wciv2/readings/wilson1.html. Accessed 12 May 2013.

Part II
The Current Polarization

Chapter 5
Political Polarization and the Markets vs. Government Debate

Stephen Nathanson

Abstract In this chapter, I suggest that political disagreements in the United States have been exacerbated by the conceptual scheme that we use to categorize economic/political systems. Public discussion about the proper role of markets and governments often presupposes the view that there are only two possibilities: capitalism and socialism. Even if we include the often omitted welfare state, the resulting three-way conceptualization omits many other possible political/economic systems. I suggest that a richer conceptual framework could help to diminish the U.S.'s polarized politics by making clear that we face a spectrum of many different options rather than a stark choice between capitalism and socialism. In this chapter, I label and describe four types of capitalism (anarcho-capitalism, minimal state capitalism, umpire state capitalism, and pragmatic capitalism) and three types of welfare state (emergency relief, opportunity, and decent level). My hope is that a richer vocabulary could increase awareness of multiple possibilities, improve public discussion, and help to diminish polarization.

5.1 Introduction

Many people in the United States lament the political polarization generated by disagreements about the proper role of government in relation to the economic system. In this chapter, I suggest that these disagreements are intensified by the impoverished conceptual scheme that we use to categorize economic/political systems. The crude conceptual scheme suggests that we face an either/or choice between capitalism and socialism. A richer set of concepts would call attention to

S. Nathanson (✉)
Philosophy & Religion, Northeastern University,
371 Holmes Hall, Boston, MA 02115, USA
e-mail: s.nathanson@neu.edu

A.E. Cudd and S.J. Scholz (eds.), *Philosophical Perspectives on Democracy in the 21st Century*, AMINTAPHIL: The Philosophical Foundations of Law and Justice 5,
DOI 10.1007/978-3-319-02312-0_5,

the complex spectrum of multiple options regarding the proper role of markets and governments, and greater awareness of these options would make people less likely to divide into polarized camps. With more views and less distance between them, we might have more civil, productive disagreements that would make it easier to devise reasonable compromises and policies that promote the country's well-being.

5.2 What Is Political Polarization?

Polarization occurs when large clusters of people hold views that are "poles apart." Not only are their views deeply inconsistent with one another, but they have intense feelings about their views and see no way to reconcile their views with those of people who disagree. Thus, they see their opponents as enemies and find it hard to sustain civility toward them.[1]

Polarization is not uncommon and can be destructive. The conflict over slavery led to the Civil War, the most destructive war in U.S. history. In the 1950s and 1960s, clashes over racial segregation led to vigilante-style violence, civil disobedience, riots, police attacks on protestors, and the use of federal troops to enforce laws. In the 1960s, the Vietnam War generated mass protests, hatred of the government and the military, and attacks on protesters by police and troops. Since 2000, intense hostility toward the Bush and the Obama administrations has escalated negative rhetoric and led to Congressional failure to deal with important issues. We face the specter feared by Richard Hofstadter in 1954: "a political climate in which the rational pursuit of our well-being and safety would become impossible" (1965, 65).

Given these dangers, we need to devise ways to diminish polarization. I suggest that how we conceptualize issues matters and that a richer conceptual scheme might diminish the threat that political polarization poses to civility and effective decision-making.[2]

5.2.1 The Current Conceptualization

In February 2009, at his first news conference as president, Barack Obama explained why some people opposed the policies that he thought were necessary to protect the U.S. economy. Referring to his opponents, he said, "You have some people, very sincere, who philosophically just think the government has no business interfering in the marketplace." Obama's diagnosis of opposition to his proposals is supported by the fact that his opponents describe him as a socialist who wants to undermine

[1] My account draws on Robert Dahl (1956, Chapter 4, especially 98); and Richard Hofstadter (1965, Part I).

[2] Crude concepts are not the only cause of political polarization. For others, see Bo Rothstein (2011, ch. 6).

Fig. 5.1 Obama embraces Marx

free market capitalism. This is evident in such book titles as *Radical-in-Chief: Barack Obama and the Untold Story of American Socialism* and *To Save America: Stopping Obama's Secular-Socialist Machine.* It can also be seen in a 2008 online poster (Fig. 5.1).

While many people think it absurd to claim that Barack Obama embraces Marxist socialism, this view gains force because it fits the conceptual scheme that frames Americans' thinking about government and the economy.

According to this conceptual scheme, there are two possible economic/political systems: capitalism and socialism, and many public issues are clashes over whether we want a capitalist society or a socialist one. When Medicare, for example, was proposed, the American Medical Association attacked it as socialized medicine just as President Obama's opponents have described the Affordable Health Care Act as socialism. During the 2012 presidential primaries, Republican Congresswoman Michelle Bachman attacked both Barack Obama and Republican candidate Mitt Romney for supporting "socialized medicine," claiming that they shared "the same core political philosophy." "The only difference," she said, was that Romney was a "a frugal socialist" while Obama was an "out-of-control socialist." Bachman, however, never said what she meant by capitalism and socialism (Bachman 2011).

5.2.2 What Are Capitalism and Socialism?

The first step in a serious discussion of capitalism and socialism is to provide a description of key elements. Table 5.1 displays the basic features of capitalism and socialism by identifying each system's ideal form of property ownership, its production and distribution system, and its principle for allocating goods and services (Nathanson 1998).

Capitalism is based on private property and a market system in which private individuals and groups decide what to produce and distribute, and decisions about what to purchase are made by consumers. Government plays a minimal economic role, leaving decisions about production and distribution to private

Table 5.1 Capitalism and socialism

	Capitalism	Socialism
Form of property ownership	Private ownership	Public ownership
Production and distribution system	Market system: private producers & sellers	Planned economy, public control
Allocation rule	To each according to ability to pay + gifts	To each according to need or an equal share

parties. The capitalist allocation rule is that goods should be allocated to people in accord with their ability to pay for them—although exceptions are made for personal gifts, charitable donations, and inheritance. By contrast, under socialism, the government runs the economy, deciding both what to produce and how goods are distributed. Traditionally, socialism's allocation rule aims to meet people's needs or to provide everyone an equal share.[3]

If these systems were the only options, the extreme differences between them would generate either a consensus in favor of one or radical polarization. Because there is no serious political support for socialism in the U.S., the capitalism/socialism conceptual scheme cannot make sense of the fact that we have a strong consensus against socialism but nonetheless have polarization.[4]

5.2.3 *The Welfare State*

The most striking omission from the standard conceptualization is the welfare state. Although the U.S. system is a welfare state (rather than a pure form of capitalism or socialism), the welfare state is not usually seen as a distinct system, and Americans often don't know what it is. When students of mine conducted interviews and asked people to define capitalism, socialism, and the welfare state, one interviewer found that "the respondents had…difficulty expressing their concept of the welfare state and even… grasping exactly what a welfare state is." Another student tried to explain this, noting that "Everyone knew what capitalism is because we live in a capitalist society, but people were unsure what a welfare state is." The opposite is true. We live in a welfare state but do not know what it is.

The welfare state is both invisible and right before our eyes. Its invisibility may result from the fact that when welfare state institutions were created during the New Deal, we changed our political/economic system but kept our capitalist ideology.[5]

[3] For classic discussions of socialism, see V. I. Lenin (1943, ch. 5); and Edward Bellamy (1996); (original ed., 1888).

[4] Although socialism is virtually invisible in U.S. politics, a Gallup poll (2012) suggests a surprising level of support for socialism among Americans.

[5] Richard Hofstadter (1954) stresses the central role of a capitalist ideology throughout U.S. history, viii.

Table 5.2 Three systems

System feature	Capitalism	Welfare state	Socialism
Form of property ownership	Private ownership	Primarily private ownership	Public ownership
Production and distribution system	Market system	Primarily market system + government production and/or distribution of some resources	Planned economy, public control
Allocation rule	To each according to ability to pay + gifts	To each according to ability to pay + gifts + legally guaranteed access to some resources	To each according to need or an equal share

Even supporters of the New Deal describe FDR as "saving capitalism" rather than replacing it or creating a different form of capitalism. Because our welfare state does not match our capitalist ideology, welfare state supporters have a difficult time defending programs that distribute goods to people irrespective of their ability to pay. Such actions are seen as violations of "free market" values.

Table 5.2 compares the basic features of a welfare state with capitalism and socialism.

While advocates of pure capitalism see everything that is market-generated as good and everything run by government as bad, and advocates of pure socialism see markets as evil and government—when it acts on behalf of society—as good, welfare state advocates reject both of these views. The welfare state's goal is to insure that everyone has access to the most important goods. When markets are the best means to achieve this goal, welfare state advocates embrace markets. When government is needed to achieve this goal, then government activity is used. For welfare state supporters, the question is not "Should we have capitalism or socialism?" Rather, it is "Which goods and services should be provided by government and which should be distributed using market processes?"

Advocates of capitalism may respond that the welfare state is nothing but socialism by another name. After all, they may say, isn't the welfare state a takeover of the market system by the government? Isn't it based on "to each according to their need"? And why should people who have worked hard to earn their money be taxed in order to provide goods and services to others who have not done the same?

Although criticisms like these are frequently raised, they neglect the fact that most people take it for granted that governments should provide some things to everyone irrespective of people's ability to pay.[6] The best examples of uncontroversial, government-provided services are police protection and K–12 education. These are seen as "socialized" goods that should be funded by taxes and provided to everyone rather than "marketized" goods that only go to those who are able to pay for them.

Some critics support public funding for K-12 education but oppose government-operated schools. They argue that government should stop running schools and

[6] John Stuart Mill (2006) discusses the functions of governments in Book V, Chapter 1.

instead provide parents with vouchers to pay for education in privately run schools. Even if this system were enacted, however, education would still be a "socialized" good that is paid for by taxes and distributed in accord with need rather than ability to pay.[7]

Because we take for granted government's role in providing police protection and K–12 education, people who support a non-market system for these services aren't branded as socialists. In addition, in spite of these "socialized" sectors, we don't call our overall system socialist because most goods and services are still produced and distributed by a market system. The result is a hybrid system that is neither capitalism nor socialism as those are often understood.

In making these points, my intention is not to defend or justify the welfare state. My purpose is only to show that the welfare state differs from both capitalism and socialism and that our conceptual framework should recognize it as an option.

Even if we include the welfare state as an option, our conceptual framework would still omit many other possible systems and would fail to show that there are multiple forms of capitalism, socialism, and the welfare state. The usual contrasts between these systems ignore the fact that political/economic systems can share certain essential features while differing with respect to other features. As a result, there are "sub-species" of each of these systems. For this reason, it would be better to think in the plural, i.e., in terms of capitalisms, socialisms, and welfare states rather than assuming that there is only one form of each.

Lacking terms for sub-species of these economic/political systems, we are like people who have the concept of a dog but lack words or concepts for different varieties of dogs (poodles, pit bulls, huskies, etc.). Without these concepts, people's ability to think and talk about dogs would be severely limited. In the same way, our ability to think and talk about capitalism, socialism, and the welfare state is limited by our lack of terms and concepts for the varieties of these systems.

Table 5.3 displays a spectrum of systems, each with a name to identify it. It arranges the systems according to the strength of the roles played by markets and governments.

In what follows, I will briefly describe the versions of capitalism and the welfare state listed below. I will not discuss socialist systems because of space limitations and because socialism is not a live option in contemporary U.S. politics.

My primary aim in describing these systems is to display an array of options. If there are only two choices, political disagreement is more likely to be polarized. Awareness of multiple options that are not all "poles apart" may diminish the intensity of disagreement. In addition, by comparing many different systems, we can clarify the values that different systems appeal to and the problems they confront. Since making rational choices requires comparing different options, considering a spectrum of views can promote better understanding and better choices.

[7] Milton Friedman (1962) defends publicly funded K-12 education but opposes publicly run schools, Chapter VI.

Table 5.3 A spectrum of systems

All market/100 % **No government/0 %**	Anarcho-capitalism
↕	Minimal state capitalism
	Umpire state capitalism
	Pragmatic capitalism
	Emergency welfare state
	Opportunity welfare state
	Decent level welfare state
	Market socialism
All government/100 % **No market/0 %**	State socialism

5.3 Four Forms of Capitalism

In this section, I describe four types of capitalism. As Table 5.4 shows, these capitalist systems differ from each other in significant ways.[8] (For each system, I have bolded the features that it adds to the previous system—i.e., the one to its left on the table). Although welfare states are sometimes called "welfare capitalism," I do not include that here since hostility to the welfare state unites many advocates of capitalist systems.[9]

5.3.1 Anarcho-Capitalism

While anarchism plays no role in ordinary politics, anarchists invoke the same values that market-oriented thinkers appeal to: freedom, rights, individualism, private property, and the virtues of market processes. Anarcho-capitalism is the purest form of capitalism.[10] It would be 100 % market and 0 % government. Individuals or groups would produce and sell products and services to others or, if they choose, give goods to others as gifts. Without a government, there would be no government involvement in the economy, no taxation, and no government interference with property rights or market processes.[11]

[8] Murray Rothbard (1973) discusses a related spectrum of capitalist views/systems, 12–20. For contrasting ideas about liberalism and capitalism, see Samuel Freeman (2011, 19–55).

[9] I omit what Ann Cudd calls "enlightened capitalism" because it is a robust form of welfare state. For Cudd's view, see Ann Cudd and Nancy Holmstrom (2011, 125–30).

[10] Some anarchists—such as Peter Kropotkin (1970)—support socialism rather than capitalism.

[11] For a brief description of anarchism's attractiveness, see Nathanson (2001, 46–63). David Friedman (1973) and Murray Rothbard (1973) are important defenses of anarcho-capitalism.

Table 5.4 Four forms of capitalism

System type	Anarcho-capitalism	Minimal state capitalism	Umpire state capitalism	Pragmatic capitalism
Role of market and government	Pure market No Government No Government services	Market system + ***Government protection against force and fraud***	Market system + Government protection from force & fraud + ***Government as economic rule-maker, umpire, definer of property rights, conflict arbiter, enforcer of rules***	Market system + Government protection from force & fraud +Government as economic rule-maker, umpire, definer of property rights, conflict arbiter, enforcer of rules, and ***provider of other important social benefits***
Allocation criterion for determining who gets what	To each according to ability to pay + gifts No guaranteed resources	To each according to ability to pay + gifts + ***guaranteed access to police/ army protection***	To each according to ability to pay + gifts + guaranteed access to police/army protection, + ***economic rule-making, adjudication, property right enforcement***	To each according to ability to pay + gifts + guaranteed access to police/ army protection + adjudication, property right enforcement + ***limited socially useful benefits [e.g., education, parks, protection from some negative externalities]***

5.3.2 Minimal State Capitalism

Defenders of minimal state capitalism reject anarchism. They support a "night watchman state" whose sole function is to protect people from force and fraud.[12] The most common argument against anarchism rests on the fear that it will lead to an unconstrained, rule-less condition in which everyone is free to act as they choose but lives in fear of being harmed by others who are equally free. This Hobbesian depiction of life in a state of nature is meant to show why people would sacrifice some freedom in exchange for a government that protects them and their property

[12] For a clear statement of this view, see Robert Nozick (1973, ix).

from attack (Hobbes 1651, ch. XIII). Minimal state capitalists accept this protective function of the state. The police and army are the paradigmatic institutions of the minimal state.

Though wary of state power and intent on protecting property, minimal state advocates entrust governments with significant power and accept the idea that they may collect taxes to pay for protective services. They also accept that these protections are provided to all people, whether or not they can pay for them. Beyond these protections, however, people must fend for themselves, meeting their needs by hunting and gathering, producing goods to barter or sell, laboring for compensation, or receiving resources at no cost from family, friends, or charitable strangers.

Though often seen as an extreme view, minimal state capitalism is a "middle" position, flanked on one side by anarchists who reject minimal state capitalism because it allows too much state activity and on the other side by people who support more extensive state activity and reject the limits of minimal statism.

Once we accept a legitimate role for government in producing and distributing protection from force and fraud, we may wonder why it is illegitimate for governments to provide other essential goods and services.[13] Minimal state advocates need to show why government protection against force and fraud is special if they are to answer anarchists who see the minimal state as involving too much government and proponents of other views who call for governments to do much more.[14]

5.3.3 Umpire State Capitalism

Defenders of "umpire state" capitalism reject the view that government should do no more than prevent force and fraud. Although umpire state capitalists strongly support the market system, they grant that market systems generate problems that the market cannot solve by itself. Contrary to the "invisible hand" view associated with Adam Smith and invoked by virtually all advocates of capitalism, umpire state defenders do not believe that market processes automatically solve all problems.[15] For that reason, market systems need government to play the role of umpire, both devising and enforcing rules to govern the actions of participants in a market system.

---

[13] Rothbard (1973, 14) criticizes the minimal state, asking rhetorically "If it is legitimate for the State to coerce the taxpayer into financing the police, then why is it not equally legitimate to coerce the taxpayer for many other activities, including building steel factories, subsidizing favored groups, etc."

[14] A minimal state need not be small. "Minimal" refers to the scope of state activity, not the size of the government. A government consisting only of military and police forces, courts, and the prison system could be quite substantial.

[15] For an exhaustive discussion that challenges standard views of Adam Smith's invisible hand doctrine, see Warren Samuels (2011).

A prime example used to support this view is the problem of monopolies. If persons or groups acquire a monopoly over particular goods or services, there will be no competition, and because competition is essential to controlling prices and motivating the production of high quality products, a monopoly-dominated market will fail to generate the good effects attributed to markets. For this reason, governments must prevent, destroy, or limit monopolies in order to preserve the market system and its virtues.

The basic idea, then, is that market systems need more government than the minimal state. Even the minimal state objective of preventing fraud requires legislatures and courts to determine what constitutes fraud and to define when a contract is violated even though there is no fraudulent intent. Governments also play a necessary role in defining property rights. As Milton Friedman notes, "just what constitutes property and what rights the ownership of property confers are complex social creations rather than self-evident propositions" (1962, 26). Without government, there is no clear definition of the property rights so valued by capitalism's advocates, and once legal definitions and rules are devised, they must be enforced. Without these governmental activities, people will lack confidence that property rights will be secure and that contracts will be honored. Without this confidence, markets cannot work.

While umpire state capitalists often use the rhetoric of limited government, they believe that markets are complex systems that need more than a minimal state in order to function.

5.3.4 Pragmatic Capitalism

While pragmatic capitalists often use the same rhetoric as defenders of less extensive government activity, they are much less ideologically rigid than minimal state advocates and support a even greater government role than umpire state advocates support. Milton Friedman, in addition to defending the functions of the umpire state, frequently appeals to utilitarian, pragmatic reasoning to defend a broader range of government activities.

Although Friedman loves markets and fears government over-reach, Friedman's pragmatism is evident in his support for some government activities simply because they produce good results that would be difficult to achieve by market processes. This tendency can be seen in his discussion of parks. While arguing against government-run national parks, Friedman does not oppose publicly run city parks. His reason is that because city parks tend to have many entrances, it would be too costly to collect entry fees from individual park users. Since it is better to have parks than not, it is okay to have government-run, tax-supported parks in cities. Friedman opposes government-run national parks, however, because he thinks that it is possible to limit the number of entrances and, therefore, that it is economically feasible for private owners to collect fees for entry and use of these park (1962, 31).

Putting aside Friedman's factual assumptions about parks, it is striking how unideological his approach is. He makes no appeal to natural rights or principles like "that government is best which governs least." Instead, he appears to support a government activity simply because it provides a valuable service for which private payment schemes are impractical. By contrast, defenders of anarcho-capitalism, the minimal state, and the umpire state would argue that if the market (or private philanthropy) cannot sustain parks, then people should do without them.

Friedman also supports publicly funded K-12 education because it is necessary to sustain a democratic society. Similarly, government-built roads are legitimate if private markets do not effectively meet this need. Friedman also believes that governments can legitimately intervene to prevent negative "neighborhood effects" (i.e., externalities) such as the polluting of streams by some persons when there is no feasible way to compensate people who are negatively affected (1962, ch. 2, ch. 6).

Pragmatic capitalists strongly prefer markets to governments, but if important goods and services cannot effectively be provided by the market system, they will support governments doing the job. Although pragmatic capitalists have guiding principles and strong preferences, these often give way to expediency. Friedman tells us that his principles "offer no hard and fast line how far it is appropriate to use government." Rather, he says, when we consider particular cases, "we must make up a balance sheet, listing separately the advantages and disadvantages" (1962, 32). Obviously, this pragmatic, utilitarian approach rejects "hard and fast" limits on government activities and allows a much broader range of governmental activities than anarcho-capitalism, the minimal state, or the umpire state.[16]

5.4 Three Forms of the Welfare State

Welfare state advocates lack both the capitalist aversion to government and the socialist aversion to market systems and private property. Welfare state advocates tend to be more concerned with outcomes than processes. If human well-being is best promoted by having governments provide certain goods and services, they see no reason to oppose government playing this role. If markets do a better job, then markets are acceptable.[17]

Welfare state advocates believe that governments should play a role in the production and distribution of at least some goods and services. Different types of

---

[16] The view that Friedrich Hayek was also a pragmatic capitalist is supported by Brian Doherty (2007), who calls Hayek "the *least* libertarian of the major libertarian influences of the twentieth century…." (98), noting that Hayek "supports sanitary laws, working-hour laws, disaster relief, provision of certain social services, and a welfare state to supply a minimum standard of living for all" (110).

[17] The unideological, result-oriented spirit of welfare state advocates echoes that of John Stuart Mill. I discuss Mill in Nathanson (2012a) and Mill (2004, ix–xxxv).

Table 5.5 Three types of welfare state

Emergency relief welfare state	Opportunity welfare state	Decent level welfare state
Market system	Market system	Market system
+ Government protection against force and fraud + **Other life-threatening emergency conditions**	+ Government protection against force, fraud + emergency, life-threatening conditions + **guaranteed access to education +other opportunity-generating resources**	+ Government protection against force, fraud + **guaranteed provision of resources required for a decent level of well-being [i.e., sufficient for the abolition of poverty]**

welfare state reflect differing views about what resources should be guaranteed to citizens and what the rationale for this guarantee should be. Table 5.5 describes three types of welfare state.

5.4.1 The Emergency Relief Welfare State

Advocates of the emergency relief welfare state agree with defenders of capitalism that people should normally take care of themselves. They should not look to government for access to resources but instead should strive to meet their own needs through market activities. Nonetheless, emergency relief state advocates argue that there are emergency circumstances in which people cannot provide for themselves and, as a result, may literally be on the brink of death. In these circumstances, governments should intervene to save them. Why? Because these are people who cannot possibly provide what they need for themselves and will die without immediate assistance.

The emergency relief state reflects a commitment to both self-reliance and compassion. It recognizes that there are conditions in which the ideal of self-reliance cannot be met and protection from the state is necessary. Nonetheless, the compassion reflected in the provision of emergency assistance is quite limited. When the emergency is over, the person who receives assistance is on his or her own. He or she must find ways to obtain what is needed, either through salary-earning work, charity, or support from family and friends (Nathanson 1998, 101–105).

In spite of its limited nature, the emergency relief state provides a level of goods and services (e.g., food, shelter, medicine) to all citizens that goes well beyond what anarcho-capitalism, the minimal state, and the umpire state would provide. While it is unclear what pragmatic capitalists would recommend in these circumstances, no other form of capitalism supports this type of guaranteed, emergency assistance. The fact that we are unsure about pragmatic capitalism suggests that there may be no clear line between it and the welfare state.[18]

[18] The lack of clarity regarding pragmatic capitalism is evident in Friedman (1962). In Chapter X, Friedman rejects state support for impoverished people while in Chapter XII, he supports it (through the use of a "negative income tax").

5.4.2 *The Opportunity Welfare State*

Supporters of an opportunity welfare state also value self-reliance, but they believe that some of the dire emergencies that the emergency relief state addresses arise from chronic conditions. Moreover, if some of these chronic conditions result from people's lack of success in market activities and if the process of market competition is itself unfair, then the chronic problems faced by many people are an injustice. What makes the process unfair is that people begin life in vastly different circumstances. As a result, different people possess undeserved advantages and disadvantages that make the likelihood of success much less for some people than for others.[19]

Defenders of the opportunity welfare state support emergency relief for people but see it as too little and too late. A just society would provide genuine opportunity to its citizens by guaranteeing both an adequate education to all as well as other opportunity-generating resources. It would aim to provide all with a decent chance to succeed in a competitive market economy. If, however, people receive fair opportunities but do not succeed, and thus find themselves in impoverished circumstances, then an opportunity welfare state will not provide them with additional resources. Advocates of the opportunity welfare state believe that members of a society deserve a chance to succeed but not success itself.

It is important to see that a commitment to genuine opportunity may require governments to provide substantial resources for individuals. Schools by themselves, even if well run, are not sufficient for creating an effective level of opportunity. Children who attend good schools but lack adequate nutrition or health care will probably be incapable of learning enough to compete effectively for economic resources. Similarly, children in impoverished households are likely to enter (and perhaps leave) schools with weaker linguistic, cognitive, and social skills than children from home environments in which they effortlessly acquire these important capacities.[20]

If the opportunity state is committed to adequate levels of competitive ability, it may have to guarantee, at least to its young citizens, a substantial array of goods and services. Advocates of the opportunity welfare state may think a weak, narrowly understood conception of opportunity is enough, but achieving their stated goal may commit them to the daunting task of overcoming the effects of children beginning life at vastly different levels of economic and social status.[21]

[19] For a powerful account of undeserved inequalities, see Brian Barry (2005, Chapter 5). For data linking income inequality with widespread social and individual ills, see Richard Wilkinson and Kate Pickett (2011).

[20] On linguistic and cognitive disparities, see Ginia Bellafante (2012).

[21] Bruce Ackerman and Anne Alstott (1999) propose a capital grant to be distributed to all at age 18. For discussion of often-unseen factors that influence success and failure, see Malcolm Gladwell, *Outliers: The Story of Success* (2008).

5.4.3 Decent Level Welfare State

The decent level welfare state aims to provide all citizens with the resources necessary for a decent level of well-being. It rejects the emergency relief state because it fails to address the chronic conditions that threaten people's well-being and also rejects the opportunity welfare state because it is unlikely to succeed in eliminating the substantial disparities in people's ability to compete effectively for success in the market. Widespread poverty is likely to continue under both of these forms of welfare state.

The decent level welfare state seeks to end poverty by severing the connection between access to the resources needed for a decent life and paid employment.[22] It aims for a decent level of well-being for all citizens, whether or not they succeed in the market competition. Because poverty is (by definition) a condition in which people lack the economic resources necessary for attaining a decent level of well-being, the goal of guaranteeing the level of resources for a decent life is equivalent to the goal of abolishing poverty.[23]

Although the decent level system is a welfare state, its guarantee of resources to all may suggest that it is a form of socialism. This claim, however, is misguided. While the decent level welfare state provides a floor on resources for people, it is unlike socialism in that it imposes no ceiling on income or wealth. Thus, it leaves intact the economic and social inequalities that socialism (with its commitment to equality and a classless society) would do away with. The decent level welfare state also retains a market system for the production and distribution of most goods and services. Although it augments the market system by guaranteeing the resources for a decent level of living, it would not be replace or destroy it.

5.5 Conclusion

My aim in this chapter has been to suggest that better conceptualizations can help to diminish the polarization that threatens democratic processes and effective governance. As the array of possible systems displayed in Table 5.6 shows, we need not be limited by the crude, polarizing conceptualization of capitalism vs. socialism.

---

[22] The link between work and access to resources is already severed for wealthy people who benefit from inheritance, have sufficient capital to live on investment income, win lotteries winners, or benefit from the altruism of friends, family or charitable strangers. For most people, however, paid labor is their ticket to resources.

[23] Nathanson discusses the meaning of "decent level" in (1998, 109–110), and (2005).

Table 5.6 The spectrum of options

Anarcho-capitalism	Minimal state capitalism	Umpire state capitalism	Pragmatic capitalism	Emergency relief welfare state	Opportunity welfare state	Decent level welfare state	Market socialism	State socialism

While I have not evaluated these systems, I have presented them in an order that displays reasons that might be used to promote more rather than less ambitious governmental systems. A full evaluation would require considering the countercharge that the more extensive governmental systems suffer from important defects. It would also require comparing the systems with each other to see whether they are better or worse than others on the spectrum.

Because each system in the spectrum appeals to some attractive values, choosing which system to support may be difficult.

5.5.1 *Postscript*

The most ambitious form of government discussed in this chapter is the decent level welfare state, which aims to abolish poverty by guaranteeing an income floor for all citizens. I have not discussed socialist systems or other systems that seek greater equality as a goal and place stronger constraints on the outcomes of market processes. I do not want to leave the impression, however, that there are no reasons for taking these systems seriously.

One such view is John Rawls's "difference principle," which goes beyond providing a floor of resources by also setting a ceiling on wealth and income. Rawls view requires that the disparity between the best and the worst off should be set at the point that will maximize the well-being of the least well-off (1971).[24] A Rawlsian state, unlike the decent level welfare state, goes beyond the goal of ending poverty and restricts upper levels so as to limit inequality.

Richard Wilkinson and Kate Pickett argue that economic inequality should be limited because greater inequalities result in worse conditions for individuals and their societies. In *The Spirit Level: Why Greater Equality Makes Societies Stronger*, they provide a wealth of empirical data to show that the degree of social ills in different societies is correlated with the degree of economic inequality (2011).[25] Societies with higher levels of economic inequality have more crime, teenage pregnancies, and mental illness as well as lower levels of social trust and lower life expectancy. They argue that these ills could be diminished by lowering the degree

[24] John Rawls (1971).

[25] Richard Wilkinson and Kate Pickett (2011).

of economic inequality within societies. If limiting income disparities would alleviate conditions that virtually everyone sees as detrimental, then people committed to "promoting the general welfare" should find the idea of diminishing inequalities worth considering.

Finally, apart from concerns about equality and inequality, the large scale damages to human life that are predicted as a result of climate change also poses a challenge to market systems and suggest the need for a greater governmental role in the economy. Since market systems allow unconstrained wealth and promote the greater production and consumption that cause climate change, unconstrained market processes pose a serious threat to future people. As a result, any evaluation of economic/political systems must give at least some weight to the well-being of future people.[26]

Even if people in the United States and other developed countries were to consider more thoughtfully the part of the spectrum of systems I focused on in this chapter, there are other, more radical views that now have little political support but that may nonetheless be worthy of our attention.

References

Ackerman, Bruce, and Anne Alstott. 1999. *The stakeholder society*. New Haven: Yale University Press.

Bachman, Michelle. 2011. Address to the Family Research Council in Washington, DC. http://www.presidency.ucsb.edu/ws/index.php?pid=98451. Accessed 18 July 2013.

Barry, Brian. 2005. *Why social justice matters*. Cambridge: Polity Press.

Bellafante, Ginia. 2012. Before a test, a poverty of words. *New York Times*, October 5.

Bellamy, Edward. 1996. *Looking backward*. New York: Dover Books.

Cudd, Ann, and Nancy Holmstrom. 2011. *Capitalism: For and against, a feminist debate*. Cambridge: Cambridge University Press.

Dahl, Robert. 1956. *A preface to democratic theory*. Chicago: University of Chicago Press.

Doherty, Brian. 2007. *Radicals for capitalism*. New York: Public Affairs.

Freeman, Samuel. 2011. Capitalism in the classical and high liberal traditions. In *Liberalism and capitalism*, ed. Ellen Frankel Paul, Fred Miller, and Jeffrey Paul. Cambridge: Cambridge University Press.

Friedman, Milton. 1962. *Capitalism and freedom*. Chicago: University of Chicago Press.

Friedman, David. 1973. *The machinery of freedom*. New York: Harper & Row.

Gallup Poll. 2012. Democrats, Republicans diverge on capitalism, federal government. http://www.gallup.com/poll/158978/democrats-republicans-diverge-capitalism-federal-gov.aspx. Accessed 18 July 2013.

Gladwell, Malcolm. 2008. *Outliers: The story of success*. Boston: Little, Brown.

Hobbes, Thomas. 1651. *Leviathan*. Indianapolis: Hackett Publishing.

Hofstadter, Richard. 1954. *The American political tradition*. New York: Vintage Books.

Hofstadter, Richard. 1965. *The paranoid style in American politics*. New York: Alfred Knopf.

Kropotkin, Peter. 1970. *Kropotkin's revolutionary pamphlets*, ed. Roger Baldwin. New York: Dover Publications.

[26] Tim Mulgan (2011) discusses private ownership from the perspective of future people who suffer from the effects climate change. Nathanson (2012b) discusses Mulgan's book.

Lenin, V.I. 1943. *State and revolution*. New York: International Publishers.
Mill, John Stuart. 2004. *Principles of political economy, abridged*, ed. Stephen Nathanson. Indianapolis: Hackett Publishing.
Mill, John Stuart. 2006. *Principles of political economy*. Indianapolis: Liberty Fund.
Mulgan, Tim. 2011. *Ethics for a broken world: Imagining philosophy after catastrophe*. Durham: Acumen Press.
Nathanson, Stephen. 1998. *Economic justice*. Englewood Cliffs: Prentice Hall.
Nathanson, Stephen. 2001. *Should we consent to be governed?* Belmont: Wadsworth/Thomson.
Nathanson, Stephen. 2005. Equality, sufficiency, decency: Three criteria of economic justice. In *Ethical issues for the twenty-first century*, ed. F. Adams. Charlottesville: Philosophy Documentation Center.
Nathanson, Stephen. 2012a. John Stuart Mill on economic justice and the alleviation of poverty. *Journal of Social Philosophy* XLIII(2): 161–176.
Nathanson, Stephen. 2012b. Review of Tim Mulgan, ethics for a broken world. *Notre Dame Philosophical Review*. http://ndpr.nd.edu/news/archives. Accessed 5 Nov 2013.
Nozick, Robert. 1973. *Anarchy, state, and utopia*. New York: Basic Books.
Rawls, John. 1971. *A theory of justice*. Cambridge, MA: Harvard University Press.
Rothbard, Murray. 1973. *For a new liberty*. New York: Macmillan.
Rothstein, Bo. 2011. *The quality of government*. Chicago: University of Chicago Press.
Samuels, Warren J. 2011. *Erasing the invisible hand: Essays on an elusive and misused concept in economics*. Cambridge: Cambridge University Press.
Wilkinson, Richard, and Kate Pickett. 2011. *The spirit level: Why greater equality makes societies better*. New York: Bloomsbury Press.

Chapter 6
Two Visions of Democracy

Richard Barron Parker

Abstract The current gridlock in the American federal government is caused by the equal political strength of two competing visions of democracy. The first vision, call it Type A democracy, is based on the ideal of a free self-governing individual who voluntarily contracts with other self-governing individuals to form a self-governing political association. This first vision takes individual freedom and political equality as its main ideals. The second vision of democracy, call it Type B democracy, takes economic and social equality within a nation as its main ideals. It is what emerges when the members of a pre-existing nation overcome a pre-existing hierarchical authoritarian patriarchal order and install a democratic government. Section 6.2 explores the differences between the two visions. Sections 6.3 and 6.4 sketch the historical roots of the two visions in America. Section 6.5 suggests ways of resolving the conflict between the two visions in the American political system and points out the need for Type A and Type B democrats to cooperate in opposing the hierarchical authoritarians who are the enemies of both visions of democracy.

6.1 Introduction[1]

The current gridlock in the American federal government is caused by the equal political strength of two competing visions of democracy and democratic citizenship, each vision having tens of millions of adherents. My aim in this essay is to describe these two visions, not to argue for one or the other.

---

[1] Versions of this essay were given as lectures at the University of Kiel and the University of Luneburg in Germany on June 6th and June 12th, 2012. Those lectures were sponsored by the Hamburg Consulate of the United States State Department and the German-American Society of Kiel. I am grateful for their support and for the questions and comments received from the

R.B. Parker (✉)
Law, Hiroshima Shudo University, 12 Merrill Road, Falmouth, ME 04105, USA
e-mail: rbarronparker@yahoo.com

A.E. Cudd and S.J. Scholz (eds.), *Philosophical Perspectives on Democracy in the 21st Century*, AMINTAPHIL: The Philosophical Foundations of Law and Justice 5,
DOI 10.1007/978-3-319-02312-0_6,

Three initial points should be kept in mind. First, the assertions in this essay are at best statistically true as in the example: men are taller than women. That statement is statistically true even though there are billions of women taller than billions of men. Second, this essay takes a distant, high altitude view of political conflict in the United States. Just as a high altitude view of a landscape reveals the relationship of the entire forest to the mountains and the sea but not the details of particular trees, so the high-altitude view taken in this essay reveals only the largest contrasts between the two visions but not the details of all the various mixtures of the two visions. Third, although I use the issue of the government provision of individual welfare as my main illustration of the conflict between the two visions of democracy, other areas of conflict such as free speech, or conceptions of privacy, or national security could have been used.

The first vision, call it Type A democracy, takes the individual citizen as its starting point. The ideal democratic citizen is a free self-governing individual who voluntarily contracts with other equally free self-governing individuals to form a free self-governing political association. Individual freedom and political equality are primary values. As explained below, Type A democracy is rooted in Protestant Christianity. The archetypal Type A democracy is the New England town meeting where people come together as free and politically equal citizens with an equal right to speak and to vote. At town meeting, citizens collectively decide how much to tax themselves and how to spend those tax revenues on common projects and public goods. Ideally, there is no supervision from a higher political authority, or State. The town meeting does not guarantee a minimum standard of living to its members. It has no mandate to redistribute personal wealth from some town meeting members to other members. *For Type A democrats, individual poverty is the personal business of the poor person, and the poor person's family and friends.* Type A democracy is the majority view in many regions of the United States but often needs to be explained to the rest of the world.

Type A democracy is not the "individualism" that Tocqueville regarded as a serious threat to democracy (Tocqueville 1994a, 98). On the contrary, Tocqueville saw the local civic engagement required by Type A democracy as the antidote to the evils of "individualism" (1994b, 102).

Nor is Type A democracy the libertarianism which views all government as a necessary evil. Type A democrats are enthusiastic about the right kind of cooperative self-government among political equals and have historically been very skilled in substituting politics for violence and using government to advance common goals.

The second vision, call it Type B democracy, begins with a pre-existing national community of which the individual is a constituent part. The economic and social equality of individuals in that national community is the primary value. Type B

audience at each lecture. I am also indebted for their incisive comments to David Bergman, Anne Parker Bergman, Ann Cudd, Taylor Dark, Susan Gesing, Tom Ginsberg, David Kolb, David Ledbetter, Judy Ledbetter, David Parker, Jonas Parker, Annie Popkin, Dan Rosen, Sally Scholz, Nancy Schwenker and Kenneth Winston.

democracy typically emerges when the members of a pre-existing nation overcome a pre-existing patriarchal authoritarian hierarchical order and install a government that makes its primary goal the social and economic welfare of the common man and woman. *In a Type B democracy, as in a family, every member of society is entitled to a minimum standard of living.*

Type B democracy is widespread around the world. It is what the Japanese and British, French, Egyptians, Germans, and Chinese generally mean by democracy. At its core, it is the abolition of pre-existing inequalities. Paternalism by government is more acceptable to Type B democrats because they see themselves as part of a nation and are used to being governed by a State comprised of the best and brightest of their fellow nationals. *The Type B ideal is good government rather than self-government – government for the people rather than government by the people.* As explained below, the strength of Type B democracy in the United States dates only from the early twentieth century.

Type B democracy is not communism or even socialism. Type B democracy does not advocate communal ownership of property or even government ownership of the means of production. Type B democracy always includes ways by which a government unsatisfactory to the majority can be replaced without violence. The archetypal Type B democracy is the modern European nation-state in which traditional economic and social inequalities have been overcome by democracy.

Both types of democracy take equality as fundamental. Type A democracy favors political equality. Type B democracy favors social and economic equality. Both types of democracy are sophisticated forms of government concerned with the common good, but they define the common good in very different ways.

6.2 Type A and Type B Democracy Contrasted

Although it is possible to find evidence of Type A democracy in countries other than the United States, the United States is an outlier compared with other major democracies in that only in the United States is Type A democracy a major political force. The differences between Type A and Type B democracy are easiest to see in the American context.

One dramatic difference between the two types of democracy is that Type A democrats draw a sharp distinction between the personal duties and obligations they owe to their families and close friends, and the civic duties they owe to their fellow citizens. To their fellow citizens, they owe the duty to participate in the self-governing political associations they belong to as fellow citizens. They have a duty to follow the laws created by agreed-upon procedures, to pay taxes, to vote, and to serve on juries. In extreme cases, they may have a civic duty to die in defense of their country.

To their own families and close friends, Type A democrats believe that they have much more extensive duties of care. Depending on the personal relationship, they may have duties of care to provide housing, food, education, medical care, and emotional support to children, parents, relatives, and close friends. Their civic duties to their fellow citizens do not include meeting those needs.

Type A democrats do not lack compassion for the poor and needy; rather, they believe that compassion should be exercised by private individuals performing charitable acts, or by charitable organizations and religious institutions. Local government might also provide temporary assistance to local needy people for the public good of forestalling local crime or homelessness.

Type A democrats take pride in not being objects of charity. Typically, they feel ashamed to be on welfare. Even being supported by unemployment insurance makes them feel guilty for not being a fully responsible citizen able to take care of themselves. In America, programs such as Social Security (federal old age pensions) and Medicare (federal old age medical care) are rationalized by older Type A democrats as benefits they have paid for themselves rather than as transfer payments to them from younger Americans.

For Type A democrats, a democracy is similar to a voluntary club that free, responsible, and self-governing individuals establish with their fellow citizens to do the things they cannot do by themselves. Citizens hire the president, senators, representatives, judges, bureaucrats, and soldiers to serve the public as employees, as public servants. At the local level, the citizens hire police, firemen, teachers, and other public employees to serve their immediate local needs. Whom the citizens hire is determined by elections and other agreed-upon procedures. There is no concept of The State as the Europeans, Japanese, or most of the rest of the world, defines The State.

Type A democrats are willing to tax themselves and spend public money on public goods such as roads or parks, law enforcement, and national defense and often see free or inexpensive elementary, secondary, and university education as a public good. But Type A democrats draw a sharp distinction between a civil right that all citizens have to equal access to public schools established as public goods and a personal right to be educated. It is parents, family, and close friends that have the duty to see that the individual child is educated. Education is a privilege that the polity can choose to offer because an educated citizenry benefits the entire polity, but Type A democrats do not think that each individual has a right to an education that the democratic polity is duty-bound to provide at public expense. The same applies to housing, food, medical care, and emotional support.

Type A democrats can endorse governmental rules and regulations that benefit poor people. For example, the Tenement Law passed in New York City in the year 1901, requiring that indoor toilets be available to all tenement dwellers, transformed the lives of tens of thousands of people for the better (Wikipedia 2013e, New York State Tenement Law). The Tenement Law benefitted not only those tenement dwellers. It sharply reduced the incidence of infectious diseases such as cholera in the entire city. Type A democrats can support public improvements that may benefit people unequally. What is anathema to Type A democrats is using public funds to pay people's rent. Type A democrats argue that paying some peoples' rent is to treat them as dependents rather than as self-respecting politically equal citizens. Type A democrats would argue that if a paternalistic New York City government had supplied public housing in 1901 rather than just regulate housing as it did, that provision of a basic necessity to some of the poor but not all of the poor would have destroyed community unity and the ability of the tenement dwellers to band together in Type A style to help themselves as in fact they did.

Unlike Type A democracy, Type B democracy is founded on a pre-existing nation or community of which the individual is a constituent part. For Type B democrats, the welfare of the community is inseparable from the basic welfare of each individual member of the community. Type B democrats see the provision, or at least the guarantee, of education, housing, food, medical care, and emotional support for the individual as one of the chief purposes of government. Type B democratic political leaders often use metaphors of family to describe democracy. As Barack Obama, a Type B democrat, said on the night after he was first elected president, "[Americans share]…the belief that while each of us will pursue our own individual dreams, we are an American family, and we rise or fall together as one nation and as one people" Obama (2008).

Type A democrats see political metaphors of family as inherently hierarchical and undemocratic. Type B democrats are fond of saying that one can judge a democratic government by how the poorest fare under its rule. Type A democrats see governmental paternalism as a direct threat to political equality.

6.3 The Origins of Type A Democracy in America

It is easy to understand why the rest of the world defines democracy as social and economic equality and the elimination of pre-existing inequalities. The hard question is why so many Americans are so wedded to Type A democracy. Why is political equality more important to many Americans than economic equality? *Why are so many Americans so accepting of the economic inequalities that result from their democratic practices?*

To find an answer to these questions, we must return to a time 150 years before the writing of the United States Constitution. When the English colonies on the East Coast of North America were founded in the early 1600s, they were replicas of the English societies of their time. Even in the Puritan colonies of New England, high-born people sat in the front pews and the low-born sat in the back of the church. Many leaders of the separate 13 colonies, especially in the Puritan colonies of New England and the Quaker colony of Pennsylvania, were religious dissenters who believed in the direct relationship of each individual to a judgmental God, with each individual responsible only to God for the state of his or her immortal soul. No intervening church or secular authority which could assume that responsibility for the individual. Individual freedom of conscience and freedom to act in accord with one's conscience were essential to eternal salvation. This deep belief in the necessity of freedom of conscience for every person was the basis for a social order in which individuals had extraordinary freedom to shape their own lives. Seven generations (140 years) of isolation from England and virtually unlimited land and economic opportunity eroded social hierarchy and produced colonial societies often wealthier than England itself and yet characterized by a social and economic equality unique in the 1770s.

Although there were important social and economic differences between the 13 colonies—and a great deal of anti-democratic patriarchal authoritarian hierarchy embedded in their institutions—all of the colonies could be characterized as self-governing communities comprised of self-governing individuals. Slaves, the very poor, and most women excepted, people were accustomed to running their individual lives. They were also used to coming together in open town meetings in New England, and in elected councils and legislatures in the other colonies, to govern themselves collectively. These traditions of individual self-determination and collective self-government came into fundamental conflict with a more hierarchical authoritarian non-democratic England. The result was the American Revolution and political independence.

The American Revolution was not a rising of the poor against the rich. It bore little resemblance to the French Revolution of 1789, the Russian Revolution of 1917, the Communist Revolution in China, or to any rising of the oppressed against the oppressor. It was a war for independence led by the richest and most influential men of the colonies fighting against rule by the richest and most influential men in a distant mother country. It was not an attempt to found a Type B democracy, or to establish social and economic equality (Arendt 1963).

After seven perilous years under the Articles of Confederation, many of the richest and most influential citizens of the newly independent 13 American States recognized the need for closer cooperation. The problem was how to have an effective government on a continental scale that would not threaten the individual liberty and local self-government they had grown used to and had fought England to maintain. The answer to this question was the Constitution of the United States.

The Constitution of the United States establishes a Type A democracy. There are no guarantees in the United States Constitution of a basic standard of living, education, housing, or health care for each individual. There are no guarantees of economic or social equality.

This founding of a new political entity uniting the 13 newly independent states under a new Constitution was more like the formation of the European Union than the foundation of a new social and economic order. People already had Type A democracy in their several states. They felt no need for Type B democracy. They needed to give limited powers to a central government for certain limited purposes. The federal government was not intended to replace the government they had in their own states.

Because land was plentiful and economic opportunity great, and because the United States was an artificial entity, a political association, it has been possible to add tens of millions of new members over the past 220 years. New Americans were not asked to renounce their religion, their customs, or their history. They were not asked to become members of a tightly-knit community other than the ethnic or religious communities to which they already belonged. They were asked to subscribe to Type A democracy and to support the Constitution. Their connection to the United States was primarily a matter of political allegiance. The overarching system of Type A democracy allowed many of the more communal groups of immigrants, whether Mennonites, Chinese, Irish Roman Catholics, Sicilian Italians, Russian Jews, or Japanese Buddhists to live together as separate groups in relative peace.

In most nation-states, for example, Japan, China, England, France, Germany, or Sweden, it is a common cultural nationality that holds the country together. Because the people of the United States have no common cultural nationality, the United States is little more than the American legal-political system.

If the Constitution were overthrown, and American democracy replaced by a national dictatorship that destroyed democracy at the federal, state, and local levels, all that would be left would be disparate ethnic groups with their own customs, a number of regional cultures, a variety of economic marketplaces, private families, and individual lives, all bound together by an authoritarian government. The result would resemble the Hapsburg Empire more than a modern nation-state (Woodard 2012).

6.4 The Origins of Type B Democracy in America

If Type A democracy has historically been the primary form of democracy in America, why is Type B democracy now so powerful? The modern Democratic Party and President Obama are primarily Type B democrats. What is the origin of the power of Type B democracy in America?

Between the Civil War and the First World War, the United States underwent industrialization on a massive scale. There was a tsunami of immigration, mostly from Europe, of more than 25,000,000 people between the end of the Civil War and the outbreak of World War I. The population grew from 31,000,000 in 1860 to 92,000,000 in 1910 (Wikipedia 2013a, *Demographic*). The total GDP grew by a factor of 5 (Wikipedia 2013c, *List*). The GDP per capita more than doubled (Wikipedia 2013b, *File*).

This huge increase in wealth was distributed very unequally. The period of the 1890's was called the Gilded Age. And the Gilded Age led to the Progressive Era, the historic root of Type B Democracy in America.

Virtually all of the tens of millions of immigrants who flocked to America before the First World War were escaping patriarchal hierarchical authoritarian social orders and many were seeking what they could not hope to establish in their homelands, Type B democracy, social and economic equality within a pre-existing community. Although socialism and communism did not find fertile soil in the United States, by the 1920s, Type B democrats comprised a majority of the electorate in highly industrialized, immigrant heavy states such as New York. The rise of Al Smith, an Irish Catholic, Governor of New York from 1923 to 1928 and the Democratic Party's nominee for president in 1928, represented the growing political power of the new immigrant citizens and their descendants.

The Great Depression brought about the election in 1932 of Franklin Delano Roosevelt, also the Governor of New York, as president. FDR's election marked the beginning of the success of the New Deal Coalition, a Type B democratic movement that was to dominate American politics for 36 years. To understand the power of the New Deal Coalition we must go back to the American Civil War which was fought from 1861 to 1865.

The two major modern American political parties were on opposite sides of the Civil War. The Republicans generally represented the winning Northern States. (Abraham Lincoln was the first president ever elected by the modern Republican Party.) The Democratic Party represented the southern states that tried and failed to secede from the United States.

As a result of the Civil War, the Republicans in the north became the dominant party in the United States from the election of Lincoln in 1860 until 1932, when Roosevelt and the New Deal Coalition took power. During that 72 year period, the minority Democratic Party held the presidency for only 16 years.

It was the Great Depression that allowed Franklin Delano Roosevelt to forge the New Deal Coalition in 1932. The Depression was for many a failure of Type A democracy. Localities and states were overwhelmed by the magnitude of the economic disaster. The New Deal Coalition was a combination of the communally minded Type B democrats descended from recent immigrants *plus* the often hierarchical anti-democratic southern Democrats who, as a result of the Civil War, were so opposed to the Republican Party that it was said that they would vote for a yellow dog before they would vote for a Republican (Wikipedia 2013d, *Yellow*). Neither wing of the New Deal Coalition was a majority of the American people, but together they dominated. During this period of dominance of Type B democracy, Social Security (the federal old-age pension plan) was enacted in 1934, and Medicare and Medicaid (the federal medical insurance plans for the old and the poor) were enacted in 1965.

With the discrediting of the Democratic Party by the Vietnam War and the upheaval of the Civil Rights Movement in the 1960's in which southern blacks in a non-violent movement under Martin Luther King Junior asserted their Type A civil rights, the New Deal coalition of the Type B immigrant party of the north and the losers of the Civil War in the South broke up. The Republican Party pursued a Southern Strategy of appealing to white voters upset by the successful Civil Rights Movement, combining Southerners with the more traditional Type A Republicans in the North. Initially under Richard Nixon in 1968, and then under Ronald Reagan in 1980, Type A democracy, assisted by a good measure of Southern patriarchal hierarchical authoritarianism, reasserted itself. In the period of 24 years from 1968 until 1992, only Democrat Jimmy Carter in 1976 broke the Republican hold on the White House which he held for only 4 years. His election was in part due to the disgrace of the Watergate Scandal and the fact that Carter was from Georgia.

In 1992, Democrat Bill Clinton, also from the South, won the presidency. Since 1992, neither Type A or Type B democracy has been dominant. The Democratic Party has lost the Solid South. African-Americans, the major victims of pre-existing inequalities in American history, have combined with the descendants of Irish,

Italian, Jewish and, more recently, Hispanic immigrants, to form an enduring Democratic Party that is strongly Type B. The moderate Type A Republican Party that traditionally represented the West Coast States, the upper Midwest, and the Northern New England States—the heartlands of traditional Type A democracy—has faded away. The Republican Party has become the party of the old South, resisting Type B democracy but lacking the enthusiasm for collective self-government that characterized Type A democracy, to some degree realizing the fears of Tocqueville concerning "individualism."

As the New Deal Coalition broke down, there was less and less overlap between the two parties in the House and the Senate. The moderate Type A Republican Party members from the north and the moderate Type A Democrat Party members from the South retired or were defeated in party primaries and in general elections. Traditional Type A democrats, while perhaps still a majority in the country as a whole, are now under-represented in Washington. Since 1992, both the Democratic and Republican parties have become increasingly national and disciplined and increasingly hierarchical. The national parties more closely resemble British parliamentary parties rather than the loose coalitions of state parties they used to be (Mann and Ornstein 2012).

Americans now have gridlock in the federal government between Republicans who insofar as they are not hierarchical authoritarians are Type A democrats, and Democrats who insofar as they are not hierarchical authoritarians are Type B democrats. The Type A US Constitution is designed to prevent action when the people are evenly divided. The result is a federal government in gridlock.

6.5 A Way Out of Gridlock?

No democracy of either Type A or Type B can long survive the loss of the trust and confidence of a majority of its citizens. Polling by the Pew Research Center For The People and The Press has shown the percentage of Americans trusting in the Federal Government "to do the right thing all or most of the time" has fallen from 73 % in 1958 to 26 % in 2013 (Pew 2013a, *Public Trust*).

Unfortunately, Type A and Type B democrats are often fighting one another more than their common enemies. The problem is how to find the common ground between Type A and Type B democrats so that they can ally against the patriarchy, hierarchy, and authoritarianism that still abound in the United States. I have three brief suggestions.

First, the most important common ground between Type A and Type B democrats is the concept of public goods. Take, for example, health care. Type A democrats can accept publicly funded health care for the individual if it is for the common good. For example, guaranteed health care for the young from pre-natal to age 26 can easily be viewed as a public good because a healthy population is conducive to a healthy politics and economic prosperity. The parallel is with public education.

To make possible compromise on how much individual health care can be considered a public good, Type B democrats need to abandon their position that health care is a fundamental right, not a privilege (Pear and Baker 2013).

Second, Type A democrats need to strengthen their traditional commitment to funding public goods by taxes freely self-imposed. Type A resistance to Type B democracy that takes the form of asserting that all government is waste and that taxes can never be raised plays into the hands of hierarchical authoritarians who wish to weaken democracy of either type.

Third, Type B democrats need to get over their nostalgia for the federal government of the New Deal Coalition. Type B democrats need to agree with Type A democrats that local and state governments are inherently less hierarchical and more democratic than the federal government. Recent polling by the Pew Research Center For The People and The Press shows a far greater trust in local and state government than in the federal government.[2] The United States is a collection of regional cultures and ethnic groups (Woodard 2012; Fischer 1989; Garreau 1981). Whenever possible, especially on the level of the welfare of the individual, local solutions tailored to local public opinion are likely to be more successful than one national solution.

For example, the United States has the best collection of colleges and universities in the world, in part because the United States has never had a system of national universities. Individual states such as California, Wisconsin, and Michigan were able to forge ahead to establish large high-quality public research universities without convincing the voters in Alabama, Wyoming, or Mississippi of the value of such public universities. In time, the success of large public research universities in the states that first adopted them caused some other states such as New York and Texas to follow suit. Some states have never funded first-rate public universities, but at least those reluctant states have not held back the states willing to forge ahead.

In the same way, well-designed single payer public health programs in some of the states with an electoral majority of Type B democrats will, if successful, encourage other states to follow suit. Health care is similar to university education in that it does not have be on a federal scale to be successful. Indeed, trying to do universal health care for the first time as a federal initiative is likely to produce an unfortunate hybrid such as the current Obamacare (Patient Protection and Affordable Care Act), riddled with special interest compromises. The argument that a morality of "good government" requires the federal government to impose a health care system on unwilling states or localities is essentially an argument for authoritarian hierarchy.

In sum, the solution to gridlock in the federal government is for Type B democrats to stop trying to use the federal government to impose Type B national

[2] "Even as public views of the federal government in Washington have fallen to another new low, the public continues to see their state and local governments in a favorable light. Overall, 63 % say they have a favorable opinion of their local government, virtually unchanged over recent years. And 57 % express a favorable view of their state government – a five-point uptick from last year. By contrast, just 28 % rate the federal government in Washington favorably. That is down five points from a year ago and the lowest percentage ever in a Pew Research Center survey" (Pew 2013b, *State*).

solutions on states with a majority of Type A democrats. Type B democrats have a much better chance of succeeding if they focus their efforts in the states where they have an electoral majority, and where they can demonstrate that their solutions are conducive to the common good. If Type A democrats feel less threatened by Type B democrats at the federal level, Type A democrats will be more willing to work with Type B democrats to combat the forces of inequality hostile to both types of democracy.

Both Type A and Type B democrats are advocates of democracy. They differ in the sorts of equality they think are most important. Each type of democrat tends to see only one side of their common enemies. Type B democrats, typically Democrat Party members, see clearly the danger to economic and social equality of the concentration of economic power in large corporations and the super-rich (Freeland 2012). For the United States, the dangerous concentration of wealth in the upper 10 % (or 1 %) of the population has been attacked from both the political right (Murray 2012) and the political left (Hayes 2012). Type A democrats, typically Republican Party members, see clearly the dangers of the concentration of power and the danger to political equality and personal freedom in a powerful federal welfare state. Both Type A and Type B democrats occasionally see the danger of a federal national security state (Maddow 2012; Thomas 2012). Unfortunately, Type A and Type B Democrats are often fighting one another rather than their common enemy. Those who threaten economic equality usually also threaten political equality, and vice versa. They are the same people and are the common enemy of any type of democracy.

References

Arendt, H. 1963. *On revolution*. New York: Viking.

Fischer, D.H. 1989. *Albion's seed: Four British folkways in America*. New York: Oxford University Press.

Freeland, C. 2012. *Plutocrats: The rise of the new global super-rich and the fall of everyone else*. London: Penguin Press HC.

Garreau, J. 1981. *The nine nations of North America*. Boston: Houghton Mifflin.

Hayes, C. 2012. *Twilight of the elites: America after meritocracy*. New York: Crown.

Maddow, R. 2012. *Drift: The unmooring of American military power*. New York: Crown.

Mann, T.E., and Norman J. Ornstein. 2012. *It's even worse than it looks: How the American constitutional system collided with the new politics of extremism*. New York: Basic Books.

Murray, C. 2012. *Coming apart: The state of white America, 1960–2010*. New York: Crown Forum.

Obama, B. 2008. Election night speech. http://www.nytimes.com/2012/11/07/us/politics/transcript-of-president-obamas-election-night-speech.html?pagewanted=all&_r=0. Accessed 20 July 2013.

Pear, R., and Peter Baker. 2013. Health law is defended with vigor by President. The New York Times Online. http://www.nytimes.com/2013/05/11/us/politics/obama-to-makes-new-pitch-on-health-care-law.html?_r=0. Accessed on 20 July 2013.

Pew Research Center for the People & the Press. 2013a. Public trust in government: 1958–2013 http://www.people-press.org/2013/01/31/trust-in-government-interactive/. Accessed 20 July 2013.

Pew Research Center for the People & the Press. 2013b. State governments viewed favorably as federal rating hits new low. http://www.people-press.org/2013/04/15/state-govermnents-viewed-favorably-as-federal-rating-hits-new-low/. Accessed on 20 July 2013.

Thomas, E. 2012. *Ike's Bluff: President Eisenhower's secret battle to save the world.* Boston: Little Brown.

Tocqueville, A. 1994a (1840). *Of individualism in democratic countries. Democracy in America*, vol. 2. New York: Knopf, Everyman's Library.

Tocqueville, A. 1994b (1840). *That the Americans combat the effects of individualism by free institutions. Democracy in America*, vol. 2. New York: Knopf, Everyman's Library.

Wikipedia. 2013a. Demographic history of the United States http://en.wikipedia.org/wiki/Demographic_history_of_the_United_States. Accessed 20 July 2013.

Wikipedia. 2013b. File:US-GNP-per-capita-1869-1918.png. http://commons.wikimedia.org/wiki/File:US-GNP-per-capita-1869-1918.png. Accessed 20 July 2013.

Wikipedia. 2013c. List of regions by past GDP (PPP). http://en.wikipedia.org/wiki/List_of_regions_by_past_GDP_(PPP). Accessed 20 July 2013.

Wikipedia. 2013d. Yellow dog Democrat. http://en.wikipedia.org/wiki/Yellow_dog_Democrat. Accessed 20 July 2013.

Wikipedia. 2013e. http://wikipedia.org/wiki/New_York_State_Tenement_House_Act. Accessed 6 Nov 2013.

Woodard, C. 2012. *American nations: A history of the eleven rival regional cultures of North America.* London: Penguin Books.

Chapter 7
Proportional Representation, the Single Transferable Vote, and Electoral Pragmatism

Richard Nunan

> *If we're able to stop Obama on [health care reform], it will be his Waterloo. It will break him.*
>
> —Jim DeMint (Smith 2009)

> *The single most important thing we want to achieve is for President Obama to be a one-term president.*
>
> —Mitch McConnell (Garrett 2010)

Abstract An exploration of competing electoral systems—single-member district plurality systems (predominant in the U.S.) versus proportional representation systems (STV in particular)—and competing theories of participatory democracy: J.S. Mill's optimistic deliberative democracy model, and Richard Posner's more pessimistic elite democracy model. Mill assumes voters are politically educable, capable of making informed contributions to legislative processes through electoral action. Posner assumes voters are too narrowly self-interested to be substantively educable. Elections, consequently, serve merely as a crude form of quality control and smooth succession of political authority. It is argued that the latter theory is plausible only under single-member district plurality electoral systems like ours, so that the electoral system grounds the theory, not the other way around. Under a single transferable vote system (Mill's preferred system), in which voters' ordinal preferences among candidates govern the outcomes in multi-member districts, Mill's deliberative democracy model has a realistic prospect of success.

R. Nunan (✉)
Philosophy Department, College of Charleston,
66 Charles St., 29424 Charleston, SC, USA
e-mail: nunanr@cofc.edu

A.E. Cudd and S.J. Scholz (eds.), *Philosophical Perspectives on Democracy in the 21st Century*, AMINTAPHIL: The Philosophical Foundations of Law and Justice 5,
DOI 10.1007/978-3-319-02312-0_7, © Springer International Publishing Switzerland 2014

When federal legislators openly recommend obstructionism for its own sake as a partisan strategy, as was certainly the case with DeMint's call to arms (since the bill he wished to repudiate was originally a Republican health care initiative, before suffering the misfortune of being endorsed by a Democratic President), we know that American political institutions have become seriously dysfunctional. Indeed, the rhetoric and the visceral hostility continued unabated even after President Obama's reelection. Why? Vestigial racism is one hypothesis that has been offered to explain this phenomenon in the context of the Obama Presidency. But while the symptoms have been more dramatic in recent years, they did not suddenly emerge in the wake of President Obama's first election.

Kurt Vonnegut, referring to some of the principal players during the G.W. Bush Presidency, once suggested that our governmental dysfunctionality might be a matter of the sort of personality types attracted to higher office in political systems like ours: President Bush's collection of "upper-crust C-students who know no history or geography, plus not-so-closeted white supremacists, aka Christians, and plus, most frighteningly, psychopathic personalities, or PPs, the medical term for smart, personable people who have no consciences." The explanation is doubtless more complicated, not simply a case of Vonnegut's assertion that our Constitution harbors "a tragic flaw," the consequence that "only nut cases want to be president" (Vonnegut 2005, 99–102). Federal political office-holders are not *all* psychopaths.

Nonetheless, recent evidence does suggest that electorates, as currently constructed, are demonstrably bad at distinguishing between suitable and psychopathic candidates for public office. They often reward Vonnegut's "nut cases" for their public campaign behavior, and for misrepresentations of their performances while in office. To some extent, this can be attributed to ideological fervor of the hopelessly unreflective. But that can't explain majoritarian support for psychopathic personalities, since most voters are not ideologically driven. I suggest that our electoral system is a more pernicious—because more permanent—contributor to the erosion of effective government. Vestigial racism is (hopefully) more temporary, and the magnetic attraction of psychopathic personalities to public office merely contingent upon the root problem: their ability to succeed in single-member plurality systems.

We voters are, of course, often quite inattentive. We have our own lives to pursue, which makes misleading campaign tactics more effective, as does the escalating reliance on campaign money to fund televised propaganda. But the obfuscation and irrational voting behavior is significantly magnified, I will argue, by our single-member district plurality ('first past the post') electoral system for selecting candidates for legislative office, whereby all federal and state-level elections involve voting directly on one seat per election, determined by plurality victories, or sometimes by majority vote in two-candidate run-offs. We have, like Vonnegut, forgotten that constitutionally permissible alternatives are available, at least one of which, I contend, might ameliorate our current predicament.

The alternative I have in mind is proportional representation by single transferable vote (STV), which invites voters to rank candidates (ordinally) for multi-member district seats, and employs a vote-counting mechanism in which the surplus votes of each winning candidate (those which exceed the minimum number necessary to secure a seat in the multi-member district[1]) are transferred to the next-ranked candidate on each of the "surplus" ballots. The net effect of the proportionate vote transfers is to elect the candidates who enjoy the highest collective rank orderings among the voters, across all political parties.[2]

This was the system advocated in 1861 by John Stuart Mill in *Considerations on Representative Government*, after first being introduced in England 4 years earlier in Thomas Hare's *The Machinery of Representation*, and 2 years before that in Denmark by Carl Andrae.[3] There is a natural intuitive link between STV and Mill's deliberative conception of representative democracy, in which the full expression of voter sentiment possesses inherent value. For STV is a more nuanced reflection of voter convictions than most other electoral systems. But whether STV more accurately reflects voter sentiment in an *appropriate* way, and whether Mill's conception of deliberative democracy is normatively superior to other justifications that we might offer for representative democracy, are both contentious claims.

Comprehensive arguments on both points are beyond the scope of this chapter. I propose instead to offer an intuitive account of how STV compares with standard U.S. electoral practices on the question of more accurately reflecting voter sentiment. I will then turn to a defense of Mill's model of deliberative democracy against one alternative currently in vogue: the pragmatic elitist theory of representative democracy offered in the last century by Schumpeter 1962, and defended in this one by Posner 2001, 2003.[4]

---

[1] The most commonly used threshold formula, known as the Droop Quota, is calculated as follows: [(# of votes)/(#of seats +1)] +1. Thus, in a 5-member district in which 12,000 valid ballots were cast, a candidate could secure 2,000 first-preference votes without being guaranteed a seat, because it is theoretically possible that five other candidates could also secure exactly 2,000 votes each, resulting in a six-candidate dead heat, necessitating a run-off. But if one of the candidates secured 2,001 votes, that candidate, having met the Droop Quota (barely), would be guaranteed a seat.

[2] In some STV systems, the surplus ballots are literally paper ballots that happen to be at the top of the pile of first-choice ballots for any candidate who meets or surpasses the Droop Quota: every ballot counted for that candidate after the Droop Quota has been met counts as an "extra" first-choice ballot for that candidate, to be transferred to the various second-choice candidates indicated, during the second round of ballot-counting. In computerized vote-counting systems, fractional portions of *all* of a winning candidate's first-choice ballots could easily be used instead. I.e., the # of second-choice ballots for candidate *y*, among *all* those cast for winning candidate *x* as first choice, will be added to *y*'s first-choice ballots during the second round of counting, but discounted by the fraction:

$$\frac{\#\text{ of candidate x's ballots exceeding Droop quota}}{\text{total }\#\text{ of first-choice ballots cast for candidate x}}$$

For detailed accounts of the mechanics of single transferable vote balloting and ballot counting, see Farrell 2011, Chapter 6, 119–152 or Amy 2000, Chapter 4 (in part), 95–106. For a specific historical example, see Sinnott 1999.

[3] Hare's initial approach, the first scholarly publication on STV (Hare 1857), was to treat the entire country as a single multi-seat district. This was dropped later as unworkable.

[4] Posner acknowledges his debt to Schumpeter in the latter work.

7.1 STV and Electoral Alternatives: Alternate Voting and At-Large Voting

How do STV elections compare with their chief competitors among electoral systems? Historically grounded empirical data on STV is, unfortunately, rather thin. STV is currently used to elect the primary legislative bodies of Tasmania (since 1907), Ireland (since 1920), Malta (since 1921), the Australian Capital Territory, Canberra (since 1993), and Northern Ireland—the NI Assembly, not Westminster MPs (since the 1998 Good Friday Agreement). STV is also, nominally, the method of electing the Australian Senate. Of these, only the Republic of Ireland and Malta constitute national assemblies.

Apart from the Republic of Ireland and Northern Ireland, with a combined population of 6.4 million (1.8 million in Northern Ireland), STV jurisdictions are tiny. Malta has a population under 400,000, as does the Australian Capital Territory. And Tasmania has only half a million. Although Australia as a whole, at 23 million, is much larger, the Australian Senate does not initiate legislation. It does wield significant veto power on House-initiated legislation. More significantly, in 1983 Australian voters were given the option of voting a party ticket instead of rank-ordering all Senate candidates individually. Most Australian voters have opted for the former ever since, effectively transforming the Australian Senate elections into a closed list system.[5]

Comparison with single-member plurality systems, dominant in U.S. politics, will be examined in more detail in the discussion of the pragmatic elitist defense of democracy in 6.3. But as a preliminary step, we should understand the distinctions between STV and two other 'plurality-majority' electoral systems bearing superficial resemblances to STV. I'm referring here to *alternative vote* (AV) and *at-large* systems. Both are, in reality, just variations on single-member plurality voting.

AV is a mechanism for securing outright majorities rather than pluralities, by devising an instant run-off mechanism between the two strongest candidates, or by serially eliminating the weakest remaining candidates. AV shares STV's use of ordinally ranked voting, but does so in single-member districts. It anticipates instant run-offs by inviting voters to select, in addition to a primary candidate, a rank ordering of one or more less favored additional candidates. If no candidate wins an absolute majority on the first round of balloting, second-preference votes are then added in, followed by third-preference votes, etc., until a single-candidate majority is achieved. But the end result is still a winner-takes-all single-member district system.

At-large voting does the opposite: it shares STV's multi-member districts, but retains the binary cardinal voting of single-member plurality elections. Voters are *allowed* as many *unranked* votes (for distinct candidates) as there are seats to be filled, effectively assigning each candidate 'one' ("approve") or 'zero' ("disapprove"—refrain

[5] On this last point, see Farrell 2011, 140–141. Closed list systems, as a proportional representation alternative to STV, are discussed in 6.2.

from voting for a candidate). In the at-large case voting again fails to reflect relative strength of electoral sentiment. Representation is still an all-or-nothing affair, as it is in single-member districts. That is why at-large voting has been particularly popular at the local level in racially and politically polarized communities in the southern U.S., as an effective method for sustaining majoritarian dominance throughout an at-large district. In an at-large county council election, for example, conducted in a racially divisive polity that is two-thirds white, one-third African-American, identity politics voting behavior might routinely result in an entirely white, entirely Republican county council, despite significant African-American and Democratic Party minorities in the county, simply because white Republican voters, using a single ticket voting strategy, overwhelm both groups of minority voters at polling places. (And the reverse form of under-representation would apply in predominantly, but not exclusively, Democratic at-large districts.)

STV systems are designed to achieve the opposite effect: insure adequate representation of otherwise disenfranchised minorities. Consider an STV scenario in which the political spectrum equivalent of U.S. Republicans field five candidates for a five-seat district, and the "Democrats" stick with two. Even with strong party loyalties, the "Republicans" will not fare better under STV voting by fielding an "excessive" number of candidates, unless the candidate slate ranges across the political spectrum supported by significant numbers of voters (as both Maltese and Tasmanian parties in fact tend to do, at least to a more significant degree than either Republicans or Democrats here in the U.S.). Even then, in a polity like Malta, party loyalty tends to undermine this strategy. In a hypothetical five-member district consisting of three-fifths "Republican" voters and two-fifths "Democratic" voters, three-fifths of the vote will now be split five ways because of first-choice variations among the "Republican" voters, so the two "Democrats" will probably reach the quota for election on the first or second count, and three of the "Republicans" will probably meet it only after the vote transfers resulting from several counts sort out which three of the five "Republicans" enjoy stronger overall voter preference. If there is a viable third (or even fourth or fifth) party, the dominant party runs a serious risk of losing one or more seats it might otherwise win, by fielding too many candidates for existing voter support to carry through to election.

It was precisely this feature of STV voting which made it so attractive a system to install at the inception of the Irish Free State in 1921: to protect minority Protestant and Unionist concerns in the South and, initially at least, minority Catholic and Nationalist interests in Northern Ireland. Conversely, upon creation of the Irish Free State, as per prior agreement on self-determination, the six counties of Northern Ireland promptly disassociated themselves from the new polity—not only from the political entity that eventually became the Republic of Ireland, but also from its electoral mechanism. Now majority Protestant, they reverted to a single-member plurality electoral system for local self-government, thus protecting majority Unionist interests at the expense of the minority Nationalists, a politically short-sighted arrangement which remained in effect until the 1998 Good Friday Agreement.[6]

[6] See Farrell 2011, 119–125, for the Irish case.

Malta's adaption of STV appears to have been more of an accident of historical parallels. No significant minority interests needed to be addressed in Malta's homogeneous electorate. But like Ireland, Malta had been agitating for self-rule since the late nineteenth century, a movement that (also like Ireland), produced violent opposition to British authority after World War I. In ceding internal self-rule to Malta in 1921, the British simply imposed STV, apparently concluding that an electoral system good enough for the Irish Free State (being established simultaneously) was good enough for Malta (another Catholic country historically subject to Protestant rule from Westminster). Over time, the Maltese became accustomed to STV, and voluntarily reaffirmed their electoral system in later constitutions (Proctor 1980).

STV systems are also designed with the intent to yield representative bodies that more accurately reflect voter sentiment on policy issues generally, regardless of the party, religious, or ethnic affiliations of those voters. The usual argument against STV, and against all proportional electoral systems, is that such nuanced reflection of the range of voter sentiment also has the dilatory effect of encouraging more fragmentation of government through party proliferation: more effective representation of diverse political perspectives at the expense of less stable government, a virtue supposedly more prominent in single-member plurality systems.

Although the body of evidence of longstanding continuous usage of STV is small—two island countries and one island province—there is simply no data to support this negative claim. Throughout its history of STV usage, Malta has remained a pure two-party system. Sporadic third party movements have foundered on the party loyalty of Maltese voters, who behave at the ballot box as if they vote in an open list system (in which multi-member district seats are filled by voting for one candidate in a party slate), plus the opportunity to rank order as many as five candidates within that party vote (if five party candidates have been fielded[7]). Maltese voters have the option to split their ticket, but most do not choose to exercise that option.[8] There is somewhat more ticket-splitting in Tasmania, but it too has remained predominantly a two-party system. Third party movements in Tasmania are simply co-opted by the two larger parties, through the expedient of fielding individual party candidates who advocate policy views similar to those motivating third-party insurrections in the first place (Hughes 2000, 159–160).

Ireland, with (perhaps unsurprisingly) a more contrarian political culture, high emphasis on constituent services and on local retail politics, exhibits significant incidence of cross-party voting for individual candidates, including third-party voting (Farrell 2011, 135–136). Governments in Ireland, including occasional coalition governments, have nonetheless been as stable as governments in most European countries, and party proliferation has been modest. Effective political power has remained largely in the hands of two major center-right parties, and one smaller

[7] Each Maltese legislative district has five seats.

[8] That is, they can use ordinally-ranked voting to favor some candidates from the rival party, but they typically vote only for a subset of the preferred party slate. (Both parties frequently offer slates in excess of the five-seat districts being contested.) See Hirczy de Miño and Lane 2000.

center-left party.[9] The chief lesson to be learned here is that, in the case of STV at least, and probably in other proportional representation systems as well, government formation depends far more on the local political culture than it does on the electoral system. The same cannot be said of plurality systems, which clearly do favor two-party structures through their all-or-nothing electoral outcomes.[10]

7.2 STV and Electoral Alternatives: Closed and Open List Proportional Systems

Apart from questions of comparing the relative merits of STV and plurality-majority systems, there is also the question: does STV constitute a more effective system for representation of divergent voter sentiment than other proportional representation systems? The two major proportional competitors to STV, at least in terms of number of countries and total number of voters using them, are the closed and open list systems, both far more common than STV.[11] Unlike STV, both of these emphasize party affiliation over individual candidates. Closed lists, the original system of party list voting, do not allow any candidate selection. Voters simply vote for a party list, with the candidates ordered for election by the party. The number of party candidates occupying contested seats in the multi-member district will then be determined by the party's proportional share of the total vote cast, starting with the first candidate listed. Open list systems allow voters to play a role in ranking the candidates on the party's slate, typically by voting for one specific candidate on one party's list.

Our core question is whether STV is more representative of voter sentiment than either list system. In terms of the basic structure, the answer is clearly 'yes': STV invites more nuanced ordinal voting among multiple candidates as individuals. Political theorists sometimes argue, however, that the answer is 'no', because actual list systems typically do better in measurements of proportional representation of minority factions than the handful of actual STV systems that exist. But that is only because of the historical accident that actual STV systems have relatively small district *size* (the number of seats in a district, which is three to five in existing STV systems) compared to list systems (frequently districts of ten or more seats). Minimum representational vote thresholds are inversely related to district size. In

[9] *Fianna Fáil*, *Fine Gael*, and *Labour*, respectively. *Labour* has been the only really significant third party, although others have, from time to time, sustained enough voter support to win a few seats. See Farrell 2011, 143–146, and Gallagher 2000.

[10] See Amy 2000, 18, 32, and Farrell 2011, Appendix Table A.2, 234–237. In Farrell's table there are two notable exceptions to two-party rule among single-member plurality nations: Canada, with an effective number of parliamentary parties average of 3, and India, the world's largest democracy, with a 5.77 average.

[11] See Farrell 2011, Figure 1.1, and accompanying discussion, 7–9. See also Farrell, Appendix Table A.1, 231–233.

electorates that contain, say, four or five significant political minorities, some of those minorities are likely to secure no direct representation in a five-seat district, but all of them will do so in a ten-seat district.[12]

So an STV system incorporating larger district size *could* be just as effective as a list system in achieving parliamentary representation for minority views, and certainly more effective at serving voter expression on the ballot. There is an inherent limit to this strategy, however. STV demands much more from voters. They have to sort through multiple candidates representing multiple party platforms, and somehow come up with at least a partial rank ordering. Too many choices can overwhelm voters with limited time to devote attention to election campaigns. List systems, by contrast, are dead simple—asking voters to make just one choice, for a single party or a single candidate. Hence the ease with which they can move to large multi-member districts.

So there is a trade-off here, although we might hope that greater voter choice attendant STV systems will ultimately produce more sophisticated voters and more rational election campaigns, particularly when compared with single-member plurality systems like ours.[13] But to make that case, we have to turn now to our second question, concerning rival defenses of representative democracy as the best means of government. More specifically, Mill's account of deliberative democracy and Posner's account of pragmatic elitism are both attempts to answer the question: what is representative democracy *for*? I contend that Posner's answer to this question is plausible (to the extent that it is) only because he assumes a single-member plurality voting system.

7.3 Deliberative Democracy vs. Pragmatic Elitism

First, a brief sketch of the difference between these two theories: both reject Rousseau's concept of the *general will*, in the sense that neither Mill nor Posner (nor Schumpeter) advocate direct democracy in which the electorate engages in legislative action, because most voters are too unreliably focused on their narrow self-interest to be entrusted with that authority. Both Mill and his competitors believe that legislation should be conducted instead by educated elites: *elected* representatives of the

[12] On this point, see Farrell and McAllister 2000, at 21–22 & 28–32.

[13] Whether this is also true when the competitor is a proportional representation system, or a mixed system involving proportional representation, is a question beyond the scope of this chapter. (Dummett 1997) in particular proposed a novel and rather complex system involving a mixture of STV and *Borda counts*, a concept not discussed here. His assessment of conventional STV systems is colored though by his oddly visceral hostility: "STV occupies an extraordinary position among electoral systems, in that it is the object of a cult. A large body of electoral reformers are committed to STV as to a religious faith." (Dummett, 90–91) Dummett's mixed STV/Borda count alternative, which has never been used anywhere, has its own problems, having to do with the issue of accurately identifying political minorities. I'm offering STV as the best option among at least the existing systems, but I am here far from making that case in any comprehensive way.

people, yes, but better informed than the people themselves. Mill, however, also believes in the possibility of instilling a measure of civic virtue in the masses, through their engagement with the machinery of participatory democracy. As they encounter views different from their own in their exposure to public political discourse, participatory democracy assumes an educative function:

> The private citizen...is called upon, while so engaged, to weigh interests not his own; to be guided, in case of conflicting claims, by another rule than his private partialities; to apply, at every turn, principles and maxims which have for their reason of existence the common good: and he usually finds associated with him in the same work minds more familiarized than his own with these ideas and operations, whose study it will be to supply reasons to his understanding, and stimulation to his feeling for the general interest. He is made to feel himself one of the public, and whatever is for their benefit to be for his benefit (Mill 1861, 70).

Posner and Schumpeter do not share Mill's optimism. They subscribe rather to John Adams' cynicism about the citizenry, an older, deeper suspicion of deliberative democracy:

> If you give more than a share of the sovereignty to the democrats, that is, if you give them command or preponderance in the legislature, they will vote all property out of the hands of you aristocrats, and if they let you escape with your lives, it will be more humanity...than any triumphant democracy displayed since the creation (Hofstadter 1948, 17).

For Posner and Schumpeter, as for Adams, it is important to contain the level of mass participation in the machinery of government, but not to eliminate it entirely. Posner does not want to "simply restrict the franchise to a well-educated *cognoscenti*," because the educated elite is just as likely to be devoid of mythic civic virtue, just as likely to vote its own interests, as the unwashed masses are to vote theirs (Posner 2001, 42). For Posner and Schumpeter, but *not* for Adams or most of his fellow-eighteenth-century "revolutionaries", *universal* citizen suffrage serves as a useful check on excesses of governing elites:

> Representative democracy is a pragmatic institution rather than the instantiation of a theorist's ideal state. Voting is a method of control, not of administration. The people do not rule in a representative democracy; they control the rulers, their delegates. For voting to perform its function of control, voters must have some minimum of political sophistication, along with a measure of independence from other people. Voting is central to the orderly succession of democratic "rulers."... American democracy is structured, formal, practical, realistic...It is not starry-eyed, carnivalesque, or insurrectionary. It is not pure or participatory democracy, and it does not consider political chaos a price worth paying to actualize the popular will. Its spirit is closer to that of Burke than to that of Rousseau (Posner 2001, 28–29).

In Posner's view, the practice of voting for those who govern, and delegating most other communal powers to those elected representatives, is simply a more effective solution to the problem of orderly succession than hereditary monarchy, the most common traditional way of addressing the succession problem. The latter offers neither quality control in selection, nor the possibility of peaceful transition when the leadership product is unacceptably substandard. Representative democracy offers both: quality control through the campaign and election process, and periodic performance review through the practice of regularly scheduled new elections (Posner 2001, 23–24; 2003, 14, and Chaps. 4 and 5, generally).

Mill, in contrast, believes the masses, as the best guardians of their own interests, actually have something to contribute to policy deliberations through their voting practices—especially when their own views of those interests are enlarged and refined by their participation in civic discourse. Posner (and Schumpeter) think democratic voting practices have nothing to do with discerning the will of the people, even in this attenuated sense of conveying their collective informed self-interest on particular policy questions.

Posner and Schumpeter may be right about the intended structure of our democracy, *in its present form.* But it now appears that they are wrong about the wisdom of that structure: our single-member district plurality approach to elections is now used, quite effectively, to insulate the governing elite from the electorate. It achieves this outcome by affording legislative bodies the opportunity to create safe party districts at both federal and state levels, by means of district gerrymandering. To a lesser degree, the Electoral College has served the same function in Presidential races by creating safe Presidential "districts" (individual states).

On one level of analysis, the end result appears to bear out the hypothesis of pragmatic elitists: the electoral masses appear to be incorrigibly self-interested in very short-sighted ways—witness the current success of the Tea Party movement in taking over the Republican Party. Voters also often appear to be incorrigibly ignorant—witness the result of the 2010 South Carolina Democratic primary for the U.S. Senate. In that primary, Alvin Greene, an unemployed African-American army veteran, an inarticulate young man of limited intellectual scope and no prior political experience living with his father in rural South Carolina, after having been involuntarily discharged from both the Air Force and the Army, and currently facing federal pornography charges, managed to defeat a career public service opponent by 30,000 votes. He achieved this with no campaign—not even a campaign website. After the primary, he was somewhat belatedly recognized to be transparently unfit to serve in the U.S. Senate, and was then overwhelmed by incumbent Republican Jim DeMint in the general election (Hutchins and Axe 2012).

Posner, Schumpeter, and Adams assume that voter incompetence and myopia are simply the natural state of the general populace, dictating the necessity of severely limiting the scope of their participation in the machinery of government. But what if the causal arrow runs in the other direction? What if voter incompetence and myopia are not evidence of immutable voter incorrigibility, but artifacts of the electoral system we now have in place? Perhaps, in so severely limiting their conception of participatory democracy—it only comes in the one flavor, single-member district plurality systems—Posner and his fellow-travelers have simply embarked on a voyage of self-fulfilling prophecy which is just now bearing its richest fruit, the outcome of which they then mistakenly regard as "natural" to the human condition. Perhaps the reality of the human condition is Mill's reality, not Posner's: electorates *are* politically educable, given both sufficiently enlightened tutors among the political elite and a sufficient stake in the political system to make the education worth their time and attention. Moreover, through this process, they will have genuinely useful information to impart to the governing elite who craft and implement legislation.

Traditional older-generation Republicans are now being eaten by their young (the Tea Party) because of the rhetoric in which they have been engaged ever since the Reagan "revolution", beginning with Reagan's campaign slogan directed against incumbent Jimmy Carter: "Are you better off now than four years ago?" This unvarnished appeal to unfiltered self-interest was striking in its contrast to John Kennedy's "starry-eyed" and perhaps even "carnivalesque" slogan two decades earlier: "Ask not what your country can do for you, but what you can do for your country." Of course Reagan's slogan did speak to a long-standing libertarian tradition of mistrust of government embedded in our culture (as discussed by Richard Parker in his contribution to this volume). But political rhetoric can have serious consequences with respect to the direction and momentum of public expectations. In this regard, Reagan's rhetoric provided the early framework for the future legitimation of the Tea Party movement, rhetoric which has been nourished and sustained because it spoke to relatively homogeneous constituencies in safe Republican districts.

In consequence, the ranks of socially and economically extremist factions have swollen to the point at which, in the 2012 Presidential primary campaigns, even relatively moderate Republicans felt compelled to engage in extremist rhetoric in order to secure the nomination. This phenomenon has validated Tea Party self-confidence still further, all of which suggests that Mill was right about at least one thing: his conviction that the masses were educable by the elite. But that doesn't preclude the precise form of the education being quite destructive, whenever the pedagogical strategy crafted by the elite is itself socially corrosive.

Similarly, the 2010 SC Senate Democratic primary indicates how Mill is also right about the need for substantive electoral participation as part of the educational process. Only 170,000 voters participated in that primary, while more than 860,000 SC voters supported Obama in 2008. The contrast can be explained in terms of the SC electorate's knowledge that, regardless of the identities of the Democratic Senate candidates, participation in that primary, and in the general Senate election, would not secure representation of their views in our single-member districts. Because of the proliferation of gerrymandered safe Congressional districts, and of reliably red and blue states in Senatorial and Presidential winner-takes-all elections, many potential voters simply don't bother going to the polls, thus magnifying the influence of inattentive voters, and fostering a different kind of more broad-based political alienation, reflected in low U.S. voter turnout generally.[14]

[14] Voter participation is routinely higher in proportional representation systems (75–90 % average voter turnout during the last two decades), with Malta topping the list at 95–98 % of the voting age population. (See Amy 2000, 39; Hirczy de Miño & Lane, 190). Tasmanian electoral turnout during the same period falls in the 80–90 % range, although voting in Australia is nominally compulsory. (Appendix B, Tasmanian Election Commission's 2007–2010 House Assembly Election Report, http://tec.tas.gov.au/pages/HouseMain.html.) Among STV constituencies, Ireland has been less impressive over the past two decades, ranging between 64 and 74 % of the voting age population (generally better than neighboring U.K.). But the U.S., together with other single-member plurality systems (see Amy, 39), has been even less impressive, occupying the 47–57 % range during Presidential year elections, and consistently below 40 % during intervening Congressional elections.

Posner offers a thin explanation for this phenomenon, comparing voting with rooting for a football team. It is, on his analysis, a form of consumption, a source of entertainment, with the added psychic benefit of imbuing voters with a sense of place through their exercise of solidarity with a like-minded group. Absent more engaging reasons to exercise the franchise, any hurdles placed in the way of voting will depress turnout significantly. Posner contends that low U.S. voter turnout can be attributed largely to two minor inconveniences: the fact that voting is scheduled on a regular workday, and the inconvenience of having to re-register every time you move from one voting jurisdiction to another (Posner 2001, 14–15).

A more plausible explanation would blame the structure of our electoral system. As various advocates of proportional representation systems have argued, it seems more likely that voters whose views go consistently unrepresented in winner-take-all districts will become increasingly discouraged by their lack of representation, and opt out of the process entirely. This is known as the *wasted vote* phenomenon. Similarly, Posner's football analogy for describing voter sentiment and practice is plausible only because, *with this kind of system*, there is little else for voters to do. Candidates rarely engage in serious policy debates because irresponsible sloganeering and mudslinging are more effective in single-member districts populated with dominant political majorities. The loop between sycophantic candidates and unreflective constituencies becomes self-perpetuating.

7.4 Electoral System Reform: The Art of the Possible in a Single-Member System

How might an STV system work in the U.S., and how might it serve to confirm Mill's views about the potential for an enlarged capacity for political sophistication among the general run of voters? It is important to bear in mind that voters are comfortable with what is customary for them. There is in fact virtually no discussion of electoral *system* reform in the U.S. There are therefore limits to how far we might reasonably expect American voters to move in this direction. List systems, for example, in which you vote primarily (or exclusively) for a party rather than an individual may seem too radical a shift to proportional representation for U.S. voters, who are accustomed to voting for individuals rather than parties under our single-member plurality voting scheme. Even the rank-ordered voting in multi-member districts required by STV would take some adjustment. But it does at least bear superficial resemblance to at large districts, with which most U.S. voters have some familiarity at the local level.

In our federal system, without radical modifications, STV could have a direct effect only in the House of Representatives. The Presidency is, by its nature, a national single-member district. Similarly, each state's two Senate seats are also

(Data from the International Institute for Democracy and Electoral Assistance [IDEA], at: http://www.idea.int/vt/survey/voter_turnout1.cfm.)

single-member districts. Changing the voting system for either of those offices would require Constitutional Amendment, in a political climate currently so polarized that it is hard to imagine any Constitutional Amendment securing approval, apart from elimination of the Electoral College. That alone would yield more effective voter participation in Presidential elections by making popular vote counts more meaningful in non-swing states. Moreover, it is achievable by non-constitutional means: mutual agreement among state legislatures to circumvent the Electoral College, either by appointing electors in a way designed to mirror popular vote distributions statewide, or by appointing electors to vote for whichever candidate has won a plurality of votes nationally. (The second strategy has gained some momentum, conditional on other states doing the same.)

But even greater levels of participation can be achieved by replacing, where practically feasible, our single-member legislative districts with multi-member districts, both in Congress and at the state level. At the federal level, this can be done without any Constitutional Amendment, since Congressional apportionment is defined in Article 1 as being allocated "among the several States" and §2 of the Fourteenth Amendment is again framed in terms of *state* populations, not in terms of maintaining comparably populated single-member districts: "Representatives shall be apportioned among the several States according to their respective numbers, counting the whole number of persons in each State, excluding Indians not taxed."[15]

Unless the U.S. Supreme Court were to ignore that "plain language" for partisan reasons, there is no *constitutional* barrier to such redistricting, only a *statutory* barrier. The practice of delegating the districting authority to the individual states (usually, but not always state legislatures[16]) was established by federal statute in language that requires single-member districts:

> In each State entitled...to more than one Representative...there shall be established by law *a number of districts equal to the number of Representatives* to which such State is so entitled, and *Representatives shall be elected only from districts so established, no district to elect more than one Representative*... [2USC2c; italics mine].

So requiring, or even permitting, multi-member districts *would* necessitate an act of Congress, and there are of course political barriers to that, given the career interests of Congressional incumbents. But that intransigence could be modified in time by the pressure of popular sentiment, if the currently extreme level of partisan gridlock continues for the foreseeable future.

If we eventually come to seriously contemplate such change, how might the redistricted landscape look? Such multi-member districts should be set at sizes of four to eight legislative seats. Fewer result in inadequate representation of minority political views, minority ethnic groups, etc. More yield ballots too cumbersome for voters to process. A large state like Texas, for example, which

[15] Here the Fourteenth Amendment superseded the corresponding passage of Article 1, §2.3 of the Constitution, by eliminating the references to "free persons" and three-fifths of "other persons."

[16] Six states (AZ, CA, HI, ID, NJ, WA) implement redistricting by means of independent bipartisan commissions. This trend may be on the rise, but the extent to which it has successfully eliminated partisan redistricting is unclear.

now contains 36 U.S. Congressional districts, could be subdivided into three predominantly urban multi-member districts (Dallas/Ft. Worth 8, Houston 7, San Antonio/Austin 5) and three predominantly rural ones (East Texas 7, El Paso/West Texas 5, and South Texas 4).

A small state like South Carolina would more sensibly be treated as a single multi-member district (consisting of seven Congressional seats), both because the range of demographic variation in different geographic regions is relatively modest compared to a state like Texas (e.g., there are no large urban centers in South Carolina), and because small multi-member districts would not insure effective proportional representation of significant political minorities. With respect to ethnicity, for example, South Carolina is 28 % black and 60 % non-Hispanic white, according to 2011 U.S. census estimates. Until very recently, South Carolina had only one African-American Congressman (Jim Clyburn, in a "safe" gerrymandered majority-black district created in 1992). Tim Scott, a conservative black Republican, was elected in 2010 in the First District, a coastal district which is, thanks to careful redistricting, only 21 % black. He was reelected in 2012. But while the resulting racial mix in the SC Congressional delegation was roughly ethnically proportional in regard to the State's racial demographic, that situation was unlikely to survive Scott's Congressional career, given South Carolina's past history under our single-member plurality system. Indeed it has not. Following Jim DeMint's resignation from the Senate to lead the Heritage Foundation just 2 years after his reelection, Scott was appointed by SC Governor Nikki Haley to replace him, and the resulting vacancy filled by a white Republican (former Governor Mark Sanford, resuming his old Congressional seat through special election early in 2013). There are currently no women in the SC Congressional delegation and, less surprisingly, no Hispanics (5.3 % of the SC population). Political party strength is even more glaringly disproportionate than ethnic representation. To judge by the results of the last three Presidential elections, the political split is roughly 56 % Republican, 42 % Democratic, yet the Congressional apportionment is 6–1 Republican. If we were to switch to STV proportional voting, a 5–2 White/African American division would probably be more stable (since the days of racial voting blocks are far from over in South Carolina), and the political split would probably moderate to 4–3 Republican.

The point of these reforms would be to encourage more meaningful participation in elections, both because there would be better prospects for representation of the views of minority voting blocks, and because the more nuanced responses of the electorate would better inform the resulting legislative bodies about citizens' needs, concerns, and desires. Campaign discourse would also be likely to become more informed, less rabid, as candidates realize that they now have to reach out to newly enfranchised voters who they do not want to alienate by saying outrageous things about fundamentally like-minded opponents to whom some potential supporters may also be attracted. In this kind of political atmosphere, it might well be reasonable to embrace Mill's greater optimism about the potential for significant political education through political participation at the ballot box.

References

Amy, Douglas J. 2000. *Behind the ballot box: A citizen's guide to voting systems*. Westport: Praeger.

Bowler, Shaun, and Bernard Grofman. 2000. *Elections in Australia, Ireland, and Malta under the single transferable vote*. Ann Arbor: University of Michigan Press.

Dummett, Michael. 1997. *Principles of electoral reform*. Oxford: Oxford University Press.

Farrell, David M. 2011. *Electoral systems: A comparative introduction*, 2nd ed. Basingstoke: Palgrave Macmillan.

Farrell, David M., and Ian McAllister. 2000. Through a glass darkly: Understanding the world of STV. In *Elections in Australia, Ireland, and Malta under the single transferable vote,* ed. Shaun Bowler, and Bernard Grofman, 17–36. Ann Arbor: University of Michigan Press.

Gallagher, Michael. 2000. The (relatively) victorious incumbent under STV: Legislative turnover in Ireland and Malta. In *Elections in Australia, Ireland, and Malta under the single transferable vote,* ed. Shaun Bowler, and Bernard Grofman, 81–113. Ann Arbor: University of Michigan Press.

Garrett, Major. 2010. After the wave. *National Journal*, October 23. http://www.nationaljournal.com/magazine/after-the-wave-20101023. Accessed 8 Nov 2013.

Hare, Thomas. 1857. The machinery of representation. *Google Books, 2009*. http://books.google.com/books?id=8SBcAAAAQAAJ&printsec=frontcover&source=gbs_ge_summary_r&cad=0#v=onepage&q&f=false. Accessed 15 June 2013.

Hirczy de Miño, Wolfgang, and John C. Lane. 2000. Malta, STV in a two-party system. In *Elections in Australia, Ireland, and Malta under the single transferable vote,* ed. Shaun Bowler, and Bernard Grofman, 178–204. Ann Arbor: University of Michigan Press.

Hofstadter, Richard. 1948. The founding fathers: An age of realism. In *The American political tradition and the men who made it*, ed. R. Hofstadter, 3–23. New York: Alfred A. Knopf.

Hughes, Colin A. 2000. STV in Australia. In *Elections in Australia, Ireland, and Malta under the single transferable vote,* ed. Shaun Bowler, and Bernard Grofman, 155–177. Ann Arbor: University of Michigan Press.

Hutchins, Corey, and David Axe. 2012. *The accidental candidate: The rise and fall of Alvin Greene*. Jefferson: McFarland.

Mill, John Stuart. 1861. *Considerations on representative government*. State College: Penn State Electronic Classics, 2004. http://www2.hn.psu.edu/faculty/jmanis/jsmill/considerations.pdf. Accessed 15 June 2013. See especially Chapter VII, "Of True and False Democracy: Representation of All, and Representation of the Majority Only," 92–107.

Posner, Richard. 2001. *Breaking the deadlock: The 2000 election, the constitution, and the courts*. Princeton: Princeton University Press.

Posner, Richard. 2003. *Law, pragmatism, and democracy*. Cambridge, MA: Harvard University Press.

Proctor, J.H. 1980. The acceptance of proportional representation in Malta. *Parliamentary Affairs* 33(1): 308–321.

Schumpeter, Joseph. 1962. *Capitalism, socialism, and democracy*, 3rd ed. New York: Harper. (Originally published 1942.)

Sinnott, Richard. 1999. The electoral system. In *Politics in the Republic of Ireland*, 3rd ed, ed. John Coakley and Michael Gallagher, 99–126. London: Routledge.

Smith, Ben. 2009. Health reform foes plan Obama's 'Waterloo'. *Politico*, July 17. http://www.politico.com/blogs/bensmith/0709/Health_reform_foes_plan_Obamas_Waterloo.html. Accessed 15 Sept 2012.

Vonnegut, Kurt. 2005. *A man without a country*. New York: Random House.

Chapter 8
The Problem of Democracy in the Context of Polarization

Imer B. Flores

Abstract Contemporary democracies are more polarized than ever and this chapter inquiries not only about the conditions of possibility for democracy in the context of polarization but also on whether the relationship is one of compatibility or incompatibility. The claim is that if democracy is possible *here* and *there*—in contexts characterized by their polarization—it is possible *everywhere* as long as certain conditions are met. Hence, the response to polarization provides a hint on the (minimal) conditions of possibility for democracy and polarization more than a problem is a great opportunity for democracy and a greater democratization.

8.1 Introduction

Exploring the conditions of possibility in a democracy is a problem that demands a great deal of attention on its own, but in contexts characterized by increasing polarization it is a must. In fact, our contemporary democracies all over the globe seem to be quite polarized or in the process of becoming even more so.[1] Let me advance,

[1] Keep in mind, the *Québéçois* bloc and the separatist movement in Canada; the presidential elections in the United States of America in 2000, including the Florida saga of butterfly ballots, hanging chads, counts, recounts and re-recounts… and the usual deadlock in Congress; the controversial presidential elections in Mexico in 2006 and the post-electoral conflict; the hang parliamentary elections in both Australia and Belgium in 2010, and the closest ones since 1992 in the United Kingdom also in 2010; the 2011 local elections in Milan with a virtual tie between the ruling party and the opposition after an absolute dominance since 1996; the fact that most systems with a *ballotage* system end up in the second round, for instance, Colombia, France and Peru in 2011; and, more recently, the ordinary and extraordinary presidential elections in Venezuela in both 2012 and 2013. Clearly, polarization is not reduced to Election Day, but too-close-to-call or hung elections do exemplify it pretty well.

I.B. Flores (✉)
Instituto de Investigaciones Jurídicas, UNAM, Circuito Mtro. Mario de la Cueva, S/N, 4510 Coyoacán-Mexico, D.F., Mexico
e-mail: imer@unam.mx

A.E. Cudd and S.J. Scholz (eds.), *Philosophical Perspectives on Democracy in the 21st Century*, AMINTAPHIL: The Philosophical Foundations of Law and Justice 5, DOI 10.1007/978-3-319-02312-0_8,

my aim is to discuss the conditions of possibility of a democracy, in general, and in polarized contexts, in particular. My hunch is that if democracy is possible *here* and *there*—in contexts characterized by their polarization—it is possible *everywhere* if certain conditions are met. Hence, the response to polarization provides a hint of the (minimal) conditions of possibility of a democracy.

Therefore, I intend to analyze such conditions, but I must first in Sect. 8.2 emphasize the relation between democracy and polarization to check whether they are compatible or incompatible. For that purpose, we will bring to mind: first, two conceptions of "democracy"; and, second, four characterizations of "polarization". Then, later on, in Sect. 8.3, we will return to democracy and its conditions of possibility: if democracy and polarization are compatible, polarization is a great opportunity for democracy and a greater democratization.

8.2 Democracy and Polarization

Let me recall that some years ago, in March 2006, a book titled *Is Democracy Possible Here? Principles for a New Political Debate* by the late Ronald Dworkin (2006) appeared, based on the Scribner Lectures that he delivered at Princeton University the previous year. Dworkin began by acknowledging an increasing polarization between the two dominant cultures in the United States of America, represented by the ideologies of the two main political parties, who not only disagree about almost everything including the scope of their disagreements, but also—and even worse—neither have nor show respect the one for the other and vice versa to the extent that he cautions: "We are no longer partners in self-government; our politics are rather a form of war" (2006, 1). In addition, Dworkin warned that the split between the two poles may become an "unbridgeable gulf" if there is "no common ground to be found and no genuine argument to be had" in order to seek and eventually reach a broad consensus. In this regard, he added:

> Democracy can be healthy with no serious political argument if there is nevertheless a broad consensus about what is to be done. It can be healthy even if there is no consensus if it does have a culture of argument. But it cannot remain healthy with deep and bitter divisions and no real argument, because it then becomes only a tyranny of numbers (2006, 6).

However, he advanced that it is possible to find some shared principles to make a political debate possible and profitable (2006, 6–7) and he purported to begin a process that might "reinvigorate the argumentative dimension of politics" (2006, 8). As mentioned above, before proceeding to analyze which are the conditions of possibility of a democracy, we must examine the relation between democracy and polarization to check their (in)compatibility, by bringing to mind: first, two conceptions of "democracy"; and, second, four characterizations of "polarization" (Flores 2009, 2010b).

8.2.1 Democracy

According to its etymology—*demos* (people) and *kratos* (government, power or rule)—"democracy" means "government, power or rule of the people". It is a form of government in contraposition to other forms. The classical typology includes three "pure" forms: (1) "autocracy" (better known as "monarchy") as the government of *one*—*i.e.* the monarch; (2) "aristocracy" as the government of *few*—*i.e.* the better ones; and (3) "democracy" as the government of *all*—*i.e.* the people. But it also includes three "impure" forms: (1) "tyranny" as the government of *one*—*i.e.* the tyrant; (2) "oligarchy" as the government of *few*—*i.e.* the rich; and (3) "demagogy" as the government of *many*—*i.e.* the poor (or the mob).

It is worth mentioning that Aristotle considered "democracy" pejoratively, an equivalent to the term "demagogy", as one vicious extreme in contraposition to "oligarchy" as the other vicious extreme, whereas his *politeia* was the virtuous middle term by comprising the government of both the poor and the rich (1988, 97–8). Unlike Aristotle, I will reserve "demagogy" for the "impure" form and "democracy" for the "pure" one. But like him, I will assume that the latter is the government of *all* the people, not only both poor and rich but also both many and few, or alternatively both majority and minority.

The problem is that for some authors, "democracy" seems to be reduced to the government of the *many* or *majority* in detriment of the *few* or *minority*, a so-called majoritarian or populist democracy. On the contrary, a true "democracy" must be neither of poor or rich, nor of many or few, nor of majority or minority, but of all: both poor and rich, both many and few, both majority and minority.

So far the notion of "democracy" as a form of government and the typology has served to emphasize the ownership (or partnership) "of" the political or sovereign power, depending on whether it corresponds to one, few, many, or all. Nevertheless, the exercise of this political or sovereign power not only must be done directly and indirectly "by" its owners (or partners) and their representatives, but also must be done "for" them and their benefit, not to their detriment. The three ideas already sketched can be put together into an integral definition, such as the one embodied in Abraham Lincoln's maxim (1863/1990, 308; the emphasis is mine) and in the "Preamble" of the Fifth French Republic's motto: "government *of* the people, *by* the people, *for* the people".

In that sense, a true "democracy" must be the government of, by and for all the people: poor and rich, many and few, majority and minority… men and women, heterosexuals and homosexuals, believers and non-believers… and so on. Hence, I will consider "democracy" as the "government *of* all the people, *by* all the people—directly on their own ("direct democracy") or indirectly through their representatives ("representative democracy")—and *for* all the people" (Flores 2005a, 154–7, 2008a, 314–9, 2010c, 76–8, 2013, 95–7).

Moreover, the problem is that there are two competing and conflicting conceptions of democracy. As far as I know the distinction can be traced all the way back to John Stuart Mill, who, in his *Considerations on Representative Government*, under the epigraph "Of True and False Democracy: Representation of All, and Representation of the Majority Only", indicated:

> Two very different ideas are usually confounded under the name democracy. The pure idea of democracy, according to its definition, is the government of the whole people by the whole people, equally represented. Democracy as commonly conceived and hitherto practiced is the government of the whole people by a mere majority of the people, exclusively represented (1861/1958, 102).

In Mill's opinion, the former is synonymous with the equality of all citizens, whereas the latter with the privilege of the numerical majority over the minority (1861/1958, 102). In Dworkin's perspective, these two competing conceptions of democracy not only coexist but also are still in conflict nowadays. On the one hand, according to the *majoritarian* view: "[D]emocracy is government by majority will, that is, in accordance with the will of the greatest number of people, expressed in elections with universal or near universal suffrage" (2006, 131). On the other hand, according to the *partnership* view:

> [D]emocracy means that the people govern themselves each as a full partner in a collective political enterprise so that a majority's decisions are democratic only when certain further conditions are met that protect the status and interests of each citizen as a full partner in that enterprise. On the partnership view, a community that steadily ignores the interests of some minority or other group is just for that reason not democratic even though it elects officials impeccably majoritarian means (2006, 131).

Actually, as Dworkin acknowledged, the United States of America is neither a pure example of the majoritarian conception of democracy nor of the partnership view. Although the bipartisan system and the majority rule reinforced the former—since the founding fathers limited the power of the majorities in various forms, by including anti-majoritarian devices, which were latter reinforced by other institutions, such as the filibuster and the judicial review (of the constitutionality) of the acts of the other (elected) branches of government—it can be said that they also supported the latter. On one side, a minority of either 34 or 41 (out of the 100 senators) can block the majority of bringing a decision to a final vote, depending on whether it is a substantive or procedural issue. And, on the other, the power of the political majorities is limited by the recognition of individual constitutional rights that legislative majorities cannot infringe and much less step over (2006, 135–7). Notwithstanding, Dworkin cautioned that the degraded state of the public debate is a serious defect that endangers the partnership conception of democracy, by neglecting the mutual attention and respect between partners, and strengthens the majoritarian one, by viewing the other as an enemy and politics as a war:

> We do not treat someone with whom we disagree as a partner—we treat him as an enemy or at best as an obstacle—when we make no effort either to understand the force of his contrary views or to develop our own opinions in a way that makes them responsive to his (2006, 132–3).

8.2.2 Polarization

Since the term "polarization" is ambiguous, we are going to reserve the verb "polarize" to the activity-process and "polarization" for the product-result of such activity-process. On one side, "polarize" means to "cause division of opinion: to make the differences between groups or ideas ever more clear-cut and extreme, hardening the opposition between them, or become ever more clear-cut and extreme in this way." On the other, "polarization" means "concentration, as of groups, forces, or interests, about two conflicting or contrasting positions" and of which a rational conciliation seems highly or near to impossible (for example, between those for and against: abortion, death penalty, euthanasia, same-sex marriage, and so on). By the same token, the polarization describes the formation of antagonistic (social) classes or groups (such as bourgeois-proletariat, capitalist-socialists, conservative-liberal, democratic-republican, left-right, moderate-radical, poor-rich, rural-urban, and so on).

We can distinguish between two main options regarding polarization: (1) *exclusion* of one group by the other or (2) *inclusion* of one group by the other. Similarly, each option can be further divided into two theses: one strong and other weak. On one side, in case of exclusion: (A) the *strong* version is characterized by the annihilation, elimination, execution, extinction, or suppression of the "different", especially if "dissident", which is considered as an "enemy", *i.e. ethnic cleansing* or *mass deportation*, and may lead to an "authoritarian or totalitarian imposition and restoration"; and (B) the *weak* version is depicted by the division, excision, fragmentation, secession, or separation into two or more parts, which are not willing to cooperate, *i.e. balkanization* for short, and may lead to a "libertarian emancipation". On the other, in case of inclusion: (C) the *strong* version is illustrated by the agitation, confrontation, convulsion, or tension between majorities-minorities and may lead to a "majoritarian or minoritarian tyrannization"[2]; and (D) the *weak* version is portrayed by the deliberation, discussion, participation or representation of all partners and may lead to a (pure or true) "democratic association".

From the preceding lines, it is possible to derive four different characterizations of "polarization": two of which are openly incompatible with a conception of democracy—(A) and (B)—and, two of which are presumably compatible with democracy: one with the *majoritarian conception* (C); and, other with the *partnership conception* (D). Since (A) and (B) are not democratic, we will analyze only the two versions presumably compatible with democracy in the search for the one that is purely or truly so. In (C) polarization is recognized either as the oppression of minorities by majorities or the opposition of minorities against majorities to the extent that it is coherent with the *majoritarian conception*, and as an historical

[2] Elsewhere I have characterized these different situations as "majoritycracy", *i.e.* "government of the majority"; and, as "minoritycracy", *i.e.* "government of the minority"; and even as "partycracy", *i.e.* "government of political parties" (Flores 2005a, 159, 2008a, 338–9).

example we can mention the case of Venice. On the contrary, in (D) polarization is renowned as the association between both majorities and minorities to the extent that it is consistent with the *partnership conception*, and as an historical example we can mention the case of Florence.[3]

Nowadays, we tend to attribute to "polarization" a negative connotation, but "democracy" has not necessarily a positive one, either. Keep in mind Winston Churchill's speech, where he characterized democracy as a "lesser evil" in the continuum: "Many forms of government have been tried, and will be tried in this world of sin and woe. No one pretends that democracy is perfect or all-wise. Indeed, it has been said that democracy is the worst form of government except all those other forms that have been tried from time to time" (1947/1979, 150). Let me elucidate: I am trying to suggest that it may be the case that at least one form of "polarization" is a "lesser evil" for democracy than other tendencies, including those of "non-polarization". Therefore, I not only conceive "polarization" as an opportunity for "democracy" and not necessarily as the problem in itself but also perceive that the partnership conception of democracy is better suited than the majoritarian to deal with polarization. In a few words, the latter by either trying to avoid or confront polarization might end up increasing or even multiplying it, whereas the former by trying to engage or face polarization through a serious public debate might wind up decreasing or reducing it.

8.3 Conditions of Possibility of Democracy

As a working hypothesis, we are going to criticize and reject any answer to the question on whether democracy is possible that runs from an absolute pessimism or even skepticism in one extreme—"*not here, nor there, nor anywhere*"—to an unlimited optimism in the other extreme—"*here, there and everywhere*". On the contrary, we assume that it is possible if and only if certain conditions are met, despite being a polarized society. Instead of being before a fatality proper of *Cassandra*, who foresees the future but can not do anything to change it, we are before a great opportunity proper of *Pollyanna*, who sees in every situation despite its bad or negative side the possibility of finding a good or positive point (Crozier et al. 1975, 3).[4]

In this part, we are going to revise the conditions of possibility of a democracy by recalling: firstly, the Report of the Trilateral Commission of mid-1970s, in general, and the part on the United States of America prepared by Samuel P. Huntington, in particular; and, secondly, the so-called "false promises of democracy", following

[3] I am grateful to Mario Conetti for pointing me to the historical cases of Venice and Florence as representative of the majoritarian and the partnership conceptions, respectively.

[4] Pollyanna is a fictional character of Eleanor H. Porter that embodies optimism, and Cassandra is the mythical Greek prophet that represents pessimism—and even fatalism.

Norberto Bobbio's characterization, which will lead us into considering some substantive ideals for democracy beside the merely procedural ones, and thus into the partnership conception beyond the majoritarian view.

8.3.1 The Crisis of Democracy (and the Third Wave of Democratization)

In the "Introductory Note" to the book published in 1975 as *The Crisis of Democracy*, but well known simply as *Report on the Governability of Democracies to the Trilateral Commission*, Zbigniew Brzezinski (1975) clarified that despite the frequency and insistence with which it is asked: Is democracy in crisis? The authors of the book considered that "democratic systems are viable". However, they deemed that it is necessary that the "people truly understands the nature of the democratic system" and for that purpose the authors reexamined its basic premises and functioning. In a nutshell, the authors of the *Report* identified three different challenges for the democratic government: (1) *Contextual (and External)*, such as a world economic crisis which can lead to serious problems for the functioning of democracy; (2) *(Contextual and) Internal*, such as the social structure and social tendencies within the country; and (3) *Intrinsic*, which are proper to the functioning of a democracy, to the extent that: "The more democratic a system is, indeed, the more likely it is to be endangered by intrinsic threats." In a few words: "The demands on democratic government grow, while the capacity of democratic government stagnates" (Crozier et al. 1975, 8–9). As Huntington observed in the part devoted to the Unites States of America:

> *The vitality of democracy in the United States in the 1960s produced a substantial increase in governmental activity and a substantial decrease in governmental authority.* By the early 1970s Americans were progressively demanding and receiving more benefits from their government and yet having less confidence in their government than they had a decade earlier (1975, 64).

In short, the increase in governmental activity led to a decrease in governmental authority, and at the same time raised questions regarding both the economical and political solvency of government: "The impulse of democracy is to make government less powerful and more active, to increase its functions, and to decrease its authority" (1975, 64). He questioned, among other things: "Does an increase in the vitality of democracy *necessarily* have to mean a decrease in the governability of democracy?" (1975, 64). Moreover, he suggested that the diminution of the governmental authority could be explained by the increase in political participation and the decrease in the levels of trust of the people toward the government. Similarly, he recalled: "During the 1960s public opinion on major issues of public policy tended to become more polarized and ideologically structured, that is, people tended to hold more consistent liberal or conservative attitudes on public policy issues" (1975, 76). Finally, he insinuated that there were two reasons for this: (1) the nature of the themes themselves, which included social, racial and military matters; and (2) the features of those who participate actively in politics tended to have consistent and systematic perspectives on matters of public policy; and hence: "The increase in political participation in the early 1960s was thus followed by heightened polarization of political opinion in the mid-1960s" (1975, 77).

In this way, Huntington explained not only the appearance of polarization in a democracy but also its causes and consequences or effects:

> The polarization over issues in the mid-1960s in part, at least, explains the major decline in trust and confidence in government of the latter 1960s. Increasingly, substantial portions of the American public took more extreme positions on policy issues; those who took more extreme positions on policy issues, in turn, tended to become more distrustful of government. Polarization over issues generated distrust about government, as those who had strong positions on issues became dissatisfied with the ambivalent, compromising policies of government (1975, 78).

In addition, he explicated that there is a cyclical process of interaction between political participation–polarization-distrust-political efficaciousness, in which (1975, 84):

(1) An increase in the political participation leads to an increase in the polarization of the public policies;
(2) An increase in the polarization of public policies leads to an increase in the distrust of the people and a decrease in the political efficaciousness of the government; and
(3) An increase in the distrust and a decrease in the political efficaciousness of the government lead to a decrease in the political participation.

The result of this cyclical process is a paradox: an increase in political participation will, at the end, lead to a decrease in political participation: "an upsurge of political participation produces conditions which favor a downswing in political participation" (1975, 85). Similarly, he pointed out that the decrease in political participation produces conditions that favor the decadence of the party system, including party-identification, party-voting and party-cohesion. Furthermore, Huntington advised: "The single most important status variable affecting political participation and attitudes is education" (1975, 110); and pointed "the governability of a democracy depends upon the relation between the authority of its governing institutions and the power of its opposition institutions" (1975, 91–2).

It seems that the way out from the tension between democracy and polarization, besides requiring greater levels of education of the citizenry, depends in the relation between the government or ruling party and its opposition; or, alternately, in the relationship between the (ruling) majority and the (opposing) minority. What's more, in the conclusion of the *Report*, the authors emphasized the necessity of searching and even reaching a common agreement or shared purpose.[5] Actually, they concluded not only that "In a democracy… purpose cannot be imposed from on high by fiat" (Crozier et al. 1975, 160) but also that "Without common purpose,

[5] Even the most polarized society can reach a common agreement or shared purpose: sometimes in the form of a common enemy either internal or external.

there is no basis for common priorities, and without priorities, there are no grounds for distinguishing among competing private interests and claims… The system becomes one of anomic democracy, in which democratic politics becomes more an arena for the assertion of conflicting interests than a process for the building of common purposes" (Crozier et al. 1975, 161).

As we have already seen, Dworkin claimed that, on one side, a democracy could be and remain healthy in non-polarization situations despite lacking a serious *public debate* as long as there is a broad *consensus* about what must be done. On the other, a democracy can be and remain healthy even in polarization situations in spite of missing a shared *consensus* about what must be done as long as there is a culture of *public debate*.

It seems that democracy is identified with a widespread *consensus* among all the participants or partners and when it is not possible to reach one with a serious *public debate*. It is the *public debate* which facilitates reaching a *consensus* by finding *ex post* a common agreement or shared purpose: first, having a public debate; and, later, if necessary, voting; and not the other way around. By the by, this view reinforces the "partnership conception" and makes democracy possible regardless of polarization.

On the contrary, if polarization is said to be so deep as to cancel the possibility of finding a momentous *consensus* via a common agreement or shared purpose and of having a serious *public debate*, it seems that the only thing left is to vote to see who has *ex ante* the bigger number: lacking a public debate and going directly into voting, as the slogan "Let's vote" puts forward.[6] But as Edmund Burke criticized: "It is said, that twenty-four millions ought to prevail over two hundred thousand. True; if the constitution of a kingdom be a problem of arithmetic" (1790/1937, 190).

Let me clarify, I claim that the logic of head counting reinforces the "majoritarian" conception and may lead to the tyranny of the majority, which in some cases is a minority after all, including not only the oppression of the minority, numerical or not, but also due to the opposition between majority and minority to even more polarization, whereas the "partnership" view does not.

8.3.2 The False Promises of Democracy (and the Future of Democracy)

When Bobbio published, in 1984, the book titled *Il futuro della democrazia* (*i.e. The Future of Democracy*), he warned about the existence of six false promises of democracy (1984/1987, 23–42):

1. The birth of the pluralist society;
2. The renewed vigor of particular interests;
3. The survival of oligarchies;

[6] Elsewhere I claim that there are limits to majority decision making and voting (Flores 2006, 2008b, 2010a), such as issuing an amnesty with absolute pardons and without truth commissions. I am grateful to Mariela Morales Antoniazzi for pointing out the last case to me.

4. The limited space to participate;
5. The subsistence of the invisible power; and
6. The uneducated citizen.

Apparently, the Italian jurist and political scientist was charging democracy of having promised:

First, to give birth to a uniformed and united society, but instead it delivered not only a diversified and divided society but also a pluralized and even a polarized or radicalized one, characterized as "poliarchy" or "poliarchical" society by Robert A. Dahl (1956, 1967, 1972, 1981; Dahl and Lindblom 1953). However, as we have already proposed, it is not necessary to achieve an ample *consensus* between all the "poles", but at least possible to initiate a serious *public debate* between all of them.

Second, to vindicate the interests of the people, but since it is impossible to have all the people permanently gathered or constantly called upon to make or take directly by themselves all the decisions ("*direct democracy*"), the one and only option became to elect their representatives, who will make or take indirectly all the decisions for them and supposedly on their behalf ("*representative democracy*"). It is worth noting that the (political) representation has relied on the principles that the representatives must resemble the constituencies and look after the general or public interests. However, representatives are not necessarily considered as agents or delegates acting "for them" and dependent of their lead, but mainly as trustees acting "on their behalf" and somehow independent of them; and, additionally, they had reinforced particular or private interests (Pitkin 1967; Flores 2005b, 30–1).[7]

Third, to control the oligarchies and or at least to reduce the economic differences, but the appearance of ruling elites or groups linked directly to them and their particular interests, reinforced the picture portrayed by Joseph A. Schumpeter (1947), who pointed out that those ruling elites and groups organized through political parties compete against each other in the hunt for votes. I am neither against the existence of such elites or groups as such, nor the fact of the competition against each other, as long as they are willing to enter into a serious public debate, not a mere *façade* and even worse a battling ground or war.

Fourth, to open and even multiply spaces for the participation (and representation) of all, but most remained close and when or where open they are still limited or restricted to a very few. The representation becomes a mere delegation, whereas the participation is reduced to its minimal expression with periodic elections, (near to) universal suffrage, and a more or less direct, free, secret and popular vote. Likewise, the very few open spaces are limited or restricted to political parties and, as a consequence, the participation (and representation) of all is reduced only to a few and mainly mediated by them. What's more, there are still vast groups of society marginalized of the political process (Flores 1998, 1999, 2002).

[7] Elsewhere I have criticized the tendency that Guillermo O'Donnell labeled as "delegative democracy" as the "government of the people by their delegates" (O'Donnell 1993a, b; and Flores 2008a: 338).

Fifth, to make the exercise of power much more transparent and visible to the citizen, who will not only participate in it, but also should know the actions of the government and check them, to the extent that democracy also means government *before* the people or accountable *to* them. Moreover, as we have already seen, the demands on the government have increased, while its capacity of response decreased, leading toward an exercise of power through bureaucratic and technical apparatus, such as bureaucracy, *i.e.* the government of the bureaucrat, and technocracy, *i.e.* the government of the technician, which are neither transparent nor visible to the citizen, who remains left out of the loop and the so-called invisible power is still in place (Weber 1922/1968, 956–1012; Flores 1998, 96–7, 1999, 202–3).

Sixth, to educate all the citizens and to guarantee equality of opportunities, but instead of having active and (well-)informed citizens, the ruling class(es) and elite(s) seem to prefer passive and non-informed ones, who remained subjects and not (truly) citizens much less partners in self-government. The lack of education is, as we have already pointed out, one of the obstacles for democracy and a pending matter if we are truly committed to democracy, especially, in the substantive partnership conception.

Let me recall that Bobbio—and a vast majority of his disciples and followers as well—emphasized the procedural conception over the substantial one and insisted on a minimal definition of democracy "characterized by a set of rules (primary or basic) which establish *who* is authorized to take collective decisions and which *procedures* are to be applied" (1984/1987, 24). Actually, the subtitle of the English translation of his book, is precisely "A Defense of the Rules of the Game" and as such an apology of the procedural conception of democracy. Notwithstanding, his conclusion was that the broken promises and obstacles are not sufficient to transform a democratic regime into an autocratic one:

> The minimal content of the democratic state has not been impaired: guarantees of the basic liberties, the existence of competing parties, periodic elections with universal suffrage, decisions which are collective or the result of compromise… or made on the basis of the majority principle, or in any event as the outcome of open debate between the different factions or allies of a government coalition (1984/1987, 40).

Surprisingly, he added to his notion of democracy, as the procedural rules of the game, a substantive appeal to values, by accepting that "ideals are necessary" (1984/1987, 41) and among them he enumerates (1984/1987, 41–2):

1. The ideal of toleration;
2. The ideal of non-violence;
3. The ideal of the gradual renewal of society via the free debate of ideas and the modification of attitudes and ways of life; and
4. The ideal of brotherhood.

The ideals of toleration (without fanaticism) and of free debate of ideas (without preconceived or predetermined truths) coincide with the serious public debate, on one hand, and the ideals of non-violence (in peaceful contexts) and brotherhood—or fraternity—(with common agreements and shared purposes) correspond to the mutual or reciprocal attention and respect that is due, on the other hand. Although Bobbio insisted openly on a procedural and as such majoritarian conception, he admitted covertly on the substantial and as such a partnership conception by adding the necessity of ideals and by appealing to values, as well as by requiring decisions to be the "outcome of open debate" between the different parts of the whole.

Let me be precise, I claim that the procedural ideals often associated with the majoritarian conception, even if necessary are not sufficient, while the substantive ideals as embodied in the partnership view are. In sum, as Dworkin emphasized "the partnership conception, democracy is a substantive, not a merely procedural, ideal". In his words:

> The majoritarian conception purports to be purely procedural and therefore independent of other dimensions of political morality; it allows us to say, as I indicated, that a decision is democratic even if it is very unjust. But the partnership conception does not make democracy independent of the rest of political morality; on that conception we need a theory of equal partnership to decide what is or is not a democratic decision, and we need to consult ideas about justice, equality, and liberty in order to construct such a theory (2006, 134).

8.4 Conclusion

As we have seen, a pure or true democracy implies not the necessity of a momentous *consensus* but the possibility of a serious *public debate*, which facilitates the quest for common agreements and shared purposes, starting with mutual and reciprocal attention and respect between all the partners in self-government. Therefore, the conditions of possibility of a true democracy require: (1) the participation and representation of all the citizens, including a better and greater education of all the people… men and women, poor and rich, religious and no-religious, old and young; (2) an open political system, not closed, characterized by the existence of political parties, but neither limited to them nor reduced to election day or voting; and (3) a closer relationship between government or ruling party and opposition, majority and minority… characterized by the collaboration of all, through deliberation and discussion of the different themes, in the name not only of general and public interest and not in the particular or private interest, but also of what unites all and not what divides them from us.

To conclude, imagine that in any given country the society is divided more or less evenly in at least two main parties and quite polarized. If, on the one hand, the prevailing conception of democracy is the majoritarian one, it is plausible that this society will remain divided along party lines and, therefore, even more polarized than before, by reinforcing either the majority imposing its will over the minority or deadlock in Congress due to the unwillingness to compromise. However, if, on the other, the prevailing conception is the partnership view, it is possible that this society will end up not being divided and, thus, even less polarized than before, by enabling the deliberation and discussion required to find common agreements and shared purposes and even by reaching broad consensus after a genuine argument between all… as partners in the enterprise of self-government.[8]

References

Aristotle. 1988. *The politics*. New York: Cambridge University Press.

Bobbio, N. 1984/1987. The future of democracy. In *The Future of Democracy: A Defense of the Rules of the Game*, 23–46. Trans. Roger Griffin. Cambridge: Polity Press.

Brzezinski, Z. 1975. Introductory note. In *The crisis of democracy. Report on the governability of democracies to the trilateral commission*, ed. Michael Crozier et al. New York: New York University Press.

Burke, E. 1790/1937. *Reflections on the revolution in France, and on the proceedings in certain societies in London relative that event in a letter intended to have been sent to gentleman in Paris*. New York: P.F. Collier & Son Corporation.

Churchill, W. 1947/1979. Parliament bill. Speech on the House of Commons, November 11, 1947. In *The Oxford dictionary of quotations*, 3rd ed., ed. Elizabeth Knowles. Oxford: Oxford University Press.

Crozier, M., et al. 1975. *The crisis of democracy. Report on the governability of democracies to the trilateral commission*. New York: New York University Press.

Dahl, R. 1956. *A preface to democratic theory*. Chicago: The University of Chicago Press.

Dahl, R. 1967. *Pluralist democracy in the United States: Conflict and consent*. Chicago: Rand McVally & Co.

Dahl, R. 1972. *Democracy in the United States: Promise and performance*. Chicago: Rand McVally & Co.

Dahl, R. 1981. *Dilemmas of pluralist democracy. Autonomy versus control*. New Haven: Yale University Press.

Dahl, R., and C. Lindblom. 1953. *Politics, economics, and welfare*. New York: Harper & Brothers.

Dworkin, R. 2006. *Is democracy possible here? Principles for a new political debate*. Princeton: Princeton University Press.

Flores, I.B. 1998. Crisis, fortalecimiento y valores de la democracia. In *Los valores de la democracia*, eds. Luis Salazar and Jose Woldemberg, 89–115. México: Instituto Federal Electoral.

Flores, I.B. 1999. Democracia y participación: Consideraciones sobre la representación política. In *Democracia y representación en el umbral del siglo XXI. Memoria del Tercer Congreso*

[8] I have presented different versions of this chapter in many places: Facultad de Derecho, UNAM (Mexico); Universidad Carlos III de Madrid (Spain); Instituto Federal Electoral (Mexico); McMaster University, Hamilton, Ontario (Canada); Instituto de Investigaciones Jurídicas, UNAM (Mexico); Center for Transnational Legal Studies, London (UK); Universita'Degli Studi Dell'Insubria, Como (Italy); Max-Planck-Institut für ausländisches öffentliches Recht und Völkerrecht, Heidelberg (Germany); and AMINTAPHIL Conference, Baltimore, Maryland (USA); and have incurred in a great debt with many individuals: Edgar R. Aguilera, Armin von Bogdandy, Giuseppe D'Elia, Matthew Grellette, César Jauregui Robles, Giorgio La Rosa, Luis J. Molina Piñeiro, Mariela Morales Antoniazzi, Arturo Nuñez Jiménez, José Fernando Ojesto Martínez Porcayo, Victor V. Ramraj, Adrián Rentería Díaz, Mortimer Sellers, José María Serna de la Garza, and Wilfrid J. Waluchow for comments and critiques; Mario Conetti for a public commentary; Ann E. Cudd and Sally Scholz for helpful suggestions on editing and preparing it for publication; and, finally, Hazel Blackmore for daily deliberations and discussions. Clearly errors are mine.

Internacional de Derecho Electoral, vol. I, ed. J. Jesús Orozco Henríquez, 195–238. México: Universidad Nacional Autónoma de México.
Flores, I.B. 2002. Gobernabilidad y representatividad: Hacia un sistema democrático electoral mayoritario y proporcional. In *Memoria del VII Congreso Iberoamericano de Derecho Constitucional*, vol. IV, ed. Hugo A. Concha Cantú, 209–236. México: Universidad Nacional Autónoma de México.
Flores, I.B. 2005a. Heráclito vis-à-vis Parménides: Cambio y permanencia como la principal función del derecho en una democracia incipiente. In *Funciones del derecho en las democracias incipientes. El caso de México*, ed. Luis J. Molina Piñeiro et al., 149–171. México: Porrúa and Universidad Nacional Autónoma de México.
Flores, I.B. 2005b. The quest for legisprudence: Constitutionalism v. legalism. In *The theory and practice of legislation: Essays on legisprudence*, ed. Luc J. Wintgens, 26–52. Aldershot: Ashgate.
Flores, I.B. 2006. Sobre las formas y los límites de la legislación: A propósito de la constitucionalidad de una reforma constitucional. In *El estado constitucional contemporáneo. Culturas y sistemas jurídicos comparados*, vol. I, ed. Diego Valadés and Miguel Carbonell, 271–292. México: Universidad Nacional Autónoma de México.
Flores, I.B. 2008a. Actores, procesos e instituciones democráticas: Hacia una verdadera democracia en México. In *Instituciones, Actores y Procesos Democráticos en México 2007*, ed. Luis J. Molina Piñeiro et al., 311–340. México: Porrúa and Universidad Nacional Autónoma de México.
Flores, I.B. 2008b. Sobre los límites de las reformas constitucionales: A propósito de tres acciones de inconstitucionalidad recientes. In *La ciencia del derecho procesal constitucional. Estudios en Homenaje a Héctor Fix-Zamudio en sus cincuenta años como investigador del derecho,* vol. VIII Procesos Constitucionales Orgánicos, ed. Eduardo Ferrer Mac-Gregor and Arturo Zaldívar Lelo de Larrea, 831–856. México: Universidad Nacional Autónoma de México.
Flores, I.B. 2009. ¿Es posible la democracia en México? In *¿Polarización en las expectativas democráticas de México 2008-2009? Presidencialismo, Congreso de la Unión, órganos electorales, pluripartidismo y liderazgo*, ed. Luis J. Molina Piñeiro et al., 471–495. México: Porrúa, Universidad Nacional Autónoma de México, Instituto de Derechos Humanos "Bartolomé de las Casas"-Universidad Carlos III de Madrid and COPUEX.
Flores, I.B. 2010a. Estado de derecho y legislación: El problema de la regla de la mayoría. In *Identidad y diferencia,* vol. I "La política y la cultura", ed. Jaime Labastida and Violeta Aréchiga, 148–162. México: Siglo XXI.
Flores, I.B. 2010b. Democracia y polarización: ¿(in)compatibilidad? In *V Jornadas: Crisis y derechos humanos*, ed. Luis T. Díaz Müller, 97–116. México: Universidad Nacional Autónoma de México.
Flores, I.B. 2010c. Ronald Dworkin's justice for hedgehogs and partnership conception of democracy (With a comment to Jeremy Waldron's "A Majority in the lifeboat"). *Problema. Anuario de Filosofía y Teoría del Derecho* 4: 65–103.
Flores, I.B. 2013. Law, liberty and the rule of law (in a constitutional democracy). In *Law, liberty and the rule of law*, ed. Imer B. Flores and Kenneth E. Himma, 77–101. Dordrecht: Springer.
Huntington, S. 1975. Chapter III. The United States. In *The crisis of democracy. Report on the governability of democracies to the trilateral commission*, ed. Michael Crozier et al., 59–118. New York: New York University Press.
Lincoln, A. 1863/1990. New birth of freedom. The Gettysburg Address, November 19, 1863. In *Lincoln on democracy*, ed. Mario M. Cuomo and Harold Holzer, 307–308. New York: Harper Collins.
Mill, J.S. 1861/1958. *Considerations on representative government*. Indianapolis: The Liberal Arts Press.

O'Donnell, G. 1993a. *On the state, democratization and some conceptual problems (A Latin American view with glances at some post-communist countries)*, Kellogg Institute Working Paper, No. 192, April. In http://kellogg.nd.edu/publications/workingpapers/WPS/192.pdf.

O'Donnell, G. 1993b. *Delegative democracy?* In http://kellogg.nd.edu/publications/workingpapers/WPS/172.pdf.

Pitkin, H.F. 1967. *The concept of representation*. Berkeley: University of California Press.

Schumpeter, J. 1947. *Capitalism, socialism and democracy*. New York: Harper & Bros.

Weber, M. 1922/1968. *Economy and society. An outline of interpretative sociology*. New York: Bedminster Press.

Part III
Democracy, Capitalism, and the Influence of Big Money

Chapter 9
Is Justice Possible Under Welfare State Capitalism?

Steven P. Lee

Abstract Our current economic regime, welfare state capitalism (WSC), according to John Rawls, is unable to realize his two principles of justice. WSC is a system in which productive property (capital) is largely controlled by a relatively small number of individuals. He proposes as an alternative that could realize justice property owning democracy (POD), where productive property (capital) would be more equally distributed among citizens. I criticize his argument on two grounds. First, Rawls is likely mistaken when he argues that justice cannot be realized under WSC. Second, there is good reason to think that POD is neither a coherent notion nor a plausible alternative.

9.1 Introduction

The many problems that plague our current political and economic regime in the United States have led many to despair of our ability to achieve a greater level of social justice, indeed, even of our ability to preserve the level of partial justice achieved in the past. John Rawls seems to have shared this despair. Referring to our current system as welfare state capitalism (WSC), he argued that it could not satisfy either of his two principles of justice. This shows the mistake in the common perception that Rawls's theory of justice was meant to provide ideological justification for the welfare state. Rawls rejected WSC in favor of two, among other possible,

S.P. Lee (✉)
Department of Philosophy, Hobart and William Smith Colleges,
Geneva, NY, USA
e-mail: lee@hws.edu

A.E. Cudd and S.J. Scholz (eds.), *Philosophical Perspectives on Democracy in the 21st Century*, AMINTAPHIL: The Philosophical Foundations of Law and Justice 5,
DOI 10.1007/978-3-319-02312-0_9, © Springer International Publishing Switzerland 2014

alternative systems: liberal socialism and property owning democracy (POD).[1] In this chapter, I will focus specifically on POD and examine Rawls's argument that WSC should be abandoned in favor of POD.

As the name suggests, WSC is a form of capitalism, meaning that it concentrates productive property and natural resources in the hands of a relative few, creating a great gap in wealth between the owners and non-owners, especially the least advantaged. But it is also welfarist, meaning that it redistributes some wealth from the most advantaged to others in the society. It softens the gap between the wealthy and the rest by various social welfare programs, providing some sort of safety net, if not a more or less generous social minimum. (In the absence of such welfare measures, the regime would be some form of laissez-faire capitalism.) In contrast, in a POD, productive wealth (or capital) is still in private hands (unlike socialism), but it is much more equally distributed. Rawls says that in a POD, "the background institutions… work to disperse the ownership of wealth and capital" (Rawls 2001, 139).

In general, Rawls's argument favoring POD over WSC is subject to two lines of criticism. First, it may be that the justice-based objections to WSC can be avoided within a WSC regime, so that a switch to POD would not be necessary. Second, it may be that POD is, all things considered, either an incoherent notion or is problematic on other grounds. I consider the first of these objections in Sect. 9.2 and the second in Sect. 9.3.[2]

9.2 Can WSC Satisfy Justice?

In *Justice as Fairness*, Rawls sketches "in more detail the kind of background institutions that seem necessary when we take seriously the idea that society is a fair system of cooperation between free and equal citizens from one generation to the next." To do this, he introduces "the distinction between a property-owning democracy, which realizes all the main political values expressed by the two principles of justice, and a capitalist welfare state, which does not" (Rawls 2001, 135–136). The problem with WSC is that it "rejects the fair value of the political liberties, and while it has some concern for equality of opportunity, the policies necessary to achieve that are not followed." He continues his criticism of WSC:

> It permits very large inequalities in ownership of real property (productive assets and natural resources) so that the control of the economy and much of political life rests in few hands. And although, as the name "welfare state capitalism" suggests, welfare provisions may be quite generous and guarantee a decent social minimum covering the basic needs, a principle of reciprocity to regulate economic and social inequalities is not recognized. (Rawls 2001, 137–138).

[1] The term "property-owning democracy" was introduced by British Conservative Party intellectuals in the 1920s, and was used as a rhetorical device by subsequent Tory governments, including Margaret Thatcher's. Rawls appeals to a progressive version of the notion developed by the economist James Meade (1964) in *Efficiency, Equality, and the Ownership of Property*.

[2] I previously addressed the first of these objections in an unpublished conference presentation, "Rawls and the Crisis in Contemporary Democracy," on which the following section is partly based.

This is a strong indictment.

Let us summarize Rawls's objections to WSC, as represented in these quotations, in the following four categories.

(1) WSC does not allow the fair value of political liberties.
(2) WSC does not allow fair equality of opportunity.
(3) WSC permits too great an inequality in the ownership of property.
(4) WSC fails to recognize a principle of reciprocity to regulate inequalities.

The first of these concerns the first principle of justice—the principle of equal rights and liberties. The second concerns the first part of the second principle, which requires fair equality of opportunity (FOE). FEO mandates that each individual have a fair opportunity to develop his or her natural endowment. Objection (3) concerns the second part of the second principle—the difference principle, which stipulates that inequalities in income and wealth are justified only if they make everyone better off, especially the least advantaged.

Objection (4) is harder to categorize, but may also be connected with the difference principle. What is the failure Rawls sees when he claims that WSC does not recognize reciprocity? I suggest that this is closely connected with the important notion of self-respect, which for Rawls is a primary good and hence subject to distribution under the difference principle. To be more precise, it is not self-respect itself that is distributed (presumably its dependence on subjective elements precludes this), but rather, the "social bases of self-respect." The social bases of self-respect are "those aspects of basic institutions normally essential if citizens are to have a lively sense of their worth as persons and to be able to advance their ends with self-confidence" (Rawls 2001, 59). The connection with reciprocity is that self-respect is the basis of reciprocity; those lacking in self-respect would be unable to interact with their fellow citizens as independent equals, as reciprocity requires. Rawls has always seen a just society as "a fair system of cooperation between citizens regarded as free and equal." This requires the basic institutions "put in the hands of citizens generally, and not only of a few, sufficient productive means for them to be fully cooperating members of society on a footing of equality" (Rawls 2001, 140).

The essence of objection (4) seems to be that because the difference principle is concerned with the distribution of all the primary goods, great differences in (productive) wealth are not only unjust in themselves, which is the basis of objection (3), but also unjust because they lead to a lack of self-respect among the least advantaged. Rawls links this to a central difference between WSC and POD, which he refers to as the point at which distribution occurs. With WSC, there is a "redistribution of income to those with less at the end of each period, so to speak," while under POD, distribution ensures "the widespread ownership of productive assets and human capital (that is, education and trained skills) at the beginning of each period" (Rawls 2001, 139). This difference may be referred to as the distinction between redistribution ex post and ex ante (Krouse and McPherson 1988, 84). WSC involves ex post welfarist transfer payments (derived, for example, through progressive taxation) from the profits of productive capital owned by the few. In contrast, POD involves the distribution of that productive capital itself ex ante (for example, through sharp inheritance taxes, which limit the intergenerational transfer of economic power). It is the wide-spread ownership of capital, the characteristic difference between POD and WSC, that gives all citizens more control over their lives, the social bases of self-respect, and the ability to participate as equals with others in relationships of genuine reciprocity. Rawls seems to believe that once we have adopted ex ante distribution, there would be little need for redistribution ex post. Distribution ex ante would occur once, while redistribution ex post would need to be continuous.[3] (In the light of the last point, it is appropriate to refer to ex ante transfers as distribution, while referring to *ex post* transfers as *re*distribution).

Rawls argues that under WSC, "there may develop a discouraged and depressed underclass many of whose members are chronically dependent on welfare," an underclass that "feels left out and does not participate in the public political culture" (Rawls 2001, 140). To some extent, he shares with political conservatives arguments against the welfare state. It is not only the capitalism in WSC that Rawls finds problematic, but the welfarism as well. Capitalism makes welfarism necessary, if we are to have even a minimum of social justice. (Political conservatives would keep the capitalism largely without welfare.) Those receiving transfer payments ex post can become dependent on them and lacking in self-respect, not equals in relations of reciprocity. Samuel Freedman notes that "by focusing its attention primarily on the level of welfare of members of society, the welfare state does not encourage its citizens to take control of their lives and be actively productive and equal participants in social and political life." Under POD, the distribution of wealth "is not designed to promote individuals' welfare; instead it is designed to promote individuals' independence and an environment in which citizens cooperate as equals" (Freeman 2007, 108, 104).

Returning to Rawls's four objections to WSC, it is useful to distinguish the first three from the last. The first three objections focus on features that are not necessarily inherent in WSC, though frequently characteristic of it, or so I will argue. But objection (4) appeals to a feature of POD that distinguishes it from WSC, namely, that distribution is stipulated to be ex ante. It is the ex ante character of the distribution under POD that provides the least advantaged the social bases of self-respect and ensures genuine reciprocity among all citizens. Rawls's view seems to be that WSC cannot provide this because the ex post character of its redistribution distinguishes it, conceptually, we might say, from POD. We might put it this way: the first three objections rely on a contingent feature of WSC, while the fourth relies on a necessary feature of WSC.[3]

To show that the first group of objections appeals to what is only a contingent feature of WSC, one that is true in many of its instantiations but not all, it must be shown that there are policies that could be adopted under WSC that would avoid the objections, and that the adoption of such policies is possible (O'Neill 2009, 380–381). The policies that could avoid objection (1)—that WSC does not allow fair value of

[3] It must be admitted that part of the difficulty of criticizing Rawls's notion of POD is that he says little about it. It is mentioned only briefly in *A Theory of Justice*, not mentioned at all in *Political Liberalism*, and given only a short discussion in *Justice as Fairness*.

the political liberties—include a vigorous effort to take money out of politics through measures such as the public financing of campaigns and strict controls on lobbying. The strict controls on lobbying by the wealthy could be supplemented by subsidies provided to consumer and environmental groups to increase their lobbying presence. Of course, moneyed interests can always blackmail the rest of society by threatening to move capital abroad, but such a threat can be minimized by the imposition of capital controls. There are efficiency problems with this, but efficiency is secondary to justice.

The policies that could at least partly meet objection (2)—the inability of WSC to satisfy fair equality of opportunity—involve the funding of a public education system sufficient to approach the quality of education that wealthy people can buy for their children on the private education market.[4] Equalizing educational experiences under WSC would require a greater redistribution of wealth; perhaps a redistribution sufficient to satisfy the difference principle. If the difference principle were satisfied, this would also, ipso facto, avoid objection (3), that WSC allows for too great a wealth gap between the rich and the poor. But note that even if the difference principle were satisfied under WSC, disparities of wealth would remain considerable due to capital continuing in the hands of a relative few.

Are the policies referred to in the previous paragraphs possible under WSC? Many critics of welfare capitalism, and presumably Rawls himself, would say they are not. This view is represented by Richard Krouse and Michael McPherson, who argue against the effectiveness of a strategy that seeks to "insulat[e] the state from the influence of underlying inequalities in economy and society" (Krouse and McPherson 1988, 86). Such an "insulation strategy" is what the sorts of policies under WSC referred to above attempt to achieve. Krouse and McPherson assert that "it would be naïve indeed to believe the strategy of insulation just outlined sufficient to secure the fair value of political liberty and the autonomy of the state in the face of severe class inequality in the ownership and control of productive resources" (Krouse and McPherson 1988, 86–87). Thad Williamson and Martin O'Neill concur in this judgment, arguing that "it is all but impossible as a practical matter to allow the market to generate wide dispersions of rewards, and then to rely upon the tax system to correct the resultant inequalities to a tolerable level". Rawls asserts that "political parties [must] be autonomous with respect to private demands" (Rawls 1971, 226). This cannot be achieved under WSC, which is what makes POD necessary.

It is a controversial issue in political philosophy whether there is necessity here; that is, whether it is impossible in the face of great inequalities in wealth (such as exist under WSC) to insulate the state, keeping it autonomous from this wealth. Difficult it certainly is, but impossible? In a democracy, it seems, it is always possible for the poor, being more numerous, to outvote the rich. Critics will respond

[4] This would satisfy FEO only partly because there are many factors affecting a lack of FEO beyond the quality of a child's school experience, such as cultural factors impacting a child in its early years in the family. But such factors may be ameliorated over time under a greater redistribution of wealth.

that this is a naïve view or that WSC is incompatible with democracy—under WSC, we have a plutocracy rather than a democracy. But there are some empirical grounds for doubting the critics' claim that WSC cannot achieve the sorts of policies that would insulate the government from moneyed interests. If a particular WSC fails in this regard, the failure is contingent rather than necessary.

The empirical grounds would be a set of historical observations that there have been times in the history of the United States, and more so in other WSC states, where the people's will has prevailed over that of moneyed interests, for example the progressive era around 1900 and the New Deal in the 1930s. Of course, these victories were only partial and our current politics fill many friends of justice with despair. But there is an empirical reason, too, to think that the current rightward lurch in U.S. politics will pass, perhaps quite quickly. The speculation is that the current political movement to the right, which favors moneyed interests over the general interest, is mainly the result of an old social order trying to hold on to power, especially economic power, in the face of a major demographic shift under which it loses its majority standing. The electorate in the United States is growing increasingly non-white, and there is reason to think that the ascendency of minority voters, who are disproportionally economically disadvantaged, will once again push U.S. politics to the left. These speculations about political possibilities in the United States are bolstered by reference to the WSC regimes in Europe, especially the Scandinavian nations, which come closer to achieving the principles of justice than does the U.S.

Rawls speaks of the "tendency to equality," and this idea supports the view that to the extent that institutions are just, income inequality will decline.[5] He endorses the notion that "in a competitive economy (with or without private ownership) with an open class system excessive inequalities will not be the rule." He continues: "Given the distribution of natural assets and the laws of motivation, great disparities will not long persist" (Rawls 1971, 158). One way to understand this is that much of income inequality in our society is due not to differences in natural ability, but to lack of FEO. If we could more closely approach FEO, workers' skills would be more equal and would not drive the current excesses in income inequality. Krouse and McPherson endorse this view: "Rawls's underlying assumption is that the distribution of natural assets is sufficiently equal that it would not upset the ability of a competitive economy, with a just basic structure, to avoid great disparities in the (pretax) distribution of income and wealth" (Krouse and McPherson 1988, 93). This implies that the move toward a more just society, for example, through the success of progressive political movements, would, other things being equal, be self-reinforcing.

Now let me turn to the second kind of criticism Rawls offers of WSC, represented by objection (4), that WSC cannot provide the bases of self-respect, which is a primary good, "perhaps the most important primary good," that must be distributed across the society (Rawls 1971, 440). The objection, as we have seen, is that WSC, unlike POD, redistributes only ex post, leaving many citizens dependent and

[5] The view I ascribe here to Rawls may not be precisely what he means by the phrase "the tendency to equality," which he discusses in *A Theory of Justice*, pp. 100–108.

unable to take part in relationships of reciprocity. But notice that Rawls advocates the greater equality of wealth under POD not because that equality is valuable in itself, but because in his view it is a necessary means to independence and self-respect. As Samuel Freeman notes, Rawls promotes a liberalism of freedom rather than a liberalism of happiness (Freeman 2007, 103). Greater wealth may be correlated with greater happiness, as the idea of welfare suggests, but it cannot bring one freedom and independence, or the self-respect that follows from these. Is a greater equality of wealth necessary for the sort of freedom and independence that self-respect requires?

Are there significant bases of self-respect for the less wealthy available within WSC? Rawls denies this, but I believe that there are, or there can be. Perhaps the most obvious example is trade unionism. The iconic handshake across the negotiating table between representatives of workers and management represents this. In general, a handshake traditionally represents equality and reciprocity between the parties involved, and helps to provide self-respect for each. When that handshake seals a bargain between management and labor, it is a basis of self-respect among the workers because it shows that they can collectively exercise control over their working lives, their compensation and work environment. A strong union movement precludes the wealthy from treating labor as a mere resource to be managed, the sort of treatment that leads to alienation and lack of self-respect. Of course, the labor movement in the United States has been on the decline for decades, but a new progressive movement could bring it back. Unionism, however, is not the only example. Civil society can provide other opportunities for those who are not wealthy to organize and exert collective control over the actions of the wealthy, for example, consumer groups and environmental groups. Redistribution may come to be seen as a right, not a gift. Moreover, self-respect can arguably be achieved outside of political engagement, as in a person's private efforts as an artist, an intellectual, a sportsman, or a collector.[6] All that is required for such pursuits is a free society and a decent amount of resources.

All these things are possible within WSC, though they may not be realized at any given time. But this leads to the objection that the principles of justice require a regime under which they can be realized not from time to time, with the vicissitudes of the swings of the political pendulum, but on a continuing basis.[7] This is a serious objection, but it may, I think, be met by raising again Rawls's notion of the tendency toward equality. Should the pendulum swing far enough to the left, the processes of the tendency to equality may take over, accelerating the movement toward the realization of the principles of justice and resisting a return swing to the right.

The conclusion is that WSC can provide an environment in which the fair value of political liberties, fair equality of opportunity, a more equal distribution of wealth, and the social bases of self-respect can be realized and perhaps even sustained over time. This is not guaranteed under WSC, but it is possible. Achieving these goods need not require an ex ante distribution.

[6] I owe this point to Christian Schemmel.

[7] I owe this point to Christian Schemmel.

The question may arise, however, why not simply switch to POD, where presumably these benefits would be inherent in the institutional structure? One answer is that bringing about the switch to POD is almost certainly more politically difficult than bringing about a more just form of WSC. But a deeper difficulty is that POD may, on closer inspection, be neither a coherent notion nor, in any case, one that can lead to a plausible political regime. To this issue I now turn.

9.3 Is POD a Coherent Alternative?

We can (and should) only pursue POD, if the notion of POD is coherent and its realization is at all plausible. To raise a question of the notion's coherence is to ask whether the notion hangs together; whether it is consistent or conceivable. I will discuss three different lines of argument suggesting that POD is neither coherent nor plausible.[8]

The first line of argument finds POD to be a problematic hybrid. Under capitalism, productive property or capital is owned by a few, even though, as Marx points out, it is a social product. Socialism follows out the logic of capital's being a social product by turning it into public property. In this respect, POD tries to position itself in between capitalism and socialism. On the one hand, it rejects ownership of capital by the few, and on the other, it maintains private ownership. Rawls is clear that productive capital must be redistributed under POD; this is why the redistribution is ex ante, before the few owners of capital have been able to extract its surplus value, surplus value that under WSC is redistributed ex post, for example, through social programs supported by income taxation.[9]

In some ways, POD is one of those throwback ideas, a return to the garden, that is, a proposal to return to some supposed earlier state of innocence.[10] POD is like Jefferson's idea of equality through a society of yeoman farmers, each with a small plot of land. With land, each farmer stands before the others as an equal; ownership of the land giving him independence and creating reciprocity. (This was one of the arguments for restricting the franchise to property-owners.) Jefferson's idea never was a reality, and the rise of capitalism and industrialization destroyed it as a possibility (even agriculture became corporatized). POD could be seen as an effort to return to a pre-industrial form of equality, with the yeoman farmer being replaced by the capital owning citizen. In this sense, POD is a revolt against modernity. The idea of the yeoman farmer may have been an impractical or impossible scheme in

[8] In fairness to Rawls, note that even if POD were shown to be incoherent and implausible, he would not be stuck with WSC because there would still the other option he endorses of liberal socialism. But he would still have to deal with the argument in Sect. 9.1 above.

[9] Various questions arise about how precisely the *ex ante* redistribution would occur, but this is not an issue I raise here.

[10] Rawls may be inclined toward POD because of the influence on his thinking of Rousseau, as a reviewer of this essay pointed out to me.

any case because agricultural demands to feed an increasing population required the efficiency of larger holdings. In the same way, POD may be incoherent or implausible because industrial demands to provide a decent life for an increasing population require the concentration of capital. POD requires more than the mere ownership of stock, which can be, and to some extent is, currently widespread under WSC. POD requires that ownership include control, which stock ownership generally does not provide (Freeman 2007, 225). It is unclear whether widespread individual control of capital is consistent with the efficiency demanded by industrial production (Williamson 2009, 445).

The second line of argument against POD concerns its stability. My use of the term stability here is related to Rawls's use of the term. Rawls is concerned with the stability of a conception of justice as embodied in a political regime, whereas I am concerned with the political stability of a type of regime (such as POD) that, according to Rawls, does embody justice (which WSC does not). Specifically, it seems that a POD regime, operating under pure procedural justice, would over time revert to WSC.[11] The argument is that with citizens, in a market economy (something Rawls insists on) free to do what they want with their property, the widespread dispersion of capital would not endure. Citizens would receive their share of capital in an ex ante distribution, but, being free to do with it as they will, many would lose their capital stake due to bad economic decisions or bad luck, or simply by treating it as a liquid asset for consumption.[12] (In losing it, they will be losing what Rawls regards as the necessary social basis for their self-respect). Through such a process, capital would eventually become reconcentrated in a small number of hands and WSC would re-emerge. Any effort to avoid this through legal restrictions on how capital is disposed of would take full control of it away from individuals, denying them the independence the capital was supposed to ensure, and would probably run afoul of pure procedure justice. It should not be a condition for justice that everyone be a successful capitalist.[13]

This objection may sound like Robert Nozick's well-known Wilt Chamberlain objection to Rawls's theory (Nozick 1974, 161–163). But it is different in an important respect. Nozick argued that given the operation of human choice, any patterned theory of distributive justice (in which he included Rawls's theory) would require constant interference by government to maintain the pattern. For example, if everyone was given an equal amount of wealth (the pattern), and many people wanted to give some of their money to see Wilt Chamberlain play basketball, Wilt would become rich and the distribution would no longer be equal. One reason this is not an effective objection is that, while Rawls ensured the operations of human choice under the requirement of pure procedural justice, government interference was

[11] Some arguments supporting this view are developed by Williamson, "Who Owns What?" pp. 438, 441, 445.

[12] Williamson points out this something like this happened when the Soviet Union dissolved. Citizens received ownership vouchers in formerly state-owned enterprises, which many sold to those who consolidated them to become the new oligarchs. Williamson, "Who Owns What?" p. 442.

[13] I owe this way of putting the point to John Duncan.

limited by the need to maintain a pattern that did not guarantee outcomes for particular individuals, but for representatives of groups (such as the least advantaged). But the argument has greater traction against POD because POD focuses on distribution ex ante.[14] If rough equality in capital ownership can be achieved only by taxing capital (a tax of capital, not a tax on capital) from those whose capital stakes have grown, then the redistribution becomes ex post, as it is under WSC, and the advantage of POD, as Rawls sees it, in terms of providing the bases of self-respect, is lost. Capital becomes a form of welfare (corporate welfare, if you will, in a different sense of that term), and those to whom it is redistributed lose the sense of independence and the basis for self-respect that capital possession was supposed to provide them. They become like the least advantaged under WSC.

This challenge to the stability of POD seems like it would be part of a study that Rawls calls the "political sociology" of POD. Political sociology is "an account of the political, economic, and social elements that determine its effectiveness in achieving its public aims" (Rawls 2001, 137). Rawls explicitly precludes the political sociology as part of his account of POD in *Justice as Fairness*, but if the argument above is correct, he should have included it, as it poses a challenge to POD as an alternative to WSC.

The third line of argument for the problematic nature of POD is that POD may not fit the conditions Rawls imposes on an acceptable political realization of his theory of justice. Rawls argues that a political philosophy should be "realistically utopian." A theory is realistically utopian when it probes "the limits of practicable political possibility." A theory, as realistically utopian, should ask "how far in our world (given its laws and tendencies) a democratic regime can attain complete realization of its appropriate political values" (Rawls 2001, 4, 13). The third line of argument is that POD lies beyond the boundaries of a realistic utopia, that it is not realistically utopian, but utopian simpliciter. There are serious doubts about whether it could be successfully implemented. POD goes beyond the "limits of practical political possibility."

Support for this criticism may be found in an argument offered by Simone Chambers, though she directs her argument at Rawls's theory of justice in general, rather than at POD as a possible realization of this theory. She says that "Rawls's views on equality are very radical, indeed utopian, and as such are quite far ahead of prevailing public culture." The result is that his theory runs counter to "his main justificatory strategy, namely the argument that 'justice as fairness' was simply a rendering of certain core ideas central to our existing liberal order." The problem is his commitment to equality, which is "in tension with his equally deep and democratic commitment to consensus as the starting point of justice" (Chambers 2006, 81). Rawls's concern in part is that if his theory fell outside this consensus, citizens would have insufficient motivation to accord themselves with its demands. The problem lies in the second principle, with its commitment to the difference principle. Chambers sees a consensus for the first principle but not for the second, which

[14] Williamson comes to the opposite conclusion, but, I think, without appreciating the import of the ex ante/ex post distinction, in "Who Owns What?" p. 449.

has "failed to have a political life." She asks: "Can Rawls find the deep cultural resources he needs to defend egalitarianism?" She answers in the negative: "The fact is that Rawls's egalitarianism is very radical and far ahead of public culture" (Chambers 2006, 82, 84).

In Chambers' view, what the second principle requires is "a radical departure from property arrangements in contemporary America" (2006, 83). This is especially true for the *ex ante* distribution required by POD. There is a deep commitment in our political culture to a foundational notion of desert, that what I earn is mine irrespective of whether or not the rules under which I earned it are those of a just basic structure (Chambers 2006, 85). As one recent presidential candidate put it: "It's your money." This foundational notion of desert is in contrast with Rawls's mediated notion, where desert is legitimate expectation and expectation is legitimate only under the rules of a just basic structure. Connected with a foundational notion of desert is a heightened notion of individual responsibility, according to which each of us is largely responsible for our fate, even if it is the result, as Rawls argues, of morally arbitrary factors.

But Chambers' argument, as applied to Rawls's theory in general, may be too strong. There is a strain of economic egalitarian in our political culture, which exhibits itself, for example, in the widespread consensus that there should be a social safety net (as opposed to the argument that the care of the least advantaged should be left completely to private charity). Of course, people differ on how extensive the social safety net should be, but the commitment to *any* social safety net involves recognition of the need for redistribution, and if you're in for a dime, you may in for a dollar. It's not all your money because some of it is owed to government programs that seek the well-being (whether mere survival or flourishing) of the least advantaged. But Chambers' argument does seem to apply to POD because of the radical nature of the redistribution it requires. POD requires that the wealthy give up not only some of the profits of their productive property (as they are required to do under WSC), but some of that property itself. The distribution applies to wealth, not mere income. That commitment to economic egalitarianism may not be strong enough to overcome the conflicting element of the cultural commitment to a foundational notion of desert and individual responsibility. The cultural commitment to economic egalitarianism may be sufficiently strong to support a WSC regime that sought to realize the second principle of justice, but not strong enough to tolerate POD. In that case, POD would be simply utopian rather than realistically utopian.

9.4 Conclusion

Thus, there are good reasons for concluding that POD is an implausible and/or an incoherent notion. Moreover, as argued earlier in the chapter, POD is not necessary for justice because, given plausible social and political movements, both principles of justice could be realized under WSC. Taking these points together, there is a further line of argument. Were we seek to achieve POD, we would have to work from within our current WSC regimes, and we would have to do this by moving them leftward, making them, as we went, more and more in tune with Rawls's principles of justice. At some point in this leftward movement, according to the arguments in the first part of the chapter, we would realize the principles of justice while still under a WSC regime, while there was still some further political movement necessary to achieve POD. Thus, even if POD were an achievable goal, it would not be necessary to go that far to realize justice, and the less far we need to go, the easier it is and the more likely we are to get there. But if, as argued in the second part of the chapter, POD cannot be achieved, the moral requirement is simply that we take WSC as far as we can in the direction of satisfying the principles of justice, with the expectation that their full satisfaction is possible.[15]

References

Chambers, S. 2006. The politics of equality: Rawls on the barricades. *Perspectives in Politics* 4(1): 81–89.

Freeman, S. 2007. *Justice and the social contract*. Oxford: Oxford University Press.

Krouse, R., and Michael McPherson. 1988. Capitalism, 'property-owning democracy', and the welfare state. In *Democracy and the welfare state*, ed. Amy Gutmann. Princeton: Princeton University Press.

Meade, J. 1964. *Efficiency, equality, and the ownership of property*. London: G. Allen & Unwin.

Nozick, R. 1974. *Anarchy, state, and utopia*. New York: Basic Books.

O'Neill, M. 2009. Liberty, equality, and property-owning democracy. *Journal of Social Philosophy* 40(3): 379–396.

Rawls, John. 1971. *A theory of justice*. Cambridge, MA: Harvard University Press.

Rawls, J. 2001. *Justice as fairness*. Cambridge, MA: Harvard University Press.

Williamson, T. 2009. Who owns what? An egalitarian interpretation of John Rawls's idea of a property-owning democracy. *Journal of Social Philosophy* 40(3): 434–453.

[15] For comments on earlier versions of this chapter, I would like to thank Simone Chambers, John Duncan, Joseph Heath, David Lefkowitz, Dominic Martin, Jan Narveson, Christian Schemmel, the editors of this book, and some anonymous reviewers.

Chapter 10
Rawls on Inequality, Social Segregation and Democracy

Mark Navin

Abstract Latent in John Rawls's discussion of envy, resentment and voluntary social segregation is a plausible (partial) explanation of two striking features of contemporary American life: (1) widespread complacency about inequality and (2) decreased political participation, especially by the least advantaged members of society.

10.1 Inequality and Complacency

Economic inequality within the United States has increased dramatically over the past 30 years.[1] For example, while the income of the bottom 90 % of earners increased by only 15 % between 1979 and 2006, the income of the top 1 % grew by 144 % (and the income of the top 0.1 % grew by 324 %) (Mishel et al. 2009, table 3.10).[2] In 1979, the members of the top 1 % earned 8 % of the nation's income; they were earning 17 % of national income in 2007 (Congressional Budget Office 2011). The years since 2007 have seen inequalities of income (and wealth) increase even further (Saez 2008, 2012; Economic Policy Institute 2012). Furthermore, while much recent discussion of inequality has focused on the increased income and wealth of the top 1 %, members of 'the 99 %' have also seen inequalities expand among themselves. In addition to increased inequalities of wealth and income, they have experienced increased inequalities of employment, educational achievement, and access to quality public services

[1] For helpful feedback on this paper, I thank Michael Doan, the participants in the 2012 AMINTAPHIL conference and the editors of this volume.

[2] Cited in Stiglitz (2012, 8n27).

M. Navin (✉)
Department of Philosophy, Oakland University,
2200 North Squirrel Road, 48309-4401 Rochester, MI, USA
e-mail: navin@oakland.edu

A.E. Cudd and S.J. Scholz (eds.), *Philosophical Perspectives on Democracy in the 21st Century*, AMINTAPHIL: The Philosophical Foundations of Law and Justice 5,
DOI 10.1007/978-3-319-02312-0_10,

(Taylor et al. 2011; Alon 2009; Reardon and Bischoff 2011; Shapiro et al. 2013; Ditomaso 2013).

Many Americans are unaware that inequality has increased at all; those who are aware usually greatly underestimate the magnitude of recent expansions in inequality.[3] Perhaps for this reason, relatively few people seem motivated to do much about contemporary inequalities. For example, fewer Americans are voting or are participating in other forms of political activity (e.g., protest marches, door-to-door canvassing) than were engaging in these activities in prior generations (Berger 2011). The American people do not seem to be doing much to resist the destructive impact of inequality upon their public and private lives (Wilkinson and Pickett 2009; Noah 2012).

There are likely many reasons for Americans' complacency about economic inequality, and for their attendant political disengagement. Joseph Stiglitz (2012) argues that the causes of these phenomena include the rise of the corporate media, the direct disenfranchisement of the poor (e.g., through voter ID laws), and the disempowerment of voters (e.g., increased independent political expenditures in the aftermath of *Citizens United*). Others have argued that increases in inequality diminish social trust and, thereby, social engagement and political participation (Putnam 2001; Uslaner 2002). While I do not deny the significance of these explanations, I focus on a different (though related) cause of complacency about economic inequality: *social segregation*. America has become increasingly segregated in recent decades. We are more segregated by race, politics, culture, and income than we have ever been (Bishop 2009; Taylor and Fry 2012).

Much has been made of the fact that segregation *directly* contributes to group-based economic and political inequalities. For example, segregation prevents equal access to employment, retail services, health-related goods, social capital, and public services (Anderson 2010; Massey and Denton 1993). However, I focus in this paper on two different ways in which inequality and social segregation are related. First, inequality may contribute to social segregation, since many people prefer to participate in forms of social union with others who have similar life prospects. Second, social segregation may cultivate complacency about inequality and, in turn, complacency about inequality may make further increases in inequality more likely. Taking these two claims together, I argue that social segregation and inequality can be mutually-supporting: Increases in inequality generate social conditions (including social segregation) which promote complacency about inequality, and complacency about inequality may make future increases in inequality more likely (which, in turn, may generate greater social segregation, etc.).

My strategy in this paper is to develop some under-discussed ideas from the work of John Rawls to explain how social segregation and inequality relate to each other. First, I argue that, on Rawls's view, hostile feelings about inequality (which include envy and resentment) are rooted in feelings of inferiority and impotence which arise

[3] Stiglitz writes that "[o]nly 42 percent of Americans believe that inequality has increased in the past ten years…Several studies have confirmed that perceptions of social mobility are overly optimistic" (2012, 147). Consider, also, a recent experiment which showed that most Americans radically underestimate the amount of inequality in their society (Norton and Ariely 2011).

when social conditions prevent persons from equal participation in valued forms of community. Second, I argue that it follows from Rawls's claim that voluntary social segregation diminishes hostile feelings about the inequalities *permitted by distributive justice* that social segregation will also diminish hostile feelings about *unjust* inequalities. Third, I argue that the same psychological tendencies that drive the voluntary social segregation of private associations may also drive the retreat of the less advantaged from politics.

10.2 Envy and Resentment

According to Rawls, a person may manifest one of two hostile feelings towards inequality (or towards those who benefit from inequality). One is *envy*, and the other is *resentment*. I address each in turn.

Rawls says that *envy* is an antisocial vice. It is "the propensity to view with hostility the greater good of others," even when those others have not become better off as a result of immoral acts or unjust institutions (1999, 466). Envy is not a "moral feeling," since an envious person is not prepared to give reasons for thinking that the offensive inequality is unjust (1999, 467). Instead, Rawls says that envy arises when inequalities cultivate "a lack of self-confidence in our own worth combined with a sense of impotence. Our way of life is without zest and we feel powerless to alter it or to acquire the means of doing what we still want to do" (1999, 469). Envy arises when we do not feel that our life activities are valued by others and when we feel unable to make meaningful contributions to social projects. It is an expression of inferiority and powerlessness in the context of valued forms of community life.

On Rawls's view, envy is rooted in a person's failure to receive recognition from others that her contributions to the shared pursuits of her community are valuable (1999, 462). Rawls says that "what is necessary [for self-worth] is that there should be for each person at least one community of shared interests to which he belongs and where he finds his endeavors confirmed by his associates" (1999, 388). However, when associations are marked by significant internal inequalities, the better off members of the association may not value the (relatively meager) contributions that the worse off members can make. Importantly, the feeling of envy is not accompanied by reasons for thinking that the inequalities which are present within an association violate principles of social justice (e.g., the Difference Principle). Nor is envy accompanied by reasons for thinking that members of an association have wronged the envious person. Instead, envy expresses a sense of inferiority and powerlessness which the least advantaged members of associations experience when their relative deprivation prevents them from participating as equal members of associations whose activities they value.[4] This feeling is not accompanied by moral judgments—either of distributive injustice or interpersonal wrongs.

[4] Rawls says that "the discrepancy between oneself and others is made visible by the social structure and style of life of one's society. The less fortunate are therefore often forcibly reminded of

It is an important consequence of Rawls's account of envy that inequality gives rise to this hostile feeling only indirectly, i.e., through the impact inequality has on the ability of persons to make valued contributions to the common life of the associations whose activities they value. Inequality, as such, does not give rise to envy. Inferior status within a particular association is insufficient to cultivate envy, too. Rather, inequality cultivates envy only when it causes one to have inferior status within a form of social life which one values and whose activities one wishes to join as an equal member. Importantly, the mere fact that one is unable to make valued contributions to the activities of an association which one values is insufficient to generate envy. This is because one can value an association's activities even if one does not wish to be recognized as a valued contributor to those activities. For example, I value the activities of my local symphony orchestra, but I do not have a deep desire to be a member of the orchestra. (I am happy to watch and listen.) Therefore, my inability to be a member of my beloved orchestra does not lead me to be envious of the orchestra's members. Furthermore, even if I wanted to play music, my failure to gain entry to the orchestra is unlikely to generate feelings of envy, as long as some amateur musical group (albeit one with reasonably low standards) were willing to welcome me as a member.

Since different associations have different goals and activities, the conditions for equal participation (and, therefore, the conditions for envy) will differ between associations. For example, a person who cannot afford a yacht will be unable to participate equally in an activity which is valued by the members of the yacht club (i.e., sailing one's yacht). If such a person valued the activities of the yacht club and wanted to participate in them as an equal member, these circumstances might give rise to hostile feelings. In contrast, the fact that a person cannot afford a yacht is unlikely to undermine her equal membership in a book club or in her homeowner's association. Therefore, her lack of a yacht is very unlikely to cultivate envy within the context of these other associations. The social conditions which contribute to the formation of envy differ according to the activities of the associations in which one seeks equal membership.

In contrast to envy, Rawls says that *resentment* is a non-vicious moral feeling. It differs from envy because a person who is resentful is prepared to offer reasons for thinking that others' "being better off is the result of unjust institutions, or wrongful conduct" (1999, 467). At first glance, envy and resentment may seem radically dissimilar. Envy is a vicious nonmoral feeling of hostility towards those who have more. It emerges from the sense that one is an inferior member of a valued form of community. In contrast, resentment is a non-vicious (and potentially virtuous) moral feeling of hostility. It emerges in response to an unjust inequality or to wrongful conduct. The dissimilarity between envy and resentment is clear in the case of particular private associations: the conditions which generate envy in these associations need not also generate resentment. That is, one's inability to be an equal participant in the valued activities of a particular association (which generates envy) does not entail the existence of unjust inequalities or interpersonal wrongs (which cause resentment).

---

their situation, sometimes leading them to an even lower estimation of themselves and their mode of living. And … they see their social position as allowing no constructive alternative to opposing the favored circumstances of the more advantaged" (1999, 469).

In contrast, envy and resentment are not so clearly dissimilar when they emerge within the broader political community. Recall that, for Rawls, the injustice of an inequality depends on its tendency to undermine equal citizenship. Since Rawls thinks of political society as an association ('a social union of social unions') in which all should want to be equal members, it follows that hostile feelings about unjust inequalities (which generate resentment) can also be accurately described as hostile feelings about one's inferior membership in an association in which one (should) want(s) to be an equal member. That is, the conditions which suffice to generate *resentment* at one's unequal status in the political community also suffice to generate *envy*. In all other associations envy and resentment can pull apart, since unequal membership in other associations is not always evidence of injustice or wrongful acts. In contrast, unequal membership in *political society* is always unjust and, therefore, always a reason for resentment.

My claim that envy and resentment are analogous when they emerge in response to one's unequal membership in the political community finds support in Rawls's account of political society as a 'social union of social unions':

> The main idea is that a well-ordered society … is itself a form of social union. Indeed it is a social union of social unions. Both characteristic features [of social unions] are present: the successful carrying out of just institutions is the shared final end of all of the members of society, and these institutional forms are prized as good in themselves (1999, 462).

First, just as the members of a private association (e.g., a sports league) are committed to fair play within their association, so, too, are the members of a just society committed to the fair institutional structure of society-at-large. Second, just as the participants in a private association (e.g., an orchestra) realize some non-instrumental good by participating in their private association, so, too, do participants in a society which is regulated by the principles of justice realize some non-instrumental good by participating in the public life of their society. Among other reasons, this is because it is good for persons to participate with others in upholding just public institutions (Rawls 1999, 462). Furthermore, "the collective activity of justice is the preeminent form of human flourishing" (Rawls 1999, 463).

Equal citizenship confers a non-instrumental good that is analogous to the non-instrumental good conferred by equal membership in private associations: social recognition of one's participation in a valued collective activity. Resentment can arise from the realization that one is not recognized as a valued participant in political society, since unequal political membership is unjust in itself.

10.3 Envy and Resentment in Ideal Theory

By definition, resentment is not possible (or, at least, very unlikely) within Rawls's ideal theory (i.e., under conditions of (near) perfect compliance with justice).[5] It is very unlikely that one could offer good reasons for thinking that inequalities were unjust if inequalities were not unjust, and if people knew this to be the case (as Rawls's

[5] See Rawls (1999, 216) for the distinction between ideal and nonideal theory.

publicity condition requires).[6] (Of course, it would still be possible in a just society for members of associations to treat each other unfairly, but I leave aside forms of resentment which emerge from interpersonal wrongs.) In contrast, *envy* is possible within ideal theory. It is possible for persons to experience inferiority within particular associations, even if they are unable to offer reasons for thinking that social inequalities are inconsistent with distributive justice. This is because distributive justice may tolerate levels of inequality which would undermine the good functioning of some private associations, if those inequalities were present among the members of those associations. Therefore, the social conditions which cultivate envy may be present in a society governed by Rawls's principles of justice.

Envy is a vice, and vices are unwanted traits that are "to everyone's detriment" (Rawls 1999, 468). Accordingly, the parties to Rawls's original position "will surely prefer conceptions of justice the realization of which does not arouse [envy]" (1999, 468). If a society governed by Rawls's principles fostered envy among its citizens, this would count against the *congruence* of Rawls's principles of justice with persons' good.[7] Recall that Rawls argued that "the right and the good … are congruent," i.e., "justice [is] part of our good and connected with our natural sociability" (1999, 508, 511). Congruence requires that a person's "rational plan of life supports and affirms his sense of justice" (1999, 450). If a society governed by Rawls's principles generated (or tolerated) social conditions which cultivated envy (a trait that is not part of any rational plan of life), then Rawls's conception of justice might not be congruent with persons' good.

In response to this worry about congruence, Rawls offers two reasons for thinking that social conditions within a society governed by his principles of justice will mitigate the formation of envy. First, the knowledge that society-wide inequalities are regulated by the principles of justice—and the knowledge that the better off are motivated by these principles— should mitigate the tendency of society-wide inequalities to cultivate feelings of inferiority or impotence among the least-advantaged members of society. Rawls's principles of justice protect the conditions of equal citizenship:

> In the public forum each person is treated with the respect due to a sovereign equal; and everyone has the same basic rights … The members of the community have a common sense of justice and they are bound by ties of civic friendship … We can add that the greater advantages of some are in return for compensating benefits for the less favored; and no one supposes that those who have a larger share are more deserving from a moral point of view … For all these reasons *the less fortunate have no cause to consider themselves inferior and the public principles generally accepted underwrite their self-assurance* (1999, 470, emphasis added).

The social inequalities permitted by Rawls's principles of justice do not undermine the equal participation of the least advantaged in the social union of society. This is one way in which a society regulated by the principles of justice mitigates the formation of envy. (It is also a way in which the principles of justice prevent the formation of resentment, given the analogous structure of envy and resentment within the political community.)

---

[6] See Rawls (1999, 115) on the 'publicity condition'.

[7] For an instructive discussion of Rawls's 'congruence argument', see Freeman (2002).

Second, Rawls argues that members of a society regulated by 'justice as fairness' will voluntarily segregate themselves into private associations according to their levels of wealth and income (and other social goods). Even though the inequalities which the principles of justice permit might give rise to envy if they were present within private associations, the fact that people generally prefer more egalitarian forms of community life means that the painful effects of inequality (e.g., those which give rise to envy) will be less prevalent than they would if people did not self-segregate. Rawls says:

> [T]he plurality of associations in a well-ordered society, each with its secure internal life, tends to reduce the visibility, or at least the painful visibility, of variations in men's prospects. For we tend to compare our circumstances with others in the same or in a similar group as ourselves, or in positions that we regard as relevant to our aspirations. The various associations in society tend to divide it into so many noncomparing groups, the discrepancies between these divisions not attracting the kind of attention which unsettles the lives of those less well-placed (1999, 470).[8]

A "plurality of associations" reduces the "painful visibility" of inequality because persons form associations primarily with others who have similar life prospects. They form social unions—friendships, neighborhoods, schools, churches, sports teams, etc.—with people who possess similar amounts of wealth, income, and other social goods. The primary comparisons that matter for self-respect (and for painful recognitions of inequality) are those which occur *within* associations, rather than *between* them. Much of this seems to follow from Rawls's account of social union and envy (which I discuss above). Recall that Rawls believes envy arises when persons do not feel like equal members of their associations. Furthermore, since one's equal participation in a private association may be undermined by inequalities which are smaller than those which undermine equal participation in political society, the segregation of private associations may mitigate envy under ideal theory. Given the central importance of equal membership in associations for our self-respect/self-worth (Rawls's most important social primary good), people have good reason to segregate themselves into associations which are marked by greater internal equality than is present in society-at-large. Furthermore, Rawls argues that we ought to commend the phenomenon of voluntary social segregation for its tendency to mitigate the formation of envy within a just society; voluntary social segregation supports the congruence of justice and persons' good.

10.4 Envy and Resentment in Nonideal Theory

Citizens should want to be equal citizens. If one is an inferior member of the political community, one should develop hostile feelings about the inequalities which make one a less-than-equal citizen.[9] However, it follows from my discussion in the

[8] This is a provocative passage, but it has received almost no critical attention. A notable exception is Cohen (2008, 384).

[9] For a general account of the aptness of (particular) affective responses to injustice or immorality, see Gibbard (1990) and Nussbaum (2001).

Table 10.1 Inequality and associations

	Society 1	Society 2
Group A	3	2
Group B	5	6
Group C	7	10

previous section that social segregation is likely to mitigate the formation of hostile feelings about unjust inequalities. For that reason, we may have less reason to commend voluntary social segregation within nonideal theory than Rawls believes we have for commending voluntary social segregation within ideal theory.

Private associations are likely to become more segregated when inequalities increase (e.g., beyond what justice permits). This is because, on Rawls's view, social unions become segregated in response to the impact that inequalities have upon the *internal lives* of social unions, and because increases in society-wide inequality are likely to manifest themselves in existing social unions. As the difference between the holdings of the better- and worse-off members of society increases, people of different levels of income, wealth, etc., will want their social unions to reflect these changes. Consider the following distributive schemes of two imagined societies. The numbers indicate differences in the quantity of some bundle of social goods (e.g., income and wealth) (Table 10.1).

Suppose that intra-associational inequalities greater than 2 units are inconsistent with the good functioning of associations, and that such inequalities cultivate envy among the worst off members of associations. When the inequalities among the members of an association are greater than 2 units, the least advantaged members of the association often do not receive recognition that their contributions are valuable; they are often unable to participate in the association on equal terms with others. Therefore, given what Rawls says about the forces which encourage voluntary social segregation, Society 2 will manifest greater social segregation than will Society 1. In Society 1, members of Group A will form associations with themselves and members of Group B; members of Group B will form associations with themselves and members of both Groups A and C; and members of Group C will form associations with themselves and members of Group B. In Society 2, members of Groups A, B, and C will form associations only with members of their own groups.

If the good functioning of a private association is undermined by a relatively fixed amount of internal inequality (i.e., when the inequality is present within the association), then increases in society-wide inequality will lead to increased social segregation. To return to the above example: If an inequality greater than 2 units undermines the functioning of private associations, then Society 1 will become more socially segregated as it comes to resemble Society 2. When wealth and income become less equal, neighborhoods, schools, churches, and other groups will become populated by persons from increasingly narrow segments of the population. Recall that Rawls claims that social segregation reduces the 'visibility' of inequality. Therefore, increases in social inequality are (partially) self-concealing. They encourage increased social segregation which, in turn, (partially) conceals increases in social inequality.

It follows that increases in social inequality (beyond what justice permits) may not generate envy. This is because increased social inequality encourages greater social segregation, and because social segregation mitigates the formation of envy. Importantly, social segregation is insensitive to the distinction between just and unjust inequalities. Voluntary segregation is a strategy for escaping the sense of inferiority or impotence that one may experience as an unequal member of a valued association. Since both just and unjust inequalities can give rise to feelings of inferiority or impotence, and since social segregation aims only at avoiding those feelings, social segregation does not attend to the distinction between just and unjust inequalities. It follows that social segregation can help to resign persons to social injustice, i.e., by reducing the 'painful visibility' of unjust inequalities. However, it is pernicious to cultivate complacency about injustice. Therefore, we have reason to resist social segregation under nonideal conditions, even if Rawls is right to think that social segregation may be commendable within ideal theory.

Here I may face an objection: Rawls says that voluntary social segregation prevents *envy* and he says that envy is a vice. If envy is vicious, shouldn't we be glad that social segregation diminishes it, even under nonideal conditions? Surely the fact that background institutions are unjust does not make envy a virtue, or otherwise weaken the case in favor of diminishing the prevalence of this vice. Therefore (this objection concludes), we ought not to be troubled by the tendency of social segregation to undermine hostile feelings about unjust inequalities.

In response, we should be careful not to assume that because social segregation inhibits vicious envy under ideal conditions that it will inhibit *only* vicious envy under nonideal conditions. Instead, I argue that social segregation will (also) inhibit the formation of resentment under nonideal conditions. This is for two reasons. First, social segregation may *indirectly* inhibit the formation of resentment, even if social segregation has a direct impact only on the formation of envy. This is because resentment may result from reflection upon an original (unreflective) feeling of hostility towards inequality. Consider the following possible genealogy of resentment:

> A person finds himself envying some of the better off members of his society. He reflects upon this feeling. He asks himself whether he can defend his anger about the fact that some members of society possess so much more than he possesses. Eventually, this person identifies good reasons for thinking that the inequalities which offend him are unjust. In this way, he vindicates his original hostility towards these inequalities. He has transformed his envy into the moral feeling of resentment.

One reason to endorse the plausibility of this genealogy of resentment is that the phenomenon of transformation-by-reflection seems to be present in many experiences of the moral feelings. For example, I may experience a feeling of inner discomfort after performing an action. This feeling of discomfort may transform into a feeling of guilt if I conclude that the action which caused me discomfort involved treating another person wrongly. Similarly, this feeling of inner discomfort may also transform into a feeling of shame if I conclude that the action which caused me discomfort manifested a defect in my character. Or, I may conclude that my action was neither morally wrong nor a manifestation of bad character. In that case, the original (nonmoral) feeling may remain unchanged or may diminish. If resentment often arises from envy, and if social segregation mitigates the formation of envy, then social segregation also likely mitigates the formation of resentment. Furthermore, if greater (and more unjust) inequalities cause greater social segregation, then greater (and more unjust) inequalities generate the conditions under which people will become less likely to become resentful of those inequalities.

Second, social segregation may also *directly* inhibit the formation of resentment. Consider another possible genealogy of resentment:

> A person is originally emotionally indifferent to inequality. Upon reflection, she comes to realize that her society falls short of the demands of distributive justice. Her judgment that some inequalities are unjust may, in turn, generate hostility towards those inequalities (and towards the members of her society who benefit from injustice).

This process of resentment-formation does not rely upon a previous envy. Here, someone develops the moral feeling of resentment as a consequence of judging that inequalities are unjust. This direct method of resentment-formation may also be interrupted by social segregation, because a person may have to 'see' some of the detrimental effects of inequality in order to conclude that these inequalities are unjust. Recall that for Rawls, as for others who think of distributive justice as an expression of the conditions of equal citizenship, knowledge of abstract facts (e.g., Gini coefficients) is unlikely to be a sufficient basis for the conclusion that holdings within one's society are unjust. Instead, one must know something about the origin and socio-political consequences of inequality to justify such a conclusion. If a person's day-to-day social experiences consist solely (or primarily) of interactions with other similarly-situated persons, then it may be difficult to develop an accurate understanding of the origins and effects of inequality. Since social segregation hides many of the social realities of inequality, social segregation may prevent members of societies marked by unjust inequalities from acquiring the knowledge necessary to conclude that their societies' inequalities are unjust. Social segregation may mitigate the formation of resentment, even if this moral feeling does not require a prior unreflective envy.

10.5 Complacency, Politics, and Nonideal Theory

Unjust inequalities may motivate the less advantaged to withdraw from political society, for the same reasons which drive them to withdraw from private associations in which they cannot participate as equals. If the less advantaged cannot be *equal* members of political society, they may have reason to withdraw from participation in political society altogether. However, while the withdrawal of the less advantaged from particular private associations may be commended for its tendency to reduce envy, the withdrawal of the less advantaged from politics must be condemned. It is social disaster when less advantaged citizens resign themselves to the fact that political society has become just another private association—like a yacht club or the country club—in which only the most advantaged can be equal members.

One reason why the withdrawal of the less advantaged from active participation in political society is a disaster is because participation in political life is part of each person's good. While Rawls says that persons must participate as equal members of *at least one* private association in order to develop an adequate sense of self-worth, he says that persons must participate as equal members of *the* (only) political community in order to possess a proper self-respect. There is no alternative mechanism by which a citizen may acquire the goods associated with equal citizenship. Every citizen has good reason to be an equal citizen.

When inequalities exceed the limits set by principles of distributive justice, some citizens will have inferior standing in the political community. This may cause them to develop hostile feelings. Consider a few Rawlsian examples. One, if the least advantaged have fewer basic (political) liberties—or an unfair *worth* of their basic liberties—they may become hostile towards those who possess real political power. Two, if the least advantaged never have a fair opportunity to acquire privileged social positions (and, instead, see those positions distributed according to an aristocratic order), they may become hostile towards those who have acquired their positions merely through the good fortune of being born into a privileged class. Three, if the most advantaged possess a greater amount of social goods (beyond what justice permits) only by making the least advantaged worse off, this may generate hostility on the part of the least advantaged, who may feel as if they have been treated as mere means for the improved financial position of the wealthy. Unequal political liberties, unequal opportunities, and inequalities of wealth and income which do not prioritize the outcomes of the least advantaged may generate hostile feelings among the least advantaged.

There is a tension between the fact that equal participation in the political community is a necessary part of persons' good and the fact that unequal citizenship is likely to generate hostile feelings. On the one hand, everyone has good reason to seek equal citizenship, and everyone has good reason to resist forms of inequality which make them unequal members of political society. There is no substitute for equal membership in the political community. On the other hand, a person who is regularly reminded that he is an inferior member of the political community is going to become resentful, and many citizens may find it too painful to be continually reminded that they are inferior members of a community whose activities they value. These people have good reason to disengage from politics altogether, and to treat the political community as just another private club whose (equal) members include only the more advantaged members of their society.

Rawls's account of voluntary social segregation lends support to the idea that the least advantaged will often withdraw from politics when inequalities exceed the limits set by distributive justice. Recall that Rawls observes that people will abandon *private* associations in which they are not equal members. When this occurs, the least advantaged redirect their energies towards other social unions, namely, social unions in which they can be equal members. Something similar can be said about the political community. When the least advantaged members of society cannot be equal members of 'the social union of social unions', they may redirect their energies towards forms of social life which better advance their good. Of course, some may choose self-sacrificial devotion to the cause of social justice, but this may be beyond what justice demands, and it seems unlikely that more than a few people will choose this path. Importantly, a person who refuses to fight for equal citizenship may thereby give up the chance to develop the most robust conception of self-respect or self-worth possible, since equal citizenship is a necessary component of a person's good. However, if equal citizenship is not a realistic outcome of social justice activism, then it may be both rational and morally permissible for inferior members of an unjust political community to stop caring about politics, and to recommit themselves towards other forms of social life.

10.6 Reconsidering Voluntary Social Segregation

One goal of this paper has been to show that latent in Rawls's discussion of envy, resentment and voluntary social segregation is a plausible (partial) explanation of two striking features of contemporary American life: (1) widespread complacency about inequality and (2) decreased political participation (especially by the least advantaged members of society). I have argued that it follows from the claims Rawls makes about social segregation that increases in inequality beyond what justice permits will encourage citizens to participate in more segregated forms of social union. Also, increased inequality will cause the less well-off members of the political community to experience feelings of inferiority and hostility when they attempt to participate in politics. While such feelings may encourage some to fight for distributive justice, they are also likely to motivate the least advantaged to redirect their limited energies towards those private associations within which they can be equal members. Furthermore, these two phenomena—increased segregation among private associations and the withdrawal of the least advantaged from politics—will contribute to citizens' complacency about unjust inequalities.

A further goal of this paper has been to identify and explain a tension in Rawls's views about the value of social segregation. Within *ideal* theory, Rawls thinks that the tendency of persons to voluntarily self-segregate is commendable, since it makes people complacent about the inequalities that distributive justice permits. However, I have argued that the tendency of persons to self-segregate is less commendable within *nonideal* theory, since social segregation may cultivate complacency about unjust inequalities. If the citizens of a society that is marked by unjust inequalities have a duty to work for distributive justice, then a tendency towards voluntary segregation in such a society is not (entirely) commendable.

References

Alon, Sigal. 2009. The evolution of class inequality in higher education competition, exclusion, and adaptation. *American Sociological Review* 74: 731–755.

Anderson, Elizabeth. 2010. *The imperative of integration*. Princeton: Princeton University Press.

Berger, Ben. 2011. *Attention deficit democracy: The paradox of civic engagement*. Princeton: Princeton University Press.

Bishop, Bill. 2009. *The big sort: Why the clustering of like-minded America is tearing us apart*. Boston: Mariner Books.

Cohen, G.A. 2008. *Rescuing justice and equality*. Cambridge: Harvard University Press.

Congressional Budget Office. 2011. *Trends in the distribution of household income between 1979 and 2007*. Washington, DC: Congress of the United States, Congressional Budget Office.

Ditomaso, Nancy. 2013. *The American non-dilemma: Racial inequality without racism*. New York: The Russell Sage Foundation.

Economic Policy Institute. 2012. State of working America. http://stateofworkingamerica.org/

Freeman, Samuel. 2002. Congruence and the good of justice. In *The Cambridge companion to Rawls*, ed. Samuel Freeman, 277–315. Cambridge: Cambridge University Press.

Gibbard, Allan. 1990. *Wise choices, apt feelings: A theory of normative judgment*. Oxford: Oxford University Press.

Massey, Douglas, and Nancy Denton. 1993. *American apartheid: Segregation and the making of the underclass*. Cambridge: Harvard University Press.

Mishel, Lawrence, Jared Bernstein, and Heidi Shierholtz. 2009. *The state of working America 2008/2009*. Ithaca: ILR Press, an imprint of Cornell University Press.

Noah, Timothy. 2012. *The great divergence: America's growing inequality crisis and what we can do about it*. New York: Bloomsbury Publishing USA.

Norton, Michael I., and Dan Ariely. 2011. Building a better America – One wealth quintile at a time. *Perspectives on Psychological Science* 6: 9–12.

Nussbaum, Martha C. 2001. *Upheavals of thought: The intelligence of emotions*. Cambridge: Cambridge University Press.

Putnam, R.D. 2001. *Bowling alone: The collapse and revival of American community*. New York: Simon and Schuster.

Rawls, John. 1999. *A theory of justice*, rev. ed. Cambridge, MA: Belknap Press of Harvard University Press.

Reardon, Sean F., and Kendra Bischoff. 2011. Income inequality and income segregation. *American Journal of Sociology* 116: 1092–1153.

Saez, Emmanuel. 2008. Striking it richer: The evolution of top incomes in the United States. *Pathways Magazine*: 6–7.

Saez, Emmanuel. 2012. Striking it richer: The evolution of top incomes in the United States (Updated with 2009 and 2010 estimates). http://elsa.berkeley.edu/~saez/saez-UStopincomes-2010.pdf

Shapiro, Thomas, Tatjana Meschede, and Sam Osoro. 2013. *The roots of the widening racial wealth gap: Explaining the black-white economic divide*. Waltham, Mass: Institute on Assets and Social Policy.

Stiglitz, Joseph E. 2012. *The price of inequality: How today's divided society endangers our future*. New York: W. W. Norton & Company.

Taylor, P., and D.R. Fry. 2012. *The rise of residential segregation by income. Social and demographic trends*. Washington, DC: Pew Research Center.

Taylor, P., D.R. Kochhar, R. Fry, G. Velasco, and S. Motel. 2011. *Wealth gaps rise to record highs between Whites, Blacks and Hispanics. Social and demographic trends*. Washington, DC: Pew Research Center.

Uslaner, Eric M. 2002. *The moral foundations of trust*. New York: Cambridge University Press.

Wilkinson, R.G., and K. Pickett. 2009. *The spirit level: Why greater equality makes societies stronger*. New York: Bloomsbury Press.

Chapter 11
Mass Democracy in a Postfactual Market Society: *Citizens United* and the Role of Corporate Political Speech

F. Patrick Hubbard

Abstract This chapter addresses the problems underlying *Citizens United v. FEC* (2010), a case decided by the United States Supreme Court in 2010. Part I discusses political speech within a context defined by three factors: (1) electorates that are so large that speech must address them largely by using "mass media"; (2) a postfactual culture where analysis and debate often rely on distortions, misstatements, or fabrications of factual matters; and (3) a market society where effective political speech depends largely upon having the financial ability to use mass media. After discussing the legal fiction of corporate personhood, Part II argues first, that *Citizens United* has a reasoned basis and second, that critics allow their concern about the role of wealth in politics to divert them from addressing both the basis of the decision and other avenues of reform. Part III discusses measures to limit the role of money in politics and the problem that, in a market society, speech is always, to some extent, for sale.

11.1 Mass Democracy in a Postfactual Market Society

11.1.1 Mass Democracy

The choice to seek virtually universal suffrage in the United States has drawbacks, two of which are particularly relevant to questions concerning political speech. First, this broad electorate inevitably includes many voters with minimal interest in

F.P. Hubbard (✉)
School of Law, University of South Carolina, 710 Main St. Room 405,
29208 Columbia, SC, USA
e-mail: phubbard@law.sc.edu

A.E. Cudd and S.J. Scholz (eds.), *Philosophical Perspectives on Democracy in the 21st Century*, AMINTAPHIL: The Philosophical Foundations of Law and Justice 5,
DOI 10.1007/978-3-319-02312-0_11,

or understanding of the political system or the issues facing the country. Second, voters generally lack personal knowledge of candidates, particularly in federal elections. House districts contain a population of around 700,000; with the exception of very small states, Senate and Presidential races involve a much larger population (United States Census Bureau 2011).

Given these conditions, voters' knowledge of candidates and issues is very limited because it must be based on diverse print and electronic media and because many voters pay little attention. Even persons who try to understand political matters are challenged by "the comparatively meager time available in each day for paying attention to public affairs, the distortion arising because events have to be compressed into very short messages, the difficulty of making a small vocabulary express a complicated world, and finally fear of facing those facts which would seem to threaten the established routines of men's lives" (Lippmann 1922, 30; Posner 2003, 150–153, 168–169).[1] Moreover, mass media have shortcomings in educating the public because they function as profit-oriented businesses where the definition of "news" is shaped by the desire to boost revenue by increasing the number of readers, viewers, or listeners and to decrease costs by limiting expenditures on gathering and presenting news. (Bybee 1999, 38–39, 61)[2]

11.1.2 Postfactual Culture

Though rhetoric can usefully communicate in ways that accurately capture a policy position or motivate people through a common basis of shared values (Posner 2003, 84–85; Sarat and Kearns 1994, 1, 5–27), it can also be used to persuade by misleading, by manipulating shared values and symbols, and by taking advantage of misconceptions in order to be "more convincing among the ignorant than the expert" (Plato 1961, 229, 242).

[1] Lippmann also argues that ordinary people are so limited in their knowledge of political matters that their only choice is "[t]o support the Ins when things are going well; to support the Outs when they seem to be going badly" and that "this, in spite of all that has been said about tweedledum and tweedledee, is the essence of popular government" (Lippmann 1925, 126). Richard Posner adopts a similar view (Posner 2003, 150–153, 168–169). However, he argues that, despite these limits, our democracy functions relatively well (Posner 2003, 158–212). For example, he argues: "We should not take the Tweedledum-Tweedledee character of major-party competition as a sign that competition is not working. If the parties were highly dissimilar, one of them would probably be the permanent minority party" (Posner 2003, 190).

[2] News has always been a profit-oriented business. For example, the Spanish American War was the first "media war" because of the role of newspapers in using misleading accounts in order to boost circulation (PBS 2007). Similarly, the television networks were so "enthusiastic about covering" the first Iraq war that "they wanted it to take place because they knew how … large the audience would be." (McGoldrick 2004, 41).

This second type of rhetoric not only characterizes a large amount of political discussion in the United States, it is also accompanied by an approach to facts that has been characterized as "truthiness" by Stephen Colbert, the host of the satirical "news" show *Colbert Report*, as follows:

> Truthiness is sort of what you want to be true, as opposed to what the facts support.... Truthiness is a truth larger than the facts that would comprise it—if you cared about facts, which you don't, if you care about truthiness (Steinberg 2005, § 4, at 3).

Colbert's term has had an impact. It was voted the 2005 word of the year (American Dialect Society 2006). One commentator noted that the word "caught on instantaneously … precisely because we live in the age of truthiness," (Rich 2006, § 4, at 16) and the *Chicago Tribune* published an obituary for "Facts, 360 BC–A.D. 2012" (Huppke 2012).

In effect, the postmodern subjectivity of values includes a claim by some of the subjectivity of the *value of empirical claims*. This claim is used to justify a "postfactual" subjectivity of facts where both values and facts are constructed within each person's mind. This construction of facts is necessary because information about the vast "factual" world only makes sense after it has been fitted into a simpler world model within one's mind (Lippmann 1922, 3–32).[3] Not surprisingly, this modeling process can be affected by factors like limited time and a dislike of accepting unpleasant facts (See Sect. 11.1.1). For many, it is more "truthful" to reject the factual claims of "elites" and rely on common sense "facts" like: "Climate change and evolution are just theories." The effect of this factual subjectivity is that opinion, meaning, interpretation, and narrative are only loosely structured by a shared "real" world. As a result, cynicism and ends-justify-means reasoning result in a context where advertising in mass media, particularly television, has become even more important in manipulating and shaping people's subjective maps of the factual world. In the world of truthiness, "[w]hat matters most now is whether a story can be sold as truth, preferably on television." (Rich 2006)[4]. Though there is debate about the utility of using political advertising to sell their version of truth, candidates clearly believe it is useful, if not essential, in a campaign, even if it merely forces the other side to do the same (Scherer 2012, 38, 40).[5]

[3] Lippmann uses vague simplified phrases like a person "must have maps of the world" and make "a trustworthy picture inside his head of the world" (Lippmann 1922, 16, 29). Such phrases are themselves simplified models of an extremely complex process (Dennett 1991).

[4] Others have noted the use of "'symbolic politics,'" "empirically ungrounded political lore," and "iconic images" to "mold public agendas" (Haltom and McCann 2004, 270–271.)

[5] The article contains comments by Karl Rove that $75 million in advertising by the super PAC American Crossroads attacking Obama was "forcing Obama to respond … and thus draining the President's funds" and by Steve Law, CEO of Crossroads, conceding that "Crossroads has not yet fundamentally reshaped any major Senate race," but noting that "Crossroads has forced Democrats into new spending just to hold their ground." (Scherer 2012).

11.1.3 Market Society

In a market society, the right to free speech is not free where mass media are concerned. The amounts of money for political advertising and other campaign expenses[6] have reached enormous levels. The campaign expenditures in the race between Romney and Obama were estimated to cost a combined total of 2.5 billion dollars.[7] Total federal election campaign spending for the presidential and congressional races is estimated to be $5.8 billion dollars, nearly twice the 3.1 billion dollars spent in 2000.[8] (Scherer 2012)

Though funding for campaign expenditures has been characterized as "a rich man's game" (Scherer 2012, 42–45), such rhetorical phrases must be assessed in context. Money is important, but how important? Candidates who spend the most money usually win, but donors tend to give more to candidates who are already likely to win—for example, to incumbents (Wert et al. 2011, 721–722) Moreover, money comes from many sources, some of which cancel one another. Finally, because speech funded by corporations is limited in comparison to funding by wealthy individuals or other sources, it is very hard to assess the relative role of corporate speech in the complex world of political campaigns. (See section "Impact")

11.2 Corporations and Speech

11.2.1 Corporate Personhood

Corporations and partnerships have been recognized as nonnatural persons for centuries. However, because "corporate persons" lack the physical dimensions necessary to act and think like humans, their decisions and actions can only be undertaken by human agents acting on behalf of the entity. As noted centuries ago, a corporation "has no soul to be damned, and no body to be kicked" (Coffee 1981, 386).[9]

---

[6] Examples of nonadvertising campaign expenses include overhead costs and grassroots organizing, which can also be very expensive (Scherer 2012, 45).

[7] This figure includes expenditures by the candidates, the two political parties, and outside groups (Scherer 2012, 41).

[8] This figure includes expenditures by the candidates, the two political parties, and outside groups. (Scherer 2012, 41).

[9] Others have made similar comments. Justice Stevens, in his dissent in *Citizens United* (2012, 972), noted that "corporations have no consciences, no beliefs, no feelings, no thoughts, no desires." Elizabeth Wolgast argued that "it is implausible to treat a corporation as a member of the human community, a member with a personality (but not a face), intentions (but no feelings), relationships (but no family or friends), responsibility (but no conscience), and susceptibility to punishment (but no capacity for pain)" (Wolgast 1992, 86).

The rights granted to corporate persons are extremely limited in comparison to those granted to humans. For example, though both corporations and infants require humans to act for them, corporations have owners, who can buy, sell, or dissolve ("kill") a corporation with virtually no substantive restraints. Though corporations are persons under the First, Fifth, and Fourteenth Amendments, (*Citizens United* 925 2012)[10] their protections for "life, liberty, or property" are limited. For example, they have no right to life or physical liberty, no right to vote, and no rights under the Thirteenth Amendment's prohibition of slavery (Hubbard 2011, 434–435).

Corporations lack many basic rights because their personhood is simply a fictional legal status that facilitates complex legal relationships among humans (Hubbard 2011, 434–435). When corporate personhood furthers this goal, as in allowing individuals to associate and speak together as a corporation, personhood is recognized (See section "Corporate Personhood"). Where corporate personhood does not facilitate human goals, it is abandoned. For example, because buying, selling, and dissolving corporations is crucial to implementing human goals, we view the corporation as a thing, not a person.

11.2.2 Citizens United*: Corporate Rights and the Human Right of Association*

Facts

Citizens United v. FEC (2010) involved a challenge to a statutory scheme prohibiting corporations and unions from expending general treasury funds for any "electioneering communication" or for speech that expressly advocated the election or defeat of a candidate (2 United States Code § 441b 2000).[11] In January 2008, Citizens United, a nonprofit corporation, released a documentary (*Hillary*) critical of then-Senator Hillary Clinton, a candidate for her party's Presidential nomination. Concerned about possible civil and criminal penalties for violating the statutory

[10] The first case to recognize corporate constitutional rights was *Santa Clara Cnty. v. S. Pac. R.R.* (1886). In *Santa Clara*, the reported opinion states that, prior to oral argument, Chief Justice Waite said:

> The court does not wish to hear argument on the question whether the provision in the Fourteenth Amendment to the Constitution, which forbids a State to deny to any person within its jurisdiction the equal protection of the laws, applies to these corporations. We are all of opinion that it does.

Though this brief statement with no discussion or reasons has never been overruled, it has been widely criticized and is followed today (Hubbard 2011, 434–435).

[11] Section 100.29(a)(2)–(b)(3)(ii) of the Code of Federal Regulations defines "electioneering communication" as "any broadcast, cable, or satellite communication" that (1) "refers to a clearly identified candidate for Federal office" and (2) is made within 30 days of a primary election, and (3) that is "publicly distributed," which in "the case of a candidate for nomination for President... means" that the communication "[c]an be received by 50,000 or more persons in a State where a primary election... is being held within 30 days."

prohibition, Citizens United challenged the constitutionality of the prohibition in federal court. That court ruled against Citizens United, which then appealed to the Supreme Court.

Corporate Personhood

A central question in *Citizens United* was whether corporations can have the First Amendment right to free speech. The majority (5–4) opinion by Justice Kennedy stressed that "[t]he Court has recognized that First Amendment protection extends to corporations" (*Citizens United* 2012, 899). The dissenting opinion by Justice Stevens criticized the majority for adopting "[t]he conceit that corporations must be treated identically to natural persons," noted that when the framers of the Constitution "constitutionalized the right of free speech in the First Amendment, it was the free speech of individual Americans that they had in mind," and emphasized the difference between corporations and humans (*Citizens United* 2012, 930, 950, 971–972).

Justice Scalia's concurring opinion disagreed with the dissent's view of the framers' intent (*Citizens United* 2012, 925–929). His opinion also addressed the corporate right to speech issue as follows:

> All the provisions of the Bill of Rights set forth the rights of individual men and women—not, for example, of trees or polar bears. But the individual person's right to speak includes the right to speak *in association with other individual persons*. Surely the dissent does not believe that speech by the Republican Party or the Democratic Party can be censored because it is not the speech of "an individual American." It is the speech of many individual Americans, who have associated in a common cause, giving the leadership of the party the right to speak on their behalf. The association of individuals in a business corporation is no different—or at least it cannot be denied the right to speak on the simplistic ground that it is not "an individual American" (*Citizens United* 2012, 928).

Scalia's position is not novel. The Court recognized in 1958 that an inherent aspect of freedom of speech is the right to associate for the purpose of exercising the right (*NAACP v. Alabama* 1958). In 1830, Tocqueville noted in *Democracy in America* that "the right to associate almost merges with the freedom to write" (de Tocqueville 1840, 218). Moreover, Scalia's argument—i.e., that the corporate right to speech is useful because it protects the right of human persons to associate and thus exercise their right to speech more effectively—is consistent with the basic concept that the fiction of corporate personhood is recognized where necessary to further human goals (See Sect. 11.2.1).

Criticisms

The recognition of corporations' right to speech has been widely criticized. Perhaps the best known criticism is President Obama's comment during the State of the Union address that *Citizens United* "reversed a century of law" and will "open the floodgates for special interests" (Roff 2012). Senator (and former Republican presidential candidate) John McCain used similar language: "The worst decision by the Supreme Court in the 21st century. Uninformed, arrogant, naïve" (Scherer 2012, 9). Strong critical language is also used by Ronald Dworkin, who, for example, stressed similar concerns for the impact of the case and asserted that the Court's reasoning was so "simplistic," "shallow," and "poor" that it suggests "some motive other than a desire to reach the right legal result" (Dworkin 2010a, February, 2010b, May).

Such criticisms of ineptitude, dire consequences, and improper motives should be supported by extremely strong, nonconclusory arguments. However, the following assessment of the criticisms indicates that, while these critics have asserted that the majority position is disastrous and unfounded, they have not provided adequate support for the assertions.

Such support would have to be sufficiently detailed to accommodate the very complex constitutional framework the Court has developed for addressing the open-textured language of the First Amendment's restriction on government action "abridging the freedom of speech, or of the press." This framework includes a number of important, generally accepted guidelines. In particular, where political speech is involved, the Court has consistently held that "government has no power to restrict expression because of its message, its ideas, its subject matter or its content" (*Police Dep't of Chi. v. Moseley* 1972, 95–96) and that laws burdening political speech are "subject to strict scrutiny," which requires proof by the Government that the restriction "furthers a compelling interest and is narrowly tailored to achieve that interest" (*FEC v. Wisconsin Right to Life, Inc.* 2007, 464). Because vague prohibitions of speech might "chill" the expression of constitutionally protected speech, such prohibitions are impermissible (*Citizens United* 2012, 889).

Under this framework, restrictions on the content of political speech are hard to justify, though not impossible.[12] Consequently, it is interesting to note that critics of *Citizens United* have not even tried to draft a statute that is both narrowly tailored to achieve a compelling interest and sufficiently precise to avoid the problem of chilling political speech.

Failure to Limit Decision to "As Applied" Challenge

In the lower court, *Citizens United* challenged the statute on the ground that, "as applied" to it, the challenge was an unconstitutional restriction on its right to speech (*Citizens United* 2012, 888). The Court asked the parties to address whether the statute was unconstitutional "on its face"—i.e., unconstitutional no matter what the factual context (*Citizens United* 2012, 888). The decision by the majority to broaden the matter to a "facial" attack, rather than use the narrow "as applied" approach, was criticized by the dissent as an abandonment of principles of judicial

[12] For example, defamatory statements can be "restricted" by the threat of a defamation suit against the speaker if the plaintiff can satisfy the requirements of *New York Times Co. v. Sullivan* (1964).

restraint, which require using narrower grounds that limit the decision's impact on the legislative scheme (*Citizens United* 2012, 931–938).[13] The majority responded that a narrower ground would "chill" speech because of lack of clarity and that the Court had a responsibility to resolve the issue properly (*Citizens United* 2012, 888–896, 913–919). Justice Stevens responded that the majority's decision to address the facial attack, even though the trial court had not addressed it, resulted in a lack of an adequate factual record to assess whether "chilling" was likely. (*Citizens United* 2012, 933–936). Justice Kennedy countered that such a record was not necessary because the burdens and incentives of the "interpretive process [of resolving a series of as-applied challenges] itself would create an inevitable, pervasive, and serious risk of chilling protected speech…" (*Citizens United* 2012, 891).

Precedent and Stare Decisis

The majority overruled holdings in two relatively recent (1990, 2003) cases that had upheld restrictions on campaign speech (*Citizens United* 2012, 913)[14]. The dissent criticized this overruling of precedent (*Citizens United* 2012, 938–942),[15] which was defended by the majority as consistent with the accepted view that precedent should be overruled where appropriate (*Citizens United* 2012, 924–925). Whether this results in overruling a "century of law" as claimed by President Obama depends on how one reads the small number of diverse cases in this area. Whether the overruling was justified depends on the evaluation of the other criticisms of the decision.

Corporate Personhood

Scalia's concurring argument concerning corporations' rights can be summarized as follows: If thousands of people, who lack the ability to purchase a large newspaper individually, choose to pool their money and form a corporation that purchases political advertisements, why can the government restrict these advertisements but not those purchased by wealthy individuals? The dissent and other critics never provide an explicit answer to this question (*Citizens United* 2012, 949–952).[16]

---

[13] Dworkin made a similar argument. (Dworkin 2010a, February).

[14] The cases overruled are *McConnell v. FEC*, 540 U.S. 93 (2003) and *Austin v. Michigan Chamber of Commerce*, 494 U.S. 652 (1990).

[15] Dworkin made a similar argument. (Dworkin 2010b, May).

[16] Dworkin also fails to address Scalia's argument. (Dworkin 2010a, February, 2010b, May) The dissent argues that corporations can "distort" the political process (*Citizens United* 2012, 971–977). However, with the exception of the issue of speaker identity (which could be addressed by the disclosure requirements upheld by the court), the dissent fails to distinguish this from the effect of individual wealth and, except for a reference to the First Amendment's Free Press Clause (*Citizens United* 2012, 951–952) generally avoids the problems of electioneering by political parties and media corporations.

Application of "Strict Scrutiny" Test

Underlying the disagreements involved in the prior three criticisms was the issue of whether the government had successfully demonstrated that the restriction on speech: (1) furthered a compelling interest; and (2) was narrowly tailored. (See section "Criticisms") The compelling interests asserted by the dissent were prevention of "corruption" of the "integrity" of the political process, prevention of "distortion" of the process, and shareholder protection (*Citizens United* 2012 961–979). Except for shareholder protection, these concerns also apply to wealthy individuals. Thus, the dissent's concerns are undermined by Scalia's associational rationale, which is not addressed by the dissent. Moreover, as indicated in the following discussion of impact, the corruption and distortion arguments have less factual support than critics assume. As to shareholder protection, most expenditures are made by PACs, which are formed to influence political decisions, not to make profits for shareholders. (See Sect. 11.3)

Impact

In terms of political campaigns, the impact of corporate political speech is relatively limited for five reasons. First, most business corporations avoid political controversy for fear of losing customers (Epstein 2011; Wert et al. 2011, 726–727). Second, the amount spent by corporate entities formed for the purpose of political speech (like PACs) is small compared to the total amounts of time and money donated to campaigns. Third, the concept of diminishing marginal utility applies to money spent on political speech—i.e., additional expenditures on speech have a lesser effect than prior expenditures. Fourth, individuals concerned with a corporate or industry position, like employees or shareholders, already give considerable sums to support campaigns. Fifth, given the scale of campaign expenditures, the incremental impact of expenditures by entities that are independent from a candidate's campaign, including expenditures by individuals and corporations, on elections is less than generally assumed (Wert et al. 2011, 722–724).

Conclusion

As indicated above, the argument herein is that *Citizens United*, like most fundamental constitutional cases, is not indisputably **in**correct. This narrower point is important for two reasons.

First, though the case is extraordinarily important, it is, to a considerable degree, simply another difficult case where Supreme Court justices have reasoned disagreements. Consequently, unsupported ad hominem attacks like Dworkin's are, at best, not useful in addressing the issues involved. Simplistic rejections of a corporation's right to speech because corporations are not human are similarly flawed. Instead of such attacks, it would be more fruitful to criticize Congress, which has not adopted strong restrictions on campaign speech that would be constitutional (See Sect. 11.3).

Second, many of the concerns expressed by critics of *Citizens United* are based on objections to the impact of wealth on the political process rather than a narrowly focused concern for corporate speech. If wealthy individuals can purchase a newspaper, a television network, or an advertisement in either of these and "slant" political speech however they want with virtually no legal restrictions on content,[17] why is Scalia's right-to-association argument for corporate personhood invalid? It is not surprising that no critic has satisfactorily addressed Scalia's argument. Economic inequality is inherent in the classical Lockean right to private property, which has been as basic as liberties like free speech since the colonial era (Hubbard 2011, 409–410). This Lockean commitment results in distributional inequality which, in turn, results in inequality in the ability to exercise the right to free speech. As a result, people with property have advantages in terms of speech unless we make very fundamental changes in our constitutional framework concerning property, the market, wealth distribution, and speech.

11.3 Money in Politics

The impact of money on politics can be limited in some ways. For example, *Citizens United* makes it clear that wealthy individuals can be limited in their right to contribute money to candidates; such contributions are not speech (*Citizens United* 2012, 908). The effectiveness of such limits is currently restricted because of what appears to be close coordination between the campaign organizations of candidates and the "independent" expenditures by wealthy individuals or corporate entities. Realistically, however, even if the rules (or enforcement of the rules) on coordination were tightened, it will be hard to prevent "conscious parallelism" in activities.

Citizens United also makes clear that noncontent-based disclosure requirements are permissible (*Citizens United* 2012, 913–914). Thus, any flaws in disclosure rules (which currently allow, in effect, some donors to remain anonymous) are the fault of Congress, not the Court. However, it is not clear how much effect disclosure will have in terms of limiting the role of wealth per se.

In assessing the role of corporations and money in politics, it is important to note that, by and large, corporate entities that spend money supporting a candidate's campaign are *not* business enterprises like General Motors. Business corporations generally avoid the public relations problems that come with funding partisan activities (See section "Impact"). Instead, expenditures are made by entities like PACs that exist for the purpose of partisan political activities and that often rely on contributions by individuals, who already have a First Amendment right as humans to spend their money on political advertising. Thus, to a considerable extent, the problem underlying criticisms of *Citizens United* is not related to whether the funds for speech take the form of corporate or individual contributions. Instead, the problem

[17] *Buckley v. Valeo* (1976) recognized these individual rights.

is that wealth inequality among citizens makes the right to free speech very unequal in practice (See section "Conclusion").

The challenges in *Citizens United* of addressing the interconnection of money, speech, and politics are not new. Some of the analyses of media, democracy, and subjectivity of facts quoted herein were made in the 1920s (See Sect. 11.1). For at least a century, our republic has been dealing with the possible truth of the position asserted by the corporate CEO in the movie, *Network*, who asserts that business and dollars are such "primal forces of nature" that "there is no democracy." (MGM 1976)

The majority in *Citizens United* held that the impact of the primal forces of money, whether spent by individuals or corporate entities, does not justify content-based limitations on political speech in order to prevent the "corruption" or "distortion" of democracy. In effect, the Court chose to protect democracy by trusting voters rather than censors. This choice indicates an understandable fear of censorship, no matter how well motivated. (If money is the problem, how can we prevent the use of money to influence censorship—i.e., prior restraint of speech—and thus affect who will be political winners and losers?) The Court's choice also indicates a faith in the ability of voters, despite the voters' relatively limited ability to assess candidates and issues, to sort through a barrage of often conflicting messages, many of which are somewhat deceptive and manipulative, in deciding how to vote. By placing its faith in voters, the majority was demonstrating its faith in the view that, if prior generations managed to operate a democracy in a market society where political speech is for sale to those who possess these "primal forces" without resorting to censorship, so can we.

References

American Dialect Society. 2006. Truthiness voted 2005 word of the year. http://www.americandialect.org/Words_of_the_Year_2005.pdf. Accessed 10 Dec 2012.

Austin v. Michigan Chamber of Commerce, 494 U.S. 652 (1990).

Buckley v. Valeo, 424 U.S. 1. 1976.

Bybee, Carl. 1999. Can democracy survive in the post-factual age? A return to the Lippmann-Dewey debate about the politics of news. *Journalism & Communication Monographs* 1: 28–66. http://jmo.sagepub.com/content/1/1/28.citation. Accessed 10 Dec 2012.

Citizens United Corp. 2008. *Hillary*.

Citizens United v. FEC, 130 S. Ct. 876 (2010).

Code of Federal Regulations.

Coffee Jr., John C. 1981. "No soul to damn: No body to kick": An unscandalized inquiry into the problem of corporate punishment. *Michigan Law Review* 79: 386–459.

de Tocqueville, Alexis. 2003. *Democracy in America*. 1835, 1840. Trans. Gerald E. Beran. London: Penguin Books.

Dennett, Daniel C. 1991. Consciousness Explained.

Dworkin, Ronald. 2010a. The "devastating" decision. *New York Review of Books*, February 25. http://www.nybooks.com/articles/archives/2010/feb/25/the-devastating-decision/. Accessed 10 Dec 2012.

Dworkin, Ronald. 2010b. The decision that threatens democracy. *New York Review of Books*, May 13. http://www.nybooks.com/articles/archives/2010/may/13/decision-threatens-democracy/. Accessed 12 Dec 2012.

Epstein, Richard. 2011. *Citizens United v. FEC*: The constitutional right that big corporations should have but do not want. *Harvard Journal of Law and Public Policy* 34: 639–662.
FEC v. Wisconsin Right to Life, Inc., 551 U.S. 449. 2007.
Haltom, William, and Michael McCann. 2004. *Distorting the law: Politics, media, and the litigation crisis*. Chicago: The University of Chicago Press.
Hubbard, F. Patrick. 2011. "Do androids dream?" Personhood and intelligent artifacts. *Temple Law Review* 83: 405–474.
Huppke, Rex W. 2012. Facts, 360 B.C.–A.D. 2012: In memoriam: After years of health problems, facts has finally died. Chi. Tribune, April 19. http://articles.chicagotribune.com/2012-04-19/news/ct-talk-huppke-obit-facts-20120419_1_facts-philosopher-opinion. Accessed 10 Dec 2012.
Lippmann, Walter. 1922. *Public opinion*. Wilder Publications.
Lippmann, Walter. 1925. *The phantom public*. New Brunswick, N.J.: Transaction Publishers.
McConnell v. FEC, 540 U.S. 93 (2003).
McGoldrick, Dominic. 2004. *From '9-11' to the 'Iraq war 2003': International law in an age of complexity*. Portland: Hart Publishing.
MGM. 1976. *Network*.
NAACP v. Alabama, 357 U.S. 449. 1958.
New York Times Co. v. Sullivan, 376 U.S. 254. 1964.
PBS. 2007. Crucible of empire: The Spanish American war.
Plato. 1961. Gorgias. In *The collected dialogues of Plato*, ed. Edith Hamilton and Huntington Cairns, 229–242. New York: Princeton University Press.
Police Dep't of Chi. v. Moseley, 408 U.S. 92 (1972).
Posner, Richard A. 2003. *Law, pragmatism, and democracy*. New York: Harvard University Press.
Rich, Frank. 2006. Truthiness 101: From Frey to Alito. *New York Times*, January 22.
Roff, Peter. 2012. Obama's super PAC reversal is cash trumping principle. U.S. News, February 7. http://www.usnews.com/opinion/blogs/peter-roff/2012/02/07/obamas-super-pac-reversal-is-cash-trumping-principle. Accessed 10 Dec 2012.
Santa Clara Cnty. v. S. Pac. R.R., 118 U.S. 394. 1886.
Sarat, Austin, and Thomas R. Kearns. 1994. Editorial introduction. In *The rhetoric of law*, ed. Austin Sarat and Thomas R. Kearns, 5–27. Ann Arbor: The University of Michigan Press.
Scherer, Michael. 2012. A rich man's game. *Time*, August 13.
Steinberg, Jacques. 2005. Truthiness. *New York Times*, December 25.
United States Census Bureau. 2011. Congressional apportionment: 2010 census briefs (2011). http://www.census.gov/prod/cen2010/briefs/c2010br-08.pdf. Accessed 10 Dec 2012.
United States Code. 2000.
Wert, Justin J., et al. 2011. Of Benedick and Beatrice: *Citizens United* and the reign of the Laggard Court. *Cornell Journal of Law and Public Policy* 20: 719–738.
Wolgast, Elizabeth. 1992. *Ethics of an artificial person: Lost responsibility in professions and organizations*. Stanford, CA: Stanford University Press.

Chapter 12
A Tsunami of Filthy Lucre: How the Decisions of the SCOTUS Imperil American Democracy

Jonathan Schonsheck

Abstract The Supreme Court of the United States—or more precisely, a bare 5–4 majority of the justices—rendered a decision in the now-infamous case of *Citizens United* v. *Federal Election Commission*. The legal particulars of this decision, together with its unmistakable aura, endorsed a First Amendment "right" of individuals and corporations to make unlimited expenditures in the attempt to influence the outcomes of elections. In the world of political campaign financing, this was a seismic event, producing a tsunami of filthy lucre. The decision was not, however, a legal outlier; it is the logical conclusion of a *line* of cases that begins with *Buckley* v. *Valeo*. In consequence, the critic must argue for the repudiation of the entire line. This I do. I argue that the Court has adopted a primitive theory of interpretation of the law, and its reasoning has relied completely upon a fatally flawed metaphor, the "marketplace of ideas." I dismantle the metaphor, and argue for a superior theory of interpretation. The reasoning of the Court poses a threat to American democracy by impelling us towards "representative plutocracy," proxy rule by Wealth. When properly understood, I argue, Freedom of Speech does not require this legal environment, which is nothing less than the philosophical self-evisceration of the First Amendment. When properly interpreted—as safeguarding the moral autonomy of the citizenry—Freedom of Speech requires the *prohibition* of these expenditures.

J. Schonsheck (✉)
Department of Philosophy and Program in Management and Leadership,
The Madden School of Business, Le Moyne College, 1419 Salt Springs Road,
13214 Syracuse, NY, USA
e-mail: schonsjc@lemoyne.edu

A.E. Cudd and S.J. Scholz (eds.), *Philosophical Perspectives on Democracy in the 21st Century*, AMINTAPHIL: The Philosophical Foundations of Law and Justice 5,
DOI 10.1007/978-3-319-02312-0_12, © Springer International Publishing Switzerland 2014

12.1 Introduction

Among the reasons that the political campaigns in America, 2012, were memorable: we witnessed the expenditure of phenomenal amounts of money—quite unprecedented amounts of money[1]— intended to influence the outcomes of campaigns. Indeed, it is no exaggeration to characterize this election as inundated with filthy lucre. Quite naturally, a couple of questions arise. How did this come about? And what are the consequences of these expenditures for American democracy?

A significant portion of the answer to the first question, origins, is relatively straightforward—it is to be found in the now-notorious decision of the Supreme Court of the United States (SCOTUS) in the case of *Citizens United* v. *Federal Election Commission* (2010). The answer the second question—the consequences for American democracy—is not at all straightforward. Indeed, it is complex, with numerous subtleties and convoluted causal chains. And it is the subject of this article.

By tradition, historic cases are referenced by the name of the plaintiff, or some portion thereof. Following this tradition, the case at the center of this ongoing controversy has come to be called "*Citizens United.*" For sound reasons, I simply cannot abide the *tone* of that appellation. It sounds so "positive"—"citizens" has a favorable connotation, and so does "united"; combined, they must be quite *wonderful.* As I shall argue, that positive aura is entirely unwarranted. I shall refer to this case/decision by means of an acronym, which begins with the initial letters of the plaintiff's name, "C.U.," and ends with the common abbreviation of the Federal Election Commission, "F.E.C." Thus I shall reference the case as "*CUFEC.*"[2]

CUFEC gave rise to the aforementioned tsunami of filthy lucre. It has done this by making it legally permissible for corporations, unions, and wealthy individuals to flood limitless cash into political elections. This tidal wave of cash is propelling us on a precipitous slide towards a form of government called "representative plutocracy." (Schonsheck 2012) It is a *plutocracy*, because it is Wealth that wields the political power. It is *representative*, because typically the plutocrats do not *themselves* have positions of executive or legislative power. Rather, in a variety of ways, Wealth is able to influence or determine the actions of those individuals who do in fact hold political office, and the fate of other ballot measures.

In addition to the particulars of the decision itself, *CUFEC* gave rise to a discernible aura—that the First Amendment's right of Freedom of Speech

[1] According to the Center for Public Integrity, "Citizens United ruling opened door to $933 million in new election spending." NBCNews.com, January 16, 2013.

[2] This is to be pronounced with hard Cs, as if it were spelled "KUFEK". Among its other virtues, this acronym has a lovely resonance with "FUBAR," and also with "SNAFU." And Patrick Hubbard noted its resonance with "KAFKA."

countenanced virtually any expenditure whatever by those of Wealth, seeking to influence outcomes.[3]

In "Mass Democracy in a Postfactual Market Society: *Citizens United* and the Role of Corporate Political Speech," F. Patrick Hubbard locates *CUFEC* in a line of cases regarding the tensions between the freedom of speech, and legal limitations on political campaign contributions—a line that originates with Buckley *v.* Valeo. I quite agree with that placement. For Hubbard, this confers legitimacy on the decision. For me, in contrast, this is the "top count" of my philosophical indictment of the decision. *CUFEC* is not an "outlier;" indeed, it is the logical conclusion of those cases. In consequence, my concern is not with *CUFEC* narrowly, but with that entire *line* of cases.[4] What I argue is that the First Amendment jurisprudence upon which this line of cases is based is profoundly *wrongheaded.* Quite literally. It begins *wrongly*, and then *heads*, relentlessly, towards "representative plutocracy." Genuine *reform* of the ways in which political campaigns are financed, thereby thwarting the threat to American democracy, is not possible unless that entire *line* of cases is repudiated. And that requires the repudiation of the First Amendment jurisprudence that it embodies. Only such a *re-orientation* of our jurisprudence regarding Freedom of Speech has even a *chance* of slowing our slide into representative plutocracy.

To put the philosophical contrast in its starkest terms: according to the jurisprudence of the line of cases from *Buckley* to *CUFEC*, Freedom of Speech *requires* a certain legal environment—one that leads inexorably to representative plutocracy. According to the jurisprudence that I shall advance, Freedom of Speech *prohibits* creating the legal environment that leads to representative plutocracy.

12.2 A Threat to Democracy: Bribery

An obvious threat to democracy is the *bribery* of public officials. Bribery is the paradigm of *quid pro quo* corruption: this, for that. The Briber offers money, or some other commodity the Official considers valuable, in exchange for some official action (or inaction) the Briber considers valuable. Typically, the Briber has a financial interest—accumulating wealth, or retaining accumulated wealth—and the Official is in a position to advance, or to set back, those interests. Such an Official may occupy a position in *any* of the three branches of government. What unites such actions, every *quo*, is the Briber's *quid.* The Official sets aside the commonweal, the interests of the constituency one has sworn to advance, and advances the interests of the Briber. In consequence,

[3] Edsall (2013) offers an incisive analysis of the 501(c)(4)s. Among the more notorious of these is Crossroads GPS, run by Karl Rove. Formed in the aura of *CUFEC*, it raised $77 million in its first 2 years, 90 % of which was from 24 donors, allowed by law to remain anonymous.

[4] Thus, while I am sympathetic with the many who have called for *CUFEC* to be overturned, that happy event would itself be a mere "outlier."

there is no philosophical obstacle to making felonious the offering of a bribe, and the accepting of a bribe.

12.2.1 A Threat to Democracy: Political Campaign Expenditures After **Buckley** *and* **Bellotti**

At least *some* of the positions in all three branches of government are *elective* offices; of necessity, then, the hopeful must *campaign.* Campaigning costs money; with the exception of the exceptionally wealthy who can self-finance the endeavor, the solicitation of political campaign donations is quite inescapable. These facts give rise to an obvious question: *are* campaign contributions essentially *bribes?* They certainly *can* be—especially if inartfully offered. But they don't have to be. Imagine a continuum of possible contributing, with two endpoints. At one endpoint, a campaign contribution is indeed a bribe, a blatant *quid pro quo*; in this instance, "contributing" is best understood as a *mode* of bribing. Contributor says to Candidate, "I will give you $$, or even $$$$, in exchange for your promise to vote against legislation that would raise my taxes." Making this sort of exchange felonious is unproblematic.

At the other endpoint is the Contributor who is pure, and wholly innocent; contributions are devoted to advancing certain values, a particular conception of the good society. Absolutely nothing is sought in return, in exchange for these contributions. Intuitively—i.e., before doing First Amendment jurisprudence—we can agree (I think) that these donations are a mode of political expression; this action is *protected* free speech.

What lies between these endpoints? Virtually *all* of political campaign financing in America. Thus the challenge we confront is to prohibit bribery, and to protect political expression—drawing that distinction is a philosophically defensible way. We have to do this in legislative language that gives fair notice to all parties regarding permissible versus prohibited conduct. It must be codified such it can be enforced in a fair way by government officials of reasonable good will and realistically anticipated intelligence.

The US Congress sought to meet this challenge with the Federal Election Campaign Act of 1971, amended in 1974. These reforms, however, were challenged in the courts, and eventually decided by the Supreme Court in *Buckley v. Valeo*. (In a related case, *First National Bank of Boston v. Bellotti*, the Court countenanced campaign contributions by corporations.)

Now some modes of free speech are indeed "free"—one can climb on a soapbox, and proclaim one's positions to everyone who pauses to listen. One can compose pamphlets, and reproduce them for minimal cost, and can hand them out at public gatherings. And save for the price of a stamp, writing letters to the editors of newspapers is free. But it is doubtful that one can really promote one's political position in these ways.

Really *effective* speech—communication that makes full use of contemporary media—isn't free at all. Indeed, it is *very* expensive. It costs a significant amount of money to mount a successful political campaign. For example, viable candidates need to buy substantial amounts of media space (print newspapers), and media time: radio, especially television, and even the Internet. We can agree with the conclusion of the SCOTUS in *Buckley* that "virtually every means of communicating ideas in today's mass society requires the expenditure of money" (Buckley 1976, 13). Raising that kind of cash can be more time-consuming than a politician's discharging official duties.[5]

In *Buckley*, the Court sought to resolve the apparent conflict between campaign-contributions-as-*quid-pro-quo*-corruption, and the free-speech-rights-of-contributors-and-candidates, in the following way.

First, direct contributions to candidates were strictly limited to $1,000 per candidate, per election. The presumption is that a thousand bucks is not enough *quid* to get much of a *quo*; this eliminated the concern about contributions constituting bribery. These contributions were called "hard money."

Second, the Court created a new legal category, known as "soft money." Individuals and groups may collect and spend as much money as they wish to express their own political views so long as they do not "co-ordinate" their efforts with the candidates. This kind of spending is known as "independent expenditures."

Most unfortunately, neither "hard money" nor "soft money" functioned as the Court hoped.

If we are to take seriously the claim that there is a First Amendment right to financially support the candidates of one's choice, then limiting a citizen's contribution to $1,000 is woefully inadequate. While this is not enough money to *corrupt* a public official, it is also not enough money to advance the interests of that candidate in *any* meaningful way. Thus the contributor's Free Speech rights have *not* in fact been protected.

When we scrutinize the claim that *unlimited* "soft money" contributions constitute a way for individuals (and also corporations) to exercise their First Amendment rights *without* "corrupting" the political process, we can see that the claim is *utter nonsense*.

First, a supporter could simply "parrot" the candidate's own message, further promulgating the positions, and even the precise wording and slogans, of the candidate. Strictly speaking, the supporter is not "coordinating" with the campaign—despite the fact the supporter's messaging is identical to the candidate's messaging. Since it is an "independent expenditure," an instance of exercising one's own Free Speech right, there is no limit to the money a supporter could expend in "parroting."

Second, imagine that a supporter created some genuinely independent material. Further imagine that the candidate disavowed it, repudiated it, and expressed the wish that it stop. A real supporter, concerned about the (newly discovered) best interests of the candidate, would cease and desist—even without formal "co-ordination." So once again, the expenditure (or its cessation) is not so "independent" after all.

---

[5] According to an official guide provided to new Democratic members of Congress, one ought to plan to spend *4 hours a day* in fundraising (Grim 2013).

Third, and most insidiously: "independent" groups could sponsor "attack ads," targeting the opponent of the candidate one supported. Since that candidate was prohibited by Federal Law from "coordinating," the candidate could not interfere with the supporter's exercise of First Amendment rights. Arguably, this is an ideal situation for a candidate. One's opponent is savaged by groups exercising their hallowed First Amendment rights, while the candidate decries them, taking the moral "high road." Meanwhile, the candidate benefits from those attack ads in the polls. And when one's opponent protests the attack ads, the candidate acts hurt, cloaks in the First Amendment, and points out that they are "independent"—not part of the candidate's campaign. (But of course the successful candidate, upon winning the election, would indeed feel "indebted" to the people who had made those "independent" expenditures, savaging one's vanquished opponent.)

To this point, we have been supposing that neither "hard money" contributions, nor "soft money" independent expenditures, constitute actual, *quid pro quo* corruption. Supporters do not get specific "actions" in exchange for contributions or expenditures. However, what large contributors *do* get is "access" to the candidate, or official. At a minimum, this creates the *appearance* of corruption. What *does* go on behind closed doors?

To sum up my critique of *Buckley* to this point: In limiting "hard money" contributions to candidates, the Court made it impossible for a citizen donor to effectively exercise Freedom of Speech rights. In refusing to limit "soft money" expenditures, the Court thereby enabled an array of corrupt practices, imperiling democracy. But even more serious threats were evolving.

What did the Court envision as the future of political campaign financing in the aftermath of its decisions in *Buckley* and *Bellotti?*

The Court subscribed, and *continues* to subscribe, to an attractive but fatally flawed[6] metaphor: the "marketplace of ideas." In the context of that metaphor, the Court envisioned two (principal) participants, or "clusters" of participants, competing in that marketplace of ideas. The "winner" of that competition of ideas would be, by definition, the superior policies for our democracy, moving forward.

Let us suppose that some citizens subscribe to Republican ideals, some citizens subscribe to Democratic ideals. Within the adherents of each Party, many citizens are of modest means; a few are wealthy. The adherents of each party make contributions to the candidates of their respective parties ("hard money"), and make independent expenditures ("soft money"), hoping that candidates who share their philosophical ideals will be successful in the elections. The vast majority—citizens of modest means—donate modest amounts. Citizens of substance, and corporations, quickly reach the limits of direct contributions to the candidates. However, *there are no limits to "soft money" contributions*; these flow to the political parties, or fund "independent" efforts.

Now the vast majority, ordinary citizens of modest means, do feel (quite correctly) that they have exercised their First Amendment rights: they have put their money where their mouths are. But they are realistic; they know that the *real*

[6] I defend this assessment below, and much more fully in Schonsheck 2010.

competition in the marketplace of ideas is the Republican Fat Cats, together with their impecunious fellow travelers, versus the Democratic Fat Cats, together with their impecunious fellow travelers.[7]

But the Fat Cats of *both* parties quickly realized that there was a "problem" with this new arrangement. If the candidate one supported with contributions actually won the election, then one thereby gained access—at *least* access; there's still the issue of what goes on behind closed doors. *However*, if the candidate one supported with contributions were *defeated*, then one no longer had (even) that access to the person holding political office. These Fat Cats had to bide their time for 2 years (House of Representatives), or 4 years (Presidency), or 6 years (Senate), and then try again: donate money to a challenger, and hope to be victorious in that (distant) future.

However, the problem of the "interregnum," the period without access/influence for having supported the losing candidate, can be solved by having always donated campaign contributions to the winning candidate. But how to always pick the winner? A Fat Cat who makes campaign contributions to *both* candidates, and to *both* parties,—of logical necessity—will have contributed money to the winner of the election. Thus, *whoever* is elected to public office will indeed be indebted to that Fat Cat.

Under this *new* dynamic, there is no chance of a Fat Cat being out of influence by having solely backed the losing candidate. If a Fat Cat has backed them both, then the Fat Cat has backed the winner, who is *beholden* for those contributions, without which she or he might well have lost.

An extraordinary transformation has taken place here. No longer is there a competition between Republican Fat Cats, versus Democratic Fat Cats, together with their respective impecunious fellow travelers. *The impecunious have been totally left behind, have been abandoned.* The interests of traditional political ideology, Republican and Democratic, have been eclipsed by the interests that are shared by the now-merged, single set of Fat Cats: the interests of Wealth.[8] What are those interests? The accumulation and retention of money. These include low income tax rates, favorable treatment of "income" low rates of tax on capital gains, favorable treatment of estates and inheritances.

This is *not* the political world envisioned by the Court in *Buckley* and *Bellotti.* It is not a world in which market forces yield superior candidates and policies. It is not even a world in which some individuals and corporations back the winning candidate (and thus gain "special" access), while other individuals and corporations back the losing candidate, and thus fail to get special access. It's a world in which some—those with sufficient resources to back *both* candidates—get special access

[7] It is noteworthy that the Supreme Court, in both *Buckley* and *Bellotti*, talks about "sides" in a debate, "parties" in a controversy: the Court subscribed to the paradigm of ideologies competing with other ideologies, in this so-called "marketplace of ideas."

[8] The ultimate winner may or may not share the broader political views, the political philosophy, of the Wealthy. Thus, to a significant extent, broader political views have receded to the background, while the immediate economic interests of Wealth have moved to the foreground.

regardless of who gets elected. Those without the resources to back both candidates are denied special access. Those with access are uniquely positioned to advance their own, narrow interests—and as they do, that advancement will be at the expense of those *without* special access. Ordinary citizens have been *completely* shut out of the process of *governing*, after the election.

Even back then, the new political dynamic did not go unnoticed, or escape criticism. Scott Harshbarger, the President of Common Cause, argued that "[t]hese 'double givers' are the prime examples of wealthy special interests who are not contributing soft money because they're ideologically aligned with one party or the other, but because they want to ensure access with lawmakers....Our democracy is dangerously close to becoming a government of, by, and for wealthy special interests" (Harshbarger 2000).

It is difficult to overestimate the impact of this new dynamic on policy making: *Buckley* accelerated the slide from democracy to "representative plutocracy"—rule by Wealth.

12.3 A Threat to Democracy: Political Expenditures After *CUFEC*

The focus of my critique is not narrowly on *CUFEC*; the focus is on the *line* of cases running from *Buckley* and *Bellotti* to *CUFEC*. Thus I welcome arguments like Hubbard's that *CUFEC* is the logical conclusion, or at least the next logical step, in this line of cases. I am pursuing a *reductio ad absurdum* strategy. It is precisely *because* these cases lead logically to the world created by *CUFEC*—a world deeply inimical to democracy, even more unfriendly than the post-*Buckley* world—that they must be repudiated *en mass*.

Ronald Dworkin, writing in *The New York Review of Books*, assesses *CUFEC* beautifully: "The five conservative justices, on their own initiative, at the request of no party to the suit, declared that corporations and unions have a constitutional right to spend as much as they wish on television election commercials specifically supporting or targeting particular candidates" (Dworkin 2010, 63). So we must ask: Why would *corporations*, as well as unions, and plutocrats generally, be anxious to open the campaign contribution floodgates? Corporations exist to maximize stockholder value; they have only *mercantile* interests.

Economics has been called "the dismal science;" we can add to that characterization, "with dismal stipulated nomenclature." The terms "rent-seeking," and "rent-seeking behavior," are neither revealing, nor "catchy." But since they *are* the extant technical terms in the literature, we are stuck with them. So let us look briefly to the origins of the term "rent-seeking," and its definition, and then consider two (very) contemporary examples. What makes this worthwhile is its explanatory power. For we shall find the phenomenon of rent-seeking at the *intersection* of the decisions of the SCOTUS, the various threats to American democracy, and injustices in the distribution of the benefits of social cooperation.

We can begin with Joseph Stiglitz, writing about *The Price of Inequality*: "The term "rent" was originally used to describe the return to land, since the owner of land receives these payments by virtue of his ownership and not because of anything he *does*. This stands in contrast to the situation of workers, for example, whose wages are compensation for the *effort* they provide." (Stiglitz 2012, 39) Thus a "rent" is money that does not accrue due to one's effort, not due to the labor of creating value. Very much to the contrary, it is a *reallocation*, or a *redistribution*, of the value that has been created by the labor of others. Stiglitz again: "To put it baldly, there are two ways to become wealthy: to create wealth or to take wealth away from others. The former adds to society. The latter typically subtracts from it, for in the process of taking it away, wealth gets destroyed" (Stiglitz 2012, 32; Schonsheck 2009). Indeed, Stiglitz calls rent-seeking a "negative-sum game:" besides the fact that no value is created, it costs value to effectuate the transfers of wealth. And yet "our political system has increasingly been working in ways that increase the inequality of outcomes and reduce equality of opportunity…This is rent seeking, getting income not as a reward to creating wealth but by grabbing a larger share of the wealth that would otherwise have been produced without their effort" (Stiglitz 2012, 31–32).

A fine example of rent-seeking arises in the Farm Bill of 2013. Amongst its myriad provisions were these two: continued crop subsidies to farmers, and cut funding to the Supplemental Nutrition Assistance Program (SNAP), popularly known as "food stamps," by $20 billion. Food stamps, are provided to the very poorest; half of the recipients are children. Stiglitz notes: "Each poor person might have only a little, but there are so many poor that a little from each amounts to a great deal" (Stiglitz 2012, 37). Under this Bill, recipients would receive a few dollars less a day—but in an era of rising food prices, this would be felt in their stomachs, as well as in their wallets. Among the supporters of this Bill were two members of the Agriculture Committee, Stephen Fincher (R-TN), who has received $3.5 million in farm subsidies since 1999, and Doug LaMalfa (R-CA), who has received $5.1 million subsidies since 1995 (Gerard 2013).

By definition, rent-seeking is non-productive; indeed, it extracts resources from the economy. What makes this instance so galling is that farm subsidies are paid for *not* growing crops, for *not* creating value—for the "great deal" of accruing money for their own action of *refusing* to create value.

A second example of rent-seeking behavior—on a vastly larger scale—is imbedded in the Financial Markets crisis of 2008ff. Stiglitz connects it directly to our current mode of funding political campaigns.

> the form of rent seeking that is most egregious—and that has been most perfected in recent years—has been the ability of those in the financial sector to take advantage of the poor and uninformed, as they made enormous amounts of money by preying upon these groups with predatory lending and abusive credit card practices.… Any sense of social justice—or any concern about overall efficiency—would have led government to prohibit these activities. After all, considerable amounts of resources were used up in the process of moving money from the poor to the rich, which is why it's a negative-sum game. But government didn't put an end to these kind of activities… The reason was obvious. The financial sector had invested heavily in lobbying and campaign contributions. And the investments had paid off (Stiglitz 2012, 37).

Obviously, rent-seeking is not a new phenomenon; it was not birthed by *CUFEC*. But when we consider its ubiquity, and how it permeates public life, that concept enhances our understanding of much that had been obscure. In the context of Wealth donating to *both* candidates, doubling its expenditure in order to gain access to the winner, whoever it turned out to be, I asked rhetorically, "What *does* goes on behind closed doors?" I believe that we have arrived at a non-rhetorical answer. According to the Center for Public Integrity,

> Businesses, trade groups and other interests hired more than five lobbyists for each member of Congress to influence financial regulatory reform legislation pending before the Senate .... More than 850 banks, hedge funds, companies, associations and other organizations hired more than 3,000-plus lobbyists to work on the reform bills (Center).

The sheer length and complexity of the US tax code, for example, is conclusive evidence of the success of the rent-seekers.

It is becoming *most* difficult to distinguish all this intrigue from *quid pro quo* corruption.

12.4 The Jurisprudence of the Freedom of Speech

The decisions of the SCOTUS, in the line of cases from *Buckley* to *CUFEC*, have brought us to quite an astonishing place. According to the majority's reasoning, the First Amendment's right of Freedom of Speech *requires* a world in which Wealth, whether individual or corporate, must be permitted to engage in what we can call "displacement" and "inundation." Wealth must be allowed to *displace* ordinary citizens in the political dialog by using its vast resources to buy up virtually all of the space in the mass media. Ordinary citizens are effectively silenced, by being muscled out of the most effective venues. And Wealth must be allowed *drown out* the voices of ordinary citizens, buying a continuous inundation of messaging that is pro-Wealth.[9] And because of that unceasing flood, arguments that are flawed or fallacious, claims that are skewed, misleading or demonstrably false, persist, since essentially unchallenged.

How did we get here? To answer this question we must take a short excursion into a general theory of law, Ronald Dworkin's "Law as Integrity." Thereafter, we can scrutinize the theory of interpretation, and the central metaphor, that have been relied upon by the SCOTUS. Then we can reject them. Quite the opposite of *requiring* inundation and displacement, the superior understanding of the freedom of speech *prohibits* them both.

[9] As put by Stevens, critical of Scalia's dissent in *Austin*: "All the majority's theoretical arguments turn on a proposition with undeniable surface appeal but little grounding in evidence or experience, 'that there is no such thing as too much speech'" (*CUFEC*, Dissent, 83).

12.4.1 Law as Integrity

The best general theory of law is Ronald Dworkin's "Law as Integrity," developed in *Law's Empire*. The fundamental theses of Dworkin's theory of law are:

First, every "proposition of law"—every statement of what the law *is*—necessarily, unavoidably, inescapably, is an *interpretation*. Were a person—e.g. a jurist—to claim that what one is offering is simply "the law," and *not* an "interpretation," the claimant evidences a deep misunderstanding of "the law."

Second, every interpretation (i.e., every proposition of law) *presupposes* a *theory* of interpretation: a position on how judges, litigants, and philosophers ought to *go about* devising interpretations. Thus, to make a statement of law is to *both* (i) inescapably offer an interpretation, and (ii) (implicitly, but unavoidably) be committed to a particular *theory* of interpretation.

Third, according to Law as Integrity, "propositions of law are true if they figure in or follow from the principles of justice, fairness, and procedural due process that provide the best constructive interpretation of the community's legal practice" (Dworkin 1986, 225). This "is a matter of imposing purpose on an object or practice in order to make of it the best possible example of the form or genre to which it is taken to belong" (Dworkin 1986, 52).

How, then, should cases be approached and decided?

> The adjudicative principle of integrity instructs judges to identify legal rights and duties, so far as possible, on the assumption that they were all created by a single author—the community personified—expressing a coherent conception of justice and fairness (Dworkin 1986, 225).

Thus, the goal of sound adjudication is an understanding of the community's legal practice that is intelligible as the work of a single author—the community personified—and is part of a consistent conception of justice.

12.4.2 The Interpretations of the SCOTUS

My concern in this article is not a fine-grained analysis of the Court on Freedom of Speech, but with its *trope*, with its broad sweep. This is best characterized as a combination of primitive "originalism," and primitive "literalism." In reverse order: Consider the stirring first words, and then the relevant phrase, of the First Amendment: "Congress shall make no law...abridging the freedom of speech..." First Amendment "literalists" are fond of claiming that "no means no!" They claim this, despite an *array* of wholly uncontroversial, and wholly justified, exceptions to "no law." These include, most obviously, restrictions on the "time, place and manner" of speech. "No" just doesn't mean literally "no."

However, the most serious flaw in the Court's reasoning regarding this entire *line* of cases is its total reliance upon a particular metaphor, the "marketplace of ideas."

Writing for the Court, Justice Kennedy speaks of "the 'open marketplace' of ideas protected by the First Amendment" (*CUFEC*, 38).

This argument begins with an incredibly "romantic" conception of the marketplace for "commodities," a marketplace that is both *transparent* and *efficient*. This conception is wildly at variance with reality; the marketplace for commodities is *neither*.[10] It then assumes, quite uncritically, that ideas are very like commodities—which most assuredly they are not.[11] The argument ends with a "romantic" conception of an imaginary "marketplace of ideas." This is even more at variance with reality; the obliterating tsunami of filthy lucre looks *nothing* like the orderly and efficient operations of a transparent marketplace. Thus I concur with Justice Stevens, writing in dissent: "The marketplace of ideas is not actually a place where items—or laws—are meant to be bought and sold, and when we move from the realm of economics to the realm of corporate electioneering, there may be no good reason to think the market ordering is intrinsically good at all."[12]

Additionally, the market metaphor does not easily accommodate the concept of "too many" competing commodities—or ideas. As Justice Kennedy writes: "The remedies enacted by law, however, must comply with the First Amendment; and, it is our law and our tradition that more speech, not less, is the governing rule" (*CUFEC*, 45). Is "more speech" invariably superior—much less the "governing rule"? Not, I submit, when the tsunami of filthy lucre purchases a tsunami of speech, an inescapable *flood* of political advertising that overwhelms the citizenry, that overwhelms the citizens' critical and reflective faculties.

12.4.3 A Superior Interpretation of the First Amendment's Right of Free Speech

In accord with Law as Integrity, the crucial question is this: What *law* is made by the First Amendment? To answer, we must first ask: What *values* is freedom of speech designed to preserve and promote?

Freedom of Speech must be placed in a larger context of political goods. When we look to the *philosophical justifications* of the right to freedom of speech, its philosophical underpinnings, we realize that free speech is *not* an *intrinsic* good, but an

---

[10] That it is not *transparent* is proved by the fact that knowledge about prices is not distributed throughout the market — indeed, there are willing buyers, and willing sellers, of such information. That it is not *efficient* is proved by the fact that the market is permeated with anti-competitive laws and practices; these include patent protection, predatory marketing, monopolistic endeavors, and (much) more (Schonsheck 2010).

[11] This is proved conclusively by contrasting the concept of "exchanges" in the marketplace for commodities, with "exchanges" in the marketplace for ideas. They are profoundly different phenomena, in crucially relevant ways (Schonsheck 2010).

[12] Stevens, p. 85. [internal cites omitted]. Even if it is possible to rank, to "market order" commodities like toasters and tires and televisions, there can be no comparable market ordering of "ideas"—especially "conceptions of the good."

instrumental good; its role is to produce some other goods: principally, the development of citizens as morally autonomous individuals, and the promotion of citizen participation in governing—which itself, of course, further develops autonomy.

Freedom of expression promotes individual autonomy in that to have a rational plan of life, one selected with full deliberative rationality, one must thoughtfully encounter, and assess, alternative plans of life. By participating in social decisions, one exercises a variety of faculties and talents, and one raises the probability of being able to actually *live out* a chosen plan of life.

For these reasons, the *law* that is made by the First Amendment consists of those measures that contribute to the nurturing and protecting of individual citizens' moral autonomy. This position is in harmony with Justice Stevens' point that the Founders had no difficulty distinguishing between natural persons and corporations, and explains just why it is so powerful. Furthermore, "The Court's blinkered and aphoristic approach to the First Amendment may well promote corporate power at the cost of the individual and collective self-expression the Amendment was meant to serve" (*CUFEC*, Dissent, 85).

Thus, the deep philosophical problem here is that this more fundamental political good—individual autonomy—cannot be fully realized under current arrangements. The incredible benefits of Freedom of Speech will not be attained if one lives in a political regime where interests are advanced or set back depending upon whether one has the financial resources to contribute to the various candidates and officials whose actions will profoundly affect one's interests. Meaningful participation in the political process is not possible, for the average citizen, in a representative plutocracy. *Wealth* monopolizes the media, *Wealth* renders all candidates beholden, *Wealth* gains assured access to officeholders, *Wealth* overwhelms with tsunamis of data, continuous waves of "messaging."

Thus, the line of cases from *Buckley* to *CUFEC*, which ultimately permits unlimited individual expenditures, and also permits corporate expenditures, *cannot* be "the best constructive interpretation of our community's legal practice." No single author, "the community personified," *could* have written the First Amendment in order to protect and nurture the individual moral autonomy of citizens, and also to have made legally permissible the tsunami of filthy lucre, and consequent tsunami of political bombast, instigated by *CUFEC*. The best constructive interpretation of the First Amendment cannot be that Freedom of Speech is totally self-eviscerating: legally countenancing precisely the actions that obliterate its very *raison d'etre*.

12.5 A Threat to American Democracy: Stateless Plutocrats

Another way in which the political campaigns of 2012 were memorable: The electorate was subjected to verbal abuse from condescending American plutocrats. Governor Mitt Romney's remarks about "the 47%" who do not take responsibility for their own lives, and are dependent upon the government, is a paradigm. The claim was demonstrably false: the recipients of federal dollars include everyone on

Social Security, everyone on Medicare, every member of the military receiving veterans' benefits (disability, education, mortgages, etc.), and so forth. Many "constituents" of the 47% took satisfaction in the fact that the videotape—according to Romney himself—played a decisive role in his defeat (Cillizza 2013). Romney's running mate, Congressman Paul Ryan, sought to distinguish the "makers" from the "takers," evidencing disdain for the "takers." (Craw 2012) Of course he believes that the "makers" are the wealthy; the "takers" are essentially "the 47%." The most egregious "takers," as I argued above, are the rent-seeking plutocrats, who are not creating value, but are extracting value from those in society who do actually create value; they are advancing their own plutocratic interests through the government officials they have purchased.

To this point, I have relied upon a casual, commonsense conception of "democracy." Moving forward, we need to adopt a more sophisticated conception; I shall rely upon that delineated by John Rawls in *Justice as Fairness: A Restatement.* We need to consider the essentials of an enduring democracy, and then investigate the ways in which rent-seeking plutocrats fail to fulfill their duties, thereby undermining the just institutions to which all the non-plutocrats—we the people—sacrifice, attempting to sustain.

A democracy is composed of "free and equal" citizens. Plutocrats view themselves as un-equal, as superior.

In a well-ordered society, "everyone accepts and knows that everyone else accepts, the very same political conception of justice (and so the same principles of political justice)" (Rawls 2001, 8). This is of transcending importance, because

> The role of the principles of justice… is to specify the fair terms of social cooperation. These principles specify the basic rights and duties to be assigned by the main political and social institutions, and they regulate the division of the benefits arising from social cooperation and allot the burdens necessary to sustain it (Rawls 2001, 7).

Of course there will be inequalities in society—however "Social and economic inequalities are to satisfy two conditions: they are to be attached to offices and positions open to all under conditions of fair equality of opportunity; and second, they are to be to the greatest benefit of the least-advantaged members of society" (Rawls 2001, 42–43). Furthermore,

> fair equality of opportunity is said to require not merely that public offices and social positions be open in the formal sense, but that all should have a fair chance to attain them. To specify the idea of a fair chance we say: supposing that there is a distribution of native endowments, those who have the same level of talent and ability and the same willingness to use these gifts should have the same prospects of success regardless of their social class of origin (Rawls 2001, 43–44).

It must be *obvious* that our current system of political campaigning, of soliciting contributions, and reliance upon "independent" expenditures by individuals and corporations, fails to satisfy "fair equality of opportunity."

> it is crucial that the difference principle includes an idea of reciprocity: the better endowed (who have a more fortunate place in the distribution of native endowments they do not morally deserve) are encouraged to acquire still further benefits—they are already

> benefited by their fortunate place in that distribution—on condition that they train their native endowments and use them in ways that contribute to the good of the less endowed (whose less fortunate place in the distribution they also do not morally deserve). (Rawls 2001, 76–77).

Of course this is deeply contrary to the plutocratic ethos.

How is the just society to achieve this reciprocity?

> background institutions must work to keep property and wealth evenly enough shared over time to preserve the fair value of the political liberties and fair equality of opportunity over generations. They do this by laws regulating bequest and inheritance of property, and other devices such as taxes, to prevent excessive concentrations of private power (Rawls 2001, 51).

Plutocrats deride the "death tax"—"You can't even *die* without paying a tax!" To which I respond: *Precisely!* For this is essential to preserving the "fair value of political liberties," and also the "fair equality of opportunity over generations."

It is more than plausible to believe that nominally "American" plutocrats are not committed to the reciprocities essential to *bona fide* citizenship, and a sustainable just society. It is readily apparent that they are not committed to the Difference Principle of Justice as Fairness: not committed to taxation in support of just institutions, not committed to reallocation in support of those who have disadvantageous draws in the natural lottery, or who have a disadvantageous starting position in society. They are not committed to preventing unfair concentrations of wealth, and thus power, over generations—indeed, they are committed to preserving and enlarging such concentrations, by means of extractions from the economy.

12.6 Conclusions

The decisions of the SCOTUS regarding Freedom of Speech are based upon a primitive theory of interpretation, and a fatally flawed metaphor. Far from fostering individual moral autonomy, especially through participation in governing, the decisions of the SCOTUS have created a legal environment that nurtures innumerable rent-seeking activities. They have thereby propelled us on a perilous trajectory. We are becoming—if we have not already become—a representative plutocracy, proxy governing by rent-seekers.

Hubbard concludes by claiming that "the majority was demonstrating its faith in the view that, if prior generations managed to operate a democracy in a market society where political speech is for sale to those who possess these "primal forces" without resorting to censorship, so can we." (Hubbard 2013). Surely we do not have to choose between these two alternatives: either the tsunami of filthy lucre, or censorship.

When correctly understood, "the law" made by the First Amendment is consistent with—indeed, *requires*—a very different alternative: a system of publicly-financed political campaigns.

References

Buckley v. *Valeo*. 1976. 424 U.S. 1.

Cillizza, C. 2013. Why Mitt Romney's "47 percent" comment was so bad. *The Washington Post*. http://www.washingtonpost.com/blogs/the-fix/wp/2013/03/04/why-mitt-romneys-47-percent. Accessed 27 June 2013.

Citizens United v. Federal Election Commission, 130 S. Ct. 876 (2010).

Craw, B. 2012. Paul Ryan: 60 percent of Americans are 'takers,' not 'makers. http://www.huffingtonpost.com/2012/10/05/paul-ryan-60-percent-of-a_n_1943073.html. Accessed 27 June 2013.

Dworkin, R. 1986. *Law's empire*. Cambridge: Harvard University Press.

Dworkin, R. 2010. The decision that threatens democracy. *The New York Review of Books*, May 13.

Edsall, T.B. 2013. Dark money politics. *The New York Times*, June 12. http://opinionator.blogs.nytimes.com/2013/06/12/dard-money-politics. Accessed 14 June 2013.

Gerard, L.W. 2013. America feeds the rich. http://huffingtonpost.com/leo-w-gerard/america-feeds-the-rich. Accessed 23 June 2013.

Grim, R. 2013. Call time for congress shows how fundraising dominates bleak work life. *The Huffington Post*, January 8. www.huffingtonpost.com/2013/01/08/call-time. Accessed 2 July 2013.

Harshbarger, S. 2000. Common cause. Cited at www.rcrwireless.com/article/20000918/sub/telecom-industry-generous. Accessed 25 Sept 2000.

Hubbard, F.P. 2013. Mass democracy in a postfactual market society: *Citizens United* and the role of corporate political speech. In *Democracy in the 21st century*, ed. Ann Cudd and Sally Scholtz. New York: Springer.

Rawls, J. 2001. *Justice as fairness: A restatement*. Ed. Erin Kelly. Cambridge: Harvard University Press.

Schonsheck, J. 2009. Mountains of value: How America's economy lost its way when creative minds abandoned wealth-creation for wealth-shifting. *The Post-Standard*, Syracuse, New York, July 12.

Schonsheck, J. 2010. The 'marketplace of ideas': A siren song for first amendment theorists. In *Freedom of expression in a diverse world*, The philosophical foundations of law and justice book series, ed. Deirdre Golash. New York: Springer.

Schonsheck, J. 2012. Fatal flaws in the libertarian conception of the market. In *Economic justice: Philosophical and legal perspectives*, ed. Helen M. Stacy and Win-Chiat Lee. New York: Springer.

Stiglitz, J.E. 2012. *The price of inequality: How today's divided society endangers our future*. New York: W.W. Norton.

The Center for Public Integrity. www.publicintegrity.org/print/2670. Accessed 29 June 2013.

Chapter 13
Democracy and Economic Inequality

Alistair M. Macleod

The first third of your campaign is money, money, money; the second third is money, money, and press; and the last third is votes, press, and money.

(Rahm Emmanuel quoted in Overby and James 2012)

We can have democracy in this country, or we can have great wealth concentrated in the hands of a few, but we cannot have both.

(Louis Brandeis 1941)

… (W)hen inequalities in political influence become too large, democracy shades into oligarchy (rule by the few) or plutocracy (rule by the wealthy).

(Martin Gilens 2012)

Abstract The paper explores several of the ways in which economic elites can threaten the implementation of the democratic ideal through the disproportionate power they are often permitted to exercise in the political domain. They can lend their support to efforts to restrict the franchise (for example, by pruning voting lists under cover of a drive to prevent electoral fraud). They can bankroll the campaigns of candidates for electoral office in ways that undermine their ability to make independent political decisions. They can pay lobbyists to do their bidding in the corridors of power, by prevailing upon legislators to protect their private interests at the expense of the public interest. And they can use the clout they have with influential members of the political class to maintain features of the electoral system that generally shield them from the effective mobilization of anti-elitist political sentiment:

A.M. Macleod (✉)
Department of Philosophy, Queens University,
John Watson Hall, Kingston, ON, Canada K7L 3N6
e-mail: Alistair.macleod@queensu.ca

A.E. Cudd and S.J. Scholz (eds.), *Philosophical Perspectives on Democracy in the 21st Century*, AMINTAPHIL: The Philosophical Foundations of Law and Justice 5,
DOI 10.1007/978-3-319-02312-0_13,

for example, they can throw their weight behind the practice of gerrymandering in the drawing of electoral district boundaries, and they can help to fend off periodic demands for reform of the electoral system through abandonment of "first-past-the-post" rules for victory in electoral contests.

13.1 Introduction

To the question whether democracy is threatened when there is economic inequality, an answer can be returned only after at least three clarificatory issues have been settled.

First, it matters how democracy is to be understood, and in particular whether, when the focus is on the democratic *ideal*, this ideal is ambitiously or more modestly characterized.

Second, it matters *how* unequal the distribution of income and wealth in a society happens to be.

Third, the extent to which economic inequality undermines the normal working of democratic institutions depends on whether, and if so how successfully, efforts are made to protect legitimate democratic processes from distortion-generating interferences by the wealthier members of society.

Because all these are large and complex questions, I want, for the purposes of this paper, to assume certain answers to them. The first assumption I'll make is that a reasonably demanding version of the democratic ideal is the one we should endorse, a version that goes well beyond requiring that there be periodic elections with universal suffrage. Second, I'll assume that in most contemporary democratic societies, there are wide (and steadily widening) disparities of income and wealth, and that these disparities are particularly evident in the yawning gap between the very rich and all the other members. Third, I'll assume that efforts to protect the integrity and independence of a society's political decision-making processes from distortion-generating interference by economic elites are seldom seriously made and, when they are, are far from being even reasonably effective.

After providing a brief description of the fairly demanding version of the democratic ideal I shall be working with, I try to identify several ways in which effective implementation of the ideal is threatened by economic elites who undermine ordinary democratic decision-making processes by exercising their extra political "clout."

13.2 Competing Conceptions of the Democratic Ideal

On various minimalist interpretations of the democratic ideal, what it requires, crucially, is universal suffrage. That is, all the members of a democratic society must have the right to vote in periodic elections, in the understanding that their elected representatives will have the power to participate, directly or indirectly, in the formation of the government and thus to contribute to the decisions the government takes in matters of legislation and public policy. The more demanding conceptions of democracy, while incorporating the requirement of universal suffrage, go beyond minimalist conceptions in also requiring the fulfillment of various background conditions. These are the many conditions that must be fulfilled if all the members of a democratic society are to be recognized as political equals and to be afforded readily seizable opportunities to function ***as equals*** within the political system.

While there can be differences of view about some of the conditions adequate implementation of this political equality requirement would call for—and while some of these differences can be expected to reflect the economic circumstances and cultural practices of particular societies—there is broad agreement about the crucial role at least four very general background conditions play in the establishment of the sort of democratic society in which all the members are political equals.

First, all members must be guaranteed educational opportunities of all the kinds that would enable them to acquire the knowledge, the skills and the dispositions to take part on terms of equality in their society's electoral processes.

Second, in addition to enjoying credible guarantees of freedom of speech and freedom of association, they must be afforded effective opportunities to participate in political decision-making processes, opportunities that would enable them to have an equal voice in these processes.

Third, it must be possible for the members of a society to rely on the media to provide them, on an ongoing basis, not only with comprehensive and accurate reports of all the news that supplies the necessary information basis for the political judgments they are committed as citizens to making, but also to present the major issues of the day and the positions on these issues of rival political groups in a genuinely non-partisan way, as free as possible of the partisan "spin" that often makes it very difficult for citizens to form reflective political views of their own.

Fourth, the electoral system itself must be so structured as to make it possible—to the greatest degree that procedural arrangements permit—for the views and priorities of those who cast their votes in periodic elections to be reflected in the views and priorities of the elected representatives who are empowered to contribute to the making of governmental decisions about the general shape of society's laws, institutions, and policies.

Given the many differences there are between the "thin" and the "thick" conceptions of democracy I've roughly sketched, and given the greater complexity of the conditions that must be fulfilled for the thicker conceptions to be properly implemented, strategies aimed at undermining democracy can take many more forms in societies which at least profess to be committed to the more demanding versions of the ideal. There are, after all, many more points at which economic elites who are not enthusiasts for an ambitious conception of democracy can chip away at crucial features of a truly democratic system. Moreover, the democracy-undermining strategies they sponsor can often be much subtler, and thus more difficult to detect and unmask, than any frontal assault on democratic voting rights would be.

13.3 Strategies for Restricting the Franchise

I want to begin by considering some of the more direct ways in which substantial economic inequality in society can undermine familiar democratic processes. Even though thin conceptions of democracy (those that highlight the right to vote of all citizens without taking account of, let alone requiring, the many background conditions that must be fulfilled if voters are to have anything close to an "equal voice") offer an unsatisfactory account of the democratic ideal, universal suffrage is an essential feature of thicker conceptions as well. It is important, therefore, to consider some of the ways in which economic elites in societies marked by great economic inequality can manipulate electoral processes in order to generate results that serve their own interests.

1. While it's too late in the day for the franchise to be restricted to, say, property-owners (or to males, or to whites), it's still possible for a variety of *seemingly* democratic strategies—strategies that are not *obviously* at odds with the democratic ideal in a one-person one-vote political system—to *restrict* the franchise. For example, there can be tightening of the conditions under which even permanent residents qualify for voting rights. Consider the uncertain status of many immigrants, or of refugees, or of permanent residents who came initially as "guest workers" and who, despite the indispensability of their contributions to the economy, continue to be denied many of the benefits of citizenship, including voting rights.
2. Laws can be passed depriving citizens who have a criminal record of the right to vote—perhaps for life. All such laws are open to objection, since the right to vote in a democratic society ought not to be seen as a right that can be forfeited. It is, however, particularly problematic when measures of this kind are targeted at citizens who have a criminal record in jurisdictions in which minor offences (including actions that ought not to be criminalized at all[1]) are treated as criminal offences or in which discriminatory enforcement of the law disproportionately disadvantages minority groups and the poor.
3. When citizens with the right to vote must register in some particular electoral district in order to be in a position to exercise the right, registration requirements can be toughened in ways that blur the line between efforts to prevent voter fraud and suppression of voting rights. This line is crossed when registration requirements make it gratuitously burdensome for citizens in certain familiar circumstances to comply. Meeting registration requirements may be unreasonably difficult for various categories of voters. There are voters who are too poor to handle the additional expense of compliance. There are voters who are ignorant of the procedures they must follow to be in compliance. There are voters with an imperfect command of the language in which the registration rules are set out. There are voters who have unusually demanding work schedules or who lack ready access to registration centers (whether because such centers are few and

[1] Plausible examples are laws that make it a (quite serious) criminal offence to be found in possession of small quantities of marijuana for personal use.

far between or because their location makes them difficult to get to), and so on. Consider, for example, voter registration laws of the kinds that have been enacted recently in some U.S. states, laws that require presentation of special documents as proof of citizenship when it is known that "marginal" voters (voters who can't be relied on to vote for candidates or parties that provide the power-base for economic elites) will find it difficult to get hold of the documents in question. In all such contexts, efforts to suppress the voting rights of citizens who are viewed as unreliable supporters of policies that favor economic elites can be safely resorted to under cover of plausible-looking—democratically "acceptable"—appeals to the importance of preventing electoral fraud.

4. Even after lists of eligible voters in particular districts have been established, efforts can be (and often enough in fact are) made to prevent some whose names are on these lists from actually casting a ballot. While resort by unscrupulous political operatives to intimidation techniques of various sorts is a sadly familiar feature of the political experience of fledgling democracies, subtler vote suppression strategies have begun to be adopted even in well-established democracies. One of the most insidious of these is facilitated by the easy access computers provide to increasingly elaborate "banks" of data about the political predilections of identifiable individual voters who can be readily contacted by phone. So-called "robocalls" can be used to send electronically generated phone messages to voters, generally just before voting day, to "inform" them of changes in the location of voting stations. The calls are typically targeted at people who are known not to be supporters of the political candidate or party that is paying for the robocall campaign, and the hope is that this sort of misinformation will be an obstacle (for at least some of them) to turning out in time to cast a vote.

13.4 Strategies for the Manipulation of Electoral Processes

Even when the franchise cannot be restricted in ways that serve the interests of economic elites, there are many ways in which electoral processes can be manipulated to achieve broadly similar results.

1. Candidate selection procedures can be devised—and then exploited—to try to ensure that only candidates who are acceptable to economic elites are on the ballot. When political parties are responsible for the selection of candidates, there is ample potential for the shaping of these procedures in ways that serve the interests of economic elites and thereby undermine the "democratic" character of these procedures. The procedures can of course vary hugely, with demonstrably undemocratic procedures at one end of the spectrum and procedures, at the other end, that at least have the appearance of being entirely democratic. A clear example of a plainly undemocratic procedure—albeit one that is not as rare as might be supposed in professedly "democratic" jurisdictions— permits candidates for election to be simply ***named*** by officials at party headquarters, without even the formality

of a democratically structured nomination process at local district level. When crucial candidate selection decisions are made in this way, not only are voters in local electoral districts deprived of the opportunity both to stand for election and to play a role in the selection of the candidate whose name will be on the ballot, but the risk is greatly increased of undue influence in the selection process being exercised by members of economic elites, whether through infiltration of key positions within the party hierarchy or through exertion of pressure on those who occupy these positions. Even when the nomination process is ostensibly controlled by citizens at local level—with party membership being open to all, and with all being entitled, as party-members, to offer to represent the party in upcoming elections—economically powerful members of the community can use their wealth to throw their support behind "reliable" candidates. Especially in jurisdictions in which successfully nominated candidates have to compete for selection in a district-wide election (in what are sometimes known as "primary" elections), the willingness of wealthy backers to help foot election expenses can be an important factor in the success of the candidate whose name goes on the ballot.

2. Once candidates for elective office have been selected, economic elites have myriad ways of contributing to the success of the candidates whose election will serve their interests, whether by providing financial support for their campaigns, or by influencing the content of the pitch for voter support, or by helping to finance advertisements that provide indirect support for their candidacy, or by ensuring that they are provided with effective platforms for getting their message out, and so on.
3. Whether or not the candidates they have supported win election to the legislature—but especially if they do and if, as members of the government, they have votes to cast that will determine what laws are enacted and what policies adopted—economic elites can use their wealth to sponsor lobbyists to "push" their legislative and policy agenda. Consider, for example, the success with which, in the wake of the 2007–2009 economic crisis caused by reckless profit-seeking in the financial sector, the banking lobby contributed to the modification—some would say, the gutting—of U.S. legislation designed to regulate banking activities to help prevent any recurrence of this sort of irresponsible behavior. It is not uncommon for defenders of democracy to be harshly critical of putative "democracies" in which votes can be bought and sold and in which the practice of bribing public officials is rife. Yet they can be strangely silent about the role paid lobbyists often play both in determining the outcome of elections (by the kinds of well-financed strategies they employ to support or oppose candidates in crucial elections) and in influencing the content of important government decisions. Silence of this sort is particularly disturbing because there is no more than a thin line—where such a line exists at all—between (on the one hand) the sort of political "corruption" that involves the buying and selling of votes and the bribing of officials and (on the other) the sort of "lobbying" that enables wealthy individuals and organizations to exert undue influence over the content of important political decisions by prevailing on governments to protect ***their*** interests at the expense of the larger public interest.

13.5 Strategies for Undermining the Background Conditions for True Democracy

In addition to the various ways in which economic elites can distort democratic processes through participation in these processes as "heavy-weights" who can amplify their own political influence by effectively drowning out (or otherwise overwhelming) the voices of their less-affluent fellow-citizens, there are many *indirect* ways in which economic inequality in society can contribute to the undermining of democracy. To see what some of these indirect ways are, it's necessary only to recall the many background conditions that must exist for democratic practice to exemplify the democratic ideal in its more demanding versions.

13.5.1 The Role of Economic Elites in Undermining the Educational Preconditions for Democracy

As noted earlier, a society's educational institutions and practices have a key role to play in facilitating the existence and the flourishing of a truly democratic political system. For example, educational arrangements must be such as to enable all citizens to acquire an adequate knowledge, not just of the workings of the democratic system and of their roles within it, but also of the major issues of the day, so that they are in a position, on terms of equality with all other citizens, to navigate effectively in often turbulent political waters. Because this is clearly a very demanding requirement, there are myriad ways in which significant inequality of economic resources (combined with "freedom" on the part of those with ampler economic resources to use them to consolidate their privileged position in society) can make it virtually impossible for the educational preconditions of democracy to be fulfilled.

13.5.2 Adverse Impact of Economic Inequality on Opportunities for Democratic Participation

Recognition is almost universally accorded the role played by freedom of speech and freedom of association in facilitating the realization of the democratic ideal. However, participation in political decision-making processes is often undermined by an over-emphasis on prevention of *interference* with these freedoms and a concomitant failure to acknowledge the need for measures to provide citizens with readily seizable *opportunities* for the exercise of these freedoms. It is small comfort to citizens who lack the economic means to make their voices heard in the political domain—for example through the purchase of radio or television advertisements, or through the mounting of expensive campaigns—to be assured that neither the government nor individuals and organizations in the private sector are permitted to interfere with their freedom to express their political opinions or to associate with others of like mind. What they clearly need, in addition, is effective access to forums that give them a reasonable approximation to equality of opportunity to participate in political decision-making processes, the sort of equal opportunity that they are routinely denied when their voices are either not heard at all or drowned out by the many political megaphones at the disposal of economic elites.

13.5.3 The Opposition of Economic Elites to Democracy-Friendly Media

Because of the role the media would have to play in facilitating the formation and continuing effectiveness of truly democratic practices in society, it's crucial for them to play their part in providing citizens with a balanced account of the major political news of the day and also (more difficult though this no doubt is) a balanced account of the issues that divide politicians and political parties. These demanding requirements cannot be adequately met when the media are effectively controlled, directly or indirectly, by economically powerful individuals and organizations, individuals and organizations bent on using economic muscle to ensure that the media do their bidding, whether by providing tendentiously selective coverage of political events or by imparting a "spin" to the account they offer of the issues of the day and the positions on these issues of the major political parties.

13.5.4 Control of the Structure of the Electoral System by Economic Elites

The structure of the electoral system in many ostensibly "democratic" jurisdictions can play a potent (even if silent and little remarked) role in subverting the democratic ideal. The role it can play is largely unnoticed because, once institutional arrangements have been established to provide the members of a society with the means of casting their vote in elections that are free of the taint of voter intimidation and voter bribery, the electoral system—whatever its precise shape and whatever the rules by which it normally operates—is generally perceived to be so familiar a piece of a society's infrastructure that questions about its defensibility (and *a fortiori* practical questions about how needed changes in its structure are to be brought about) are hardly ever addressed. Moreover, on the relatively rare occasions on which such questions are even mooted, elites are quick to leap to the defense of the status quo.

It is both interesting and revelatory that about the only general feature of an electoral system that receives routine attention at regular intervals is the requirement for electoral districts to be of roughly equal size—not geographically, of course, but in respect of the number of voters they contain. That this is a virtually uncontroversial feature of all democratically structured electoral systems is in a way rather ironic because the principle that provides the normative basis for this requirement—which is that equal weight must be assignable, in any democratically structured electoral district, to the votes of all who have the right to vote—is a principle that is egregiously disregarded when other, less striking, features of an electoral system happen to be at issue. Thus, there is virtually unanimous agreement that in a democratically structured electoral system the votes of all who have the right to vote must be given equal weight in the drawing of the boundaries of electoral districts, which is why the number of voters in all electoral districts must be approximately equal. Nevertheless, no notice is normally taken of other ways in which this principle can be (and indeed often is) breached. Two prominent examples in many "democratic" jurisdictions are (a) the considerable measure of toleration extended to "gerrymandering" in the drawing of the boundaries of electoral districts and (b) widespread endorsement of "first-past-the-post" (or winner-take-all) electoral systems.

Tolerance for "Gerrymandering" in the Establishment of Electoral Districts

The often condoned practice of "gerrymandering" is clearly at odds with the principle that underpins the commitment to ensuring that electoral districts have approximately the same number of voters because, if electoral district boundaries can be drawn (and redrawn) by elites with the power to determine these boundaries every few years and if (as often happens) they take advantage of this power to draw the boundaries in ways that give a systematic advantage in periodic electoral contests to particular political parties, then (albeit in an indirect way) the members of the electorate are being denied an "equal voice" in determining election outcomes. The objective that is typically sought by "gerrymandering" politicians when they are given the opportunity periodically to redraw electoral boundaries is to create as many "safe" electoral districts as they can, districts that are "safe," that is, in the sense that they can be relied upon to elect representatives whose political priorities are congenial to the elites with whom they identify. Consequently, voters who might like to elect representatives committed to combating the power of these elites are systematically deprived of the opportunity to do so no matter how responsibly and assiduously they set about exercising their voting prerogatives. Since it is a foregone conclusion, in any district that has been gerrymandered to render it "safe," what the result of an election is going to be, the voice of many citizens who regularly exercise the right to vote in such districts—and who would like, through the votes they cast, to express their opposition to the interests served by gerrymandered electoral boundaries—is very far from being the "equal voice" the democratic ideal calls for it to be.

Widespread Acceptance of the First-Past-the-Post Electoral System

The power to resort to gerrymandering in the drawing of electoral boundaries is, however, far from being the only feature of ostensibly democratic electoral systems that breaches the requirement that citizens in a democratic society should have an equal voice, through the votes they cast, in the processes that determine the policy orientation of elected governments.[2] Indeed, even when electoral districts are of equal size and when gerrymandering politicians have not been at work setting their boundaries, the rules that determine the outcome of an electoral contest can be rigged in ways that serve elite interests. Thus, to take one of the most securely entrenched of the ostensibly "democratic" rules that determine election results in first-past-the-post (or "winner-take-all") jurisdictions, the candidate who secures either a majority or a plurality of the votes cast in any particular electoral district is declared the "winner" of the election, entitled by the "victory" to serve (in the legislature, say) as the representative of that district. While it is uncontroversial that the practice of gerrymandering under the auspices of the first-past-the-post system robs many voters of the opportunity to cast a vote that "makes a difference"—and while it's also plausible (even if not altogether uncontroversial) to hold that it contributes to lower participation-rates—the first-past-the-post system can itself be exploited by economic elites to subvert the democratic ideal ***without*** resort to gerrymandering. To see what some of these possibilities are, it is worth conducting a couple of simple thought experiments.

(1) Consider, first the election outcomes that are possible under first-past-the-post rules *in a single electoral district* in a contest between two candidates, X and Y.[3] If we focus attention, among the mathematically possible outcomes, on those that might be regarded as realistically foreseeable[4]—outcomes that range from those that give the victory to X by a wide margin, through outcomes in which X (or Y) wins by a narrower margin, to outcomes in which there's a "landslide" for Y—two points can be made, from the standpoint of the democratic ideal, in criticism of the first-past-the-post system.

The first is that while all the possible outcomes give voice, through the candidate who wins election, to the views and priorities of the voters who supported the

---

[2] This is of course the requirement that all members have an equal **opportunity** to participate effectively in political decision-making (including electoral) processes. It should go without saying that it is not the – clearly absurd – requirement that all members wield equal **influence** in determining the outcome of these processes.

[3] While I focus here on electoral contests under the first-past-the-post system in which there are only two candidates (or parties), the objections to the system I present are even stronger in **multi**-party democracies.

[4] These "realistically foreseeable outcomes" are bound to vary a good deal from district to district, simply because they must reflect a range of relevant "facts on the ground" in particular electoral districts – for example, facts about the likely turnout of voters on election day and facts about the expected split between supporters of X and supporters of Y, indeed facts of all the sorts that might provide a plausible basis for realistic predictions of what the outcome in some upcoming electoral contest is likely to be.

winning candidate, the views and priorities of voters who cast their votes for the loser are simply not represented at all. This feature of the outcomes is a direct (and unavoidable) consequence of the structure of the first-past-the-post electoral system even when it is operating as it is supposed to operate, without the distortions that are introduced when, for example, district boundaries are gerrymandered.

The second point is that since the first-past-the-post system presupposes that all electoral districts are single-member districts, and since chances of success in electoral contests depend on the composition of the electorate within the boundaries set for these districts (no matter how impartially these boundaries may have been drawn[5])—since, that is, chances of success depend on what the split happens to be between potential supporters of one of the candidates and potential supporters of the other—how the boundaries of districts are in fact drawn is a factor in the determination of electoral outcomes that is *independent* of the political preferences of voters. Notice that this point too has to do with a structural feature of the first-past-the-post system. It consequently loses none of its force if studious (and let it be supposed, successful) efforts are made to prohibit gerrymandering in the drawing (or redrawing) of electoral boundaries. For example, even if a reliably independent electoral commission sets the boundaries, the composition of the electorate within these boundaries is still going to be a crucial factor in determining electoral success, and (as noted) this is a factor that is independent of the political preferences of voters.

(2) A second thought experiment has to do with the impact of the first-past-the-post electoral system, not on election outcomes in a single electoral district, but on *society-wide* election outcomes. Imagine a democratic society in which the first-past-the-post electoral system is in place to determine the composition of a 100-seat legislature and that all electoral contests feature only two candidates, one standing for political party P, the other for political party Q. Since there are myriad ways in which supporters of P and Q might be distributed across a society's 100 electoral districts, P could be the governing party even if its share of the total vote falls *well below* 50 %. If P can win the 51+ seats it has to win to be the governing party, it doesn't matter how slender the margin is by which these victories are secured or how disastrously low voter support happens to be in the districts in which electoral losses are sustained. P can consequently be the governing party in elections in which its overall share of the vote falls far short of Q's share. Indeed, the smaller the margin of victory is in the seats P manages to win and the smaller its share of the vote in the seats it loses, the smaller its share of the total vote has to be for it to be in a position to form the government. For example, if political party P gets 51 % of the vote in each of the 51 districts it wins, and only 1 % of the vote in each of the other 49 districts, it can form the government even though its share of the total vote in all 100 districts has fallen to only a little more than 25 %.

[5]The basic point is that the **actual** distribution, within the electoral district, of support for the competing candidates is a crucial factor in determining who wins an election – a point that holds even if, for example, the boundaries have been set by as neutral and knowledgeable and independent a body as could have been established to draw the new boundaries.

Despite the fact that election outcomes of the kinds envisaged in both these thought-experiments are clearly a direct function of the structure of the first-past-the-post electoral system, they are difficult to square with any version of the democratic ideal for which citizens must have an equal voice in the making of political decisions. As a system that can generate such outcomes, the first-past-the-post system consequently fails a fairly elementary version of the test for democratic acceptability.

In rehearsing some (by now pretty familiar) objections to the first-past-the-post electoral system, I have been assuming that it reflects an approach to the conducting of elections in two-party democracies. However this isn't because (a) there's any special affinity between this approach and two-party political systems, or because (b) the objections lose their force when the approach is adopted in multi-party democracies. (a) is false because there's no conceptual or normative affinity between the first-past-the-post electoral system and two-party versions of the democratic ideal. (b) is false because the objections to a first-past-the-post approach to the conducting of elections I've been reviewing are if anything reinforced when the approach is adopted by multi-party democracies like Canada and the United Kingdom. It's obviously easier—not more difficult—for the members of a multi-party democracy to be robbed by the first-past-the-post electoral system of the right to an equal voice in the making of political decisions. The reason is that it's obviously much easier for a political party to win a legislature seat by securing a mere plurality (rather than a majority) of the votes cast in a particular electoral district: the lowering of the threshold for electoral victory typically increases, instead of diminishing, the proportion of voters in any particular district who have the right to feel that their vote doesn't count.

While resistance in first-past-the-post democracies to any move in the direction of some form of proportional representation is traceable to factors of many different kinds, and while the role played by economic elites in supporting this resistance is only one of these factors, it is at least clear why these elites have a stake in providing such support. Especially in multi-party democracies—though also, to a smaller extent, in democracies with a ***two***-party system—the first-past-the-post system makes it less difficult for economic elites to secure (or to maintain) some measure of effective control both over election outcomes in particular districts and over the society-wide election results that determine who has the right to govern. Thus, electoral contests *in particular districts* can be more readily influenced by economic elites because the threshold for victory in multi-candidate elections is so low. Only a third of the votes *actually cast* in a three-way contest—and only a quarter if there are four candidates—may be needed to assure victory. Moreover, since low voter turnout is a common feature of electoral contests under the first-past-the-post system, the support of a much smaller fraction of the *electorate* can suffice for victory in an election. Again, while *in a society-wide election* under the first-past-the-post system, the right to form the government requires the successful party to win either a majority or a plurality of the electoral contests in particular districts, it is a matter of no consequence how slim the margin of victory is in the districts that are won or how massive the defeat happens to be in the districts that are lost. Given the divergence there understandably is between the distinctive interests of economic elites—their interest, for example, in preserving their economically privileged position and the disproportionate political influence this position typically confers—and the interests of rank-and-file members of society,[6] the wealthy have no incentive to be in the vanguard of movements for democratization of the electoral system. While the first-past-the-post system flagrantly violates the ideal of political equality, sharp economic inequalities can more easily be preserved in societies that cling to this system.

13.6 Conclusion

One of my working assumptions in this paper has been that the democratic ideal should be understood, ambitiously, as calling for institutions and procedures that give practical effect to the political equality of all the members of a society, but I have said nothing about the normative underpinnings of the ideal. Let me conclude by drawing attention to what is at stake in the battle against those forms of (especially extreme) economic inequality that are a serious obstacle to the implementation of the ideal. While political equality may be valued by *some* members of society *for its own sake*—because participation in collective decision-making processes of the kinds that determine the content and structure of a society's institutional arrangements is held to be an important ingredient in the living of a fully autonomous life—*all* members have reason to value it as a crucial *means* of achieving justice in society. When a just society is seen as one in which all members are secured on an equal basis in the enjoyment of the opportunities they need for the living of a satisfying and fulfilling life (including those opportunities that facilitate, to the greatest degree that is feasible without social conflict, the implementation of their personal conceptions of a well-lived life), the political equality that the democratic ideal requires can be seen to be an indispensable condition of the realization of justice. The battle against many familiar forms of economic inequality in the political domain and the related battle to secure the effective implementation of the democratic ideal are thus integral parts of the larger battle for equality of opportunity in society.

---

[6] One of the most significant findings in Martin Gilens's (2012) book, ***Affluence and Influence: Economic Inequality and Political Power in America***, is that when the interests of the wealthy diverge from those of the middle classes and the poor – as they commonly do in matters of great concern to the wealthy, such as the structure of the economy and taxation policy – "only the wealthy appear(ed) to influence policy outcomes." (p. 87)

References

Brandeis, L. 1941. Cited in Irving Dilliard, *Mr. Justice Brandeis, Great American*. Saint Louis: The Modern View Press.

Gilens, M. 2012. *Affluence and influence: Economic inequality and political power in America*. Princeton: Princeton University Press.

Overby, P., and Frank James. 2012. Words wealthy democratic donors should get used to: 'It's me, Rahm.' *National Public Radio*. http://www.npr.org/blogs/itsallpolitics/2012/09/07/160770861/words-wealthy-democratic-donors-should-get-used-to-its-me-rahm. Accessed 8 Sept 2012.

Part IV
Democratic Decisions and the (Un)Informed Public

Chapter 14
Epistocracy Within Public Reason

Jason Brennan

Abstract Epistocracy—a political system in which formal political power is distributed on the basis of expertise—may produce better outcomes than democracy. Yet, David Estlund contends that epistocracy is incompatible with public reason liberalism. This essay argues that, contrary to Estlund, epistocracy can be justified within public reason, even if, as Estlund argues, reasonable people cannot all agree on just what constitutes political expertise or who the experts are.

14.1 Why Not Epistocracy?

David Estlund says, "…removing the right issues from democratic control and turning them over to the right experts would lead to better political decisions, and more justice and prosperity" (Estlund 2008, 262). Why not support epistocracy?

The most important objection to epistocracy is the *Objection from Public Reason*:

> Epistocracy violates the liberal principle of legitimacy, which holds that coercive political regimes and polices are legitimate and authoritative only if there are no reasonable objections to that regime or those policies, and if all reasonable people subject to coercion have conclusive grounds for accepting that regime or those policies. (Estlund 2008, 262).

Estlund argues epistocracy is ruled out on procedural grounds. Epistocracy is incompatible with public reason liberalism.

In this essay, I argue that the Objection from Public Reason is mistaken. Epistocracy is in fact compatible with the liberal principle of legitimacy. Epistocracy can be justified within public reason.

J. Brennan (✉)
McDonough School of Business and Department of Philosophy, Georgetown University, Hariri 504, 37th and O Streets NW, 20057 Washington, DC, USA
e-mail: jb896@georgetown.edu

A.E. Cudd and S.J. Scholz (eds.), *Philosophical Perspectives on Democracy in the 21st Century*, AMINTAPHIL: The Philosophical Foundations of Law and Justice 5,
DOI 10.1007/978-3-319-02312-0_14,

14.2 The Liberal Principle of Legitimacy

Public reason liberals hold that to justify coercive interference and coercive authority, one must produce a justification that all reasonable people, by their own lights, have strong enough grounds to accept. This idea is expressed in a moral principle called the liberal principle of legitimacy. Different public reason liberals advocate slightly different versions of the principle.

1. *Estlund's Version*: No one has legitimate coercive power over another without a justification that could be accepted by all qualified points of view (Estlund 2008, 33).
2. *Gaus's Version*: A's coercive interference with B is permissible only if there is a justification for it that B may reasonably be expected to endorse (Gaus 2003, 208).
3. *Rawls's Version*: Political power is legitimate only when it is exercised in accordance with a constitution the essentials of which all citizens as free and equal may reasonably be expected to endorse (Rawls 1996, 137).

14.3 The Argument that Epistocracy Is Incompatible with Liberal Legitimacy

Many public reason liberals, such as Gaus (2003, 223; 1996, 251–253), Corey Brettschneider (2007, 18–19), and Estlund (2008), proffer variations on the following argument.

The Controversial Expertise Argument against Epistocracy

1. *The liberal principle of legitimacy*: The distribution of coercive political power is legitimate and authoritative only if all reasonable people subject to that power have strong enough grounds to endorse a justification for that power.
2. Epistocracy imbues some citizens with greater power than others on the grounds that these citizens have greater moral and social scientific knowledge, and will use this greater knowledge in good faith.
3. Reasonable people could disagree about what counts as expertise and who the experts are.
4. If reasonable people disagree about what counts as expertise and who the experts are, then epistocracy distributes political power on terms not all reasonable people have conclusive grounds to endorse.
5. Therefore, epistocracy distributes political power on terms not all reasonable people have conclusive grounds to endorse.
6. Therefore epistocracy violates the liberal principle of legitimacy, and is not legitimate or authoritative.

Premises 3 and 4 do the argument's heavy lifting. To show that epistocracy is compatible with public reason liberalism, one would need to show that at least one of these premises is mistaken.

Regarding Premises 3 and 4, Estlund accepts that turning power over to experts would produce objectively better outcomes. He agrees epistocracy would perform better than democracy. Yet, he objects, "The trick is knowing, and publically justifying, which experts to rely on for which issues" (Estlund 2008, 262). He says, "…any *particular* person or group who might be put forward as such an expert would be subject to…qualified controversy" (Estlund 2008, 36). Estlund thinks epistocracy would be superior to democracy, if only we could publicly justify some particular, concrete criteria for distinguishing the competent from the incompetent, or experts from non-experts. He thinks we cannot publicly justify any such criteria, because reasonable people will have reasonable grounds for disputing any particular, concrete criteria.

Note that Estlund accepts the claim that some people have greater moral and social scientific expertise than others. He accepts the view that some have greater willingness to act on this expertise. He accepts that some forms of epistocracy would perform better than democracy. Estlund accepts that some people really do know more than others, and empowering the knowers would produce better outcomes. He believes all reasonable people should accept that some people really do know more than others. All reasonable people can and should accept in the *abstract* that there are real distinctions among political experts, the merely competent, and the incompetent. Estlund also thinks that citizens can agree to *abstract* claims about competence—e.g., that competent decision-makers use relevant evidence while incompetent decision-makers tend to ignore it.

Instead—and this will turn out to be crucial—the complaint is that any *concrete* way of making these distinctions will be subject to reasonable objections (Estlund 2008, 71). There is no specific, particular, concrete way of making these distinctions that all people must accept. Citizens will reasonably dispute any concrete way of distinguishing between competence and incompetence. They will reasonably dispute any concrete interpretations of terms *competence, relevant evidence,* and so on.

Premise 4 is the weak spot in the Controversial Expertise Argument. From the fact that any *concrete* way of instantiating epistocracy, or any *concrete* legal criterion of expertise would be controversial, it does not follow that epistocracy is incompatible with the liberal principle of legitimacy. Or so I will argue.

14.4 When Disputes Call for Adjudication

Estlund says that reasonable people must accept, in the abstract, that political competence and expertise matter. Yet, he claims, they cannot be expected to agree on any concrete way of making these distinctions. We cannot agree on who the experts are. We might be able to agree on *abstract* epistocratic principles, but cannot agree on any *concrete* interpretation of those principles.

This is a dangerous argument for Estlund, or any public reason liberal, to make. It is problematic because this kind of situation is ubiquitous. In general, in public reason, reasonable citizens can at best be expected to agree on abstract principles.

However, they cannot be expected to agree on any concrete interpretation of those principles. Any concrete interpretation will be subject to reasonable controversy.

So, for example, Rawls (1971) claims to have justified some broad principles of justice: the principle of fair value of political liberty, the liberty principle, the principle of fair equality of opportunity, the difference principle. However, these principles are abstract and indeterminate. They admit of many reasonable interpretations. It is implausible that all reasonable people, even after sustained deliberation, would settle on any one concrete legal interpretation of these principles. As overwhelming empirical evidence of this point, I submit all philosophical writing on Rawls since 1971, as well as every philosophy conference and class on Rawls ever held.

Yet, in the real world, a government would need to act upon (and use coercion based upon) some particular, specific, concrete interpretation of those principles. Any such concrete interpretation will be controversial. Perhaps all reasonable citizens can all agree that they accept the principle of fair equality of opportunity, but they cannot all agree on just what it takes to instantiate or realize that principle. Nor will they all agree on just what fair equality of opportunity is, except in the abstract.

To take another example, Gaus (2003, 193) argues that liberals can conclusively justify a social minimum, but they cannot conclusively justify any particular, concrete theory of the social minimum. Reasonable people will reasonably dispute whether a given legal, concrete account of the social minimum is too low or too high. Even if all reasonable people think a just basic structure must ensure, one way or another, that everyone has enough, what counts as "enough", and even what counts as "ensuring" is controversial and indeterminate from the standpoint of public reason.

Concrete interpretations of abstract principles are almost always controversial. Estlund says reasonable people can agree on abstract claims about expertise and competence, but cannot agree on concrete claims. But this situation—where reasonable citizens can agree on abstract claims but will have reasonable objections to any concrete interpretations of those claims—is ubiquitous in public reason.

Thus, consider the following three justificatory situations. In each situation, there is some principle P intended to be a justification for coercive power. The situations differ in the extent and ways in which reasonable citizens disagree about P.

1. *Inconclusive Justification*: While some citizens favor P, they cannot defeat all reasonable objections to it. Or, they cannot provide strong enough justification for P against other citizens' reasonable objections.
2. *Determinate Interpretations of Conclusively Justified Principles*: P has been publicly justified; there are no reasonable objects to it, and everyone has reason to accept it. Also, everyone has conclusive grounds to accept a specific, concrete interpretation (P_1) out of all the possible alternative interpretations of P ($P_1 \ldots P_N$). No one can reasonably reject P_1 in favor of P_2 to P_N.
3. *Indeterminate Interpretations of Conclusively Justified Principles*: P has been publicly justified; there are no reasonable objections to it, and everyone has strong reason to accept it. However, P admits of multiple interpretations $P_1, P_2, \ldots P_N$.

> No specific, concrete interpretation P_1, P_2, … P_N of P has been shown to be the right way to interpret and act upon P. While all reasonable citizens must accept P, some will reasonably accept P_1 and reject P_2, while others will reasonably accept P_2 and reject P_1, etc. (Cf. Gaus 2003, 216)

From the standpoint of public reason liberalism, situations 1 and 2 are easy cases; situation 3 is complicated.

In situation 1, P cannot be justified publicly. The liberal principle of legitimacy was formulated specifically to explain why coercion is prohibited in situation 1.

Situation 2 is also an easy case. The liberal principle of legitimacy is supposed to allow for coercive authority whenever situation 2 obtains. Situation 2 may be an easy case, but it is rare. At best, we tend to be in situation 3. That is, at best, we can conclusively justify only broad, abstract principles, but any particular concrete interpretation of those principles will be controversial in public reason. Citizens will always have reasonable objections to any concrete way of interpreting abstract principles, even when those abstract principles have been justified within public reason.

We need to know what public reason liberalism allows in situation 3. Gaus says we have three choices:

A. *Subjugation*: Whoever has power should just impose his favored interpretation of P upon everyone else.
B. *Inaction*: Do nothing. Do not act upon P at all. Act as if P were unjustified.
C. *Adjudication*: Look for a "good umpire" to adjudicate reasonable disputes about the best way to interpret P. If we can find such an umpire, and if the umpire selects a concrete interpretation of P, then we should accept that umpire's decisions and act upon that interpretation.

Choice A is unacceptable. It straightforwardly violates the liberal principle of legitimacy. So this leaves choices B and C.

Choice B—do nothing—might seem best at first glance. However, as we have just seen, situation 3—in which abstract principles can be publicly justified, but all concrete interpretations of these principles are controversial—is ubiquitous. We are rarely in situation 2—where a concrete interpretation is conclusively justified to all. So, always falling back to choice B—doing *nothing* whenever we are in situation 3—results in anarchy.

Not acting on P would be practically equivalent to treating P as if it were unjustified. However, by hypothesis, P has been conclusively justified to all reasonable people—the problem is just that we have no conclusive interpretation of P. By hypothesis, we all should agree that acting on P is required, while acting on not-P is forbidden. We just do not agree on a specific, concrete interpretation of P.

Gaus argues we should take choice C: adjudication. When we agree on abstract claims but disagree on the correct concrete interpretation of those abstract claims, this gives us grounds for seeking a fair and reliable way to adjudicate our disputes. When a general principle P has been justified in public reason, but this principle is indeterminate and all concrete interpretations are controversial, then we should submit our dispute (about the best interpretation of P) to a good umpire.[1] If that umpire then selects a particular interpretation ($P_1 \ldots P_N$) of P, then we would should all accept and abide by that interpretation of P.

According to Gaus, a good umpire is:

1. Impartial/Fair: Umpires must not be biased toward or against any particular side.
2. Reliable/Competent: Umpires must have a sufficiently high ability to make correct decisions and arrive at the truth.
3. Decisive: Umpires should reach decisions quickly.
4. Public: Those bound by the umpire's decisions should be able to recognize that the umpire has features 1–3 (Gaus 1996, 184–191).

Note that an "umpire" need not be a person or group of people. It could instead be a decision-making method. (A coin flip could be an "umpire" on Gaus's definition.)

To see why these are the virtues of a good umpire, think of a baseball umpire. A good umpire treats the Yankees and Red Sox the same. He usually makes good calls. He makes calls quickly. Finally, though players often disagree with the umpires, they recognize that the umpires are impartial, reliable, and decisive. Players thus have reason to submit to the umpires' decisions.

In light of all this, we can see where Estlund's argument against epistocracy goes wrong. He says any specific, particular, concrete legal criterion of political expertise or competence would be controversial within public reason. He concludes that epistocracy is not permissible for this very reason. However, the fact that all concrete interpretations of an abstract principle P are controversial does not show that P cannot be justified in public reason. It might instead show that people should use a fair and reliable decision procedure—a good umpire—to adjudicate their disputes about P. After all, it is *normal* for concrete interpretations of abstract principles to be controversial within public reason.

Estlund's critique of epistocracy rests on a mistake. Estlund moves illicitly from "we reasonably dispute what political expertise amounts to" to "coercive authority based on expertise cannot be publicly justified." He moves illicitly from "the concrete way to interpret epistocratic principles is controversial" to "epistocracy cannot be publicly justified." He cannot make this move without further argument.

In order to show epistocracy can be justified within public reason, I need to establish two claims:

1. Within public reason, everyone has strong enough reasons to accept, in the abstract, that greater political competence should be a pre-condition for holding political power, at least provided we can adjudicate disputes about what political competence amounts to.
2. There is a good umpire for adjudicating disputes about political competence.

---

[1] It is worth noting here that this is why Gaus prefers democracy. He believes some principles can be publicly justified, and democracy is a fair and reliable method for adjudicating among our competing interpretations of publicly justified principles.

For Estlund to undermine epistocracy, he would need to show that there is no good umpire—no fair and reliable procedure—for adjudicating disputes about political competence. He has not done so. I think I can describe such an umpire. However, even if I am mistaken—even if the potential umpires I describe are not fair and reliable—Estlund's argument is still incomplete. At this point in the dialectic, we should be *agnostic* as to whether epistocracy and public reason liberalism are compatible.

14.5 Democratic Incompetence Is a Qualified Objection

To show epistocracy is compatible with public reason liberalism, I first need to show that everyone has conclusive grounds to accept the *abstract* claim that political competence should be a pre-condition for holding political power, at least provided we can adjudicate our disputes about what counts as political competence. Estlund already accepts this conditional claim. However, some other public reason liberals do not. Here, I explain why they should.

In previous work, I argued that democracy is unjust because it exposes citizens to incompetent high-stakes decision-making (Brennan 2011). I argued that citizens have a right not to be subject to incompetent high-stakes decision-making. I argued that when high-stakes decisions are made incompetently or by an incompetent body, they are illegitimate and lack authority. In this section, I will show that even if I was *mistaken* in my previous work, I have an undefeated qualified or reasonable objection to democracy. If so, then public reason liberals—in virtue of their commitment to the liberal principle of legitimacy—must regard democracy as illegitimate.

My argument concerning democracy can be summarized as follows:

1. *The competence principle*: It is illegitimate and non-authoritative to deprive citizens of life, liberty or property, or to alter their life prospects significantly, by force and threats of force as a result of decisions made by an incompetent or morally unreasonable deliberative body, or as a result of decisions made in an incompetent and morally unreasonable way (Brennan 2011).
2. A large percentage of democratic citizens are ignorant and irrational about politics. Their irrationality and ignorance causes democracy to violate the competence principle (Brennan 2011, 709; 2012, 161–184; Caplan 2007; Althaus 2003; Kelly 2012).
3. Therefore, democracies are illegitimate and non-authoritative.

I defend premise 1—the "competence principle"—by analogy to a jury trial. Juries are charged with morally momentous decisions. They have special duties to administer justice. Jury decisions greatly affect the defendants' and others' life prospects, and they can deprive the (possibly innocent) defendant of property, liberty, and life. The jury is also part of a system that claims a monopoly on decision-making power, and which demands that the defendant and others accept and comply with its decision. Its decision will be imposed, involuntarily, through violence or threats of violence.

Suppose a jury decides a murder case in an incompetent or morally unreasonable way. The jury ignores the details of the case and finds the defendant guilty after a coin flip. Or the jury finds the defendant guilty because they subscribe to some irrational conspiracy theory; or perhaps the jurors find the defendant guilty just because he is black. In any of these cases, if we knew the jury acted so badly, we would have decisive grounds to overturn the jury's decision. A defendant would have no moral obligation to accept their authority, and we would be morally obligated not to enforce the jury decision. In fact, US law allows for decisions to be overturned if jurors are later shown to have acted maliciously or incompetently.

A jury has authority and legitimacy only when it makes decisions in a competent way. The jury should be staffed by competent people. It should make its decisions competently and in good faith. If the jury does not, then the defendant has no duty to regard it as authoritative, and the rest of us have no right to impose its decision.

Electoral decisions are morally similar to jury decisions. Electorates are charged with deciding how to apply principles of justice, and how to shape the basic institutions of society. They are one of the main vehicles through which justice is supposed to be established. The electorate's decisions are high stakes; electorates can significantly alter the life prospects of the governed, and can deprive them of life, liberty, and property. The electorate claims sole jurisdiction for making certain kinds of decisions over certain people within a geographic area. The electorate demands that the governed accept and comply with their decisions. Finally, the electorate's decisions are imposed involuntarily, upon the governed, through violence and threats of violence. The relationship of between the electorate and the governed is in these respects morally analogous to the relationship between jurors and defendants.

Citizens may reasonably demand competence from the electorate. Citizens have a right not to be subject to incompetent high-stakes decision-making. Citizens can reasonably hold that it is unjust, and violates a citizen's rights, to forcibly deprive a citizen of life, liberty, or property, or (by force) to significantly alter her life prospects, as a result of decisions made by an incompetent deliberative body, or as a result of decisions made in an incompetent way. They can reasonably hold that political decisions are legitimate and authoritative only when produced by competent political bodies in a competent way. The competence principle can thus pry open the door for epistocracy.

Gaus seems to accept the competence principle. He considers whether a given citizen, Alf, has grounds for submitting to democratic decision-making, or whether Alf instead has reasons to reject the authority of democracy. Gaus (2003, 227) says,

> …if [Alf's] fellow citizens are thoroughly irrational or immoral, Alf himself may reject democracy on deeper grounds: when placed in the hands of his fellow citizens it yields consistently unreasonable results. In this case…the incredible incompetence of some majorities would come into play. As I argued…[a decision-procedure for settling disputes] has an epistemological task at which it must be competent. One's commitment to [that procedure] is thus contingent on one's evaluation that it does a reasonable job racking the

> merits of the disputes. If Alf concludes that the [procedure] is incompetent, he will not see as furthering the Ideals of Reason and Public Justification, and so will conclude that it is not justified.

Gaus says that democracy need not make optimal decisions, but agrees it must be competent. So, Gaus accepts that if democracy is incompetent, then it lacks legitimacy and authority.[2]

My objection to democracy is controversial. A reasonable person might dispute whether the competence principle is true. A reasonable person might also dispute whether democracy actually violates the competence principle, as I allege.

However, in public reason liberalism, there is an asymmetry in what it takes to *object* to a political system versus what it takes to justify a system. The point of public reason liberalism is to make it difficult to justify coercion. The point is that coercive regimes must be justifiable to any reasonable people subject to those regimes, by their own lights. A good justification for coercion must be acceptable to all reasonable people. However, a good objection to coercion need not be accepted by or acceptable to all reasonable people.

Thus, public reason liberalism is especially vulnerable to my objection in a way other forms of liberalism are not. I need not prove definitively that my objection is true. That is, I need not prove definitively that the competence principle is true, or that democracy systematically violates that competence principle. Rather, public reason liberals who advocate democracy must prove definitively (or at least provide very strong grounds to hold) either that the competence principle is false or that democracy does not systematically violate the principle. They have not done so (Brennan 2012, 161–184).

Public reason liberals, in virtue of their commitment to public reason, face a dilemma. Because I have a qualified or reasonable objection to democracy, they either need to prove I am wrong, or act is if I am right. Thus, consider the *Reasonable Objection from Competence Argument*:

1. Some citizens will reasonably believe:
    (a) The competence principle is true.
    (b) Democracy systematically violates the competence principle.
2. If some citizens reasonably believe a–b, then they will have reasonable (or "qualified") objections to democracy.
3. We cannot conclusively defeat their objections. While there are arguments against a–b, these arguments are not decisive and a reasonable person could dispute them.
4. *The liberal principle of legitimacy*: A political regime is legitimate and authoritative only if there are no reasonable objections to that political regime and all

[2] However, Gaus (2008) denies that democracies are incompetent. This paper critiques Caplan's (2007) argument that democracies make systematic mistakes about economics. Caplan (2008) responds that Gaus focuses on high-level controversies among experts and ignores that laypeople make systematic mistakes about the uncontroversial, "low-hanging fruit" of economics.

reasonable people subject to that regime's coercive power could reasonably accept a justification for that regime.
5. Therefore, democracy is illegitimate.

The point of the liberal principle of legitimacy is that we must take citizens' reasonable objections seriously, and we must not impose a system upon them against their undefeated reasonable objections. If citizens have undefeated reasonable or qualified objections to a coercive political system, then imposing that system upon them subjugates them. The liberal principle of legitimacy says such subjugation is unjust.

The liberal principle of legitimacy has an interesting implication. If someone reasonably objects to a rule, law, or system on the basis of X, then the liberal principle of legitimacy requires all of us to care about X. We must either defeat their objections, or we must act as if X is true. So the argument continues:

6. If some citizens reasonably believe a–b, and if we cannot defeat their objections, then (by the liberal legitimacy of legitimacy) we are all required to act as if a–b are true. That is, because we cannot defeat their reasonable or qualified objections, we may not impose rules or systems upon them to which they object.
7. Therefore, all reasonable citizens have strong grounds to accept (the abstract claim) that incompetent citizens should be excluded from holding power over others.

Notice that this argument does *not* claim democracy is illegitimate because it violates the competence principle. Therefore, for this argument to have force, one need not prove that the competence principle is true or that democracy violates the competence principle.

Rather, the argument claims democracy is illegitimate because some reasonable citizens have qualified objections to democracy on the basis of the competence principle. This argument thus relies upon a weaker claim than my objection to democracy. It claims reasonable citizens could endorse the competence principle and could object to democracy on the grounds that it violates the competence principle. These citizens may be *wrong*, but we cannot conclusively show them that they are wrong. Their objections are reasonable and we cannot defeat them. Because we cannot defeat their objections, the liberal principle of legitimacy requires us all to act as if the objections are true. This means that a commitment to liberal legitimacy requires us not to empower the incompetent, unless we could show that doing so would not violate the competence principle.

The Reasonable Objection Argument is *not* an argument for epistocracy. It does not purport to justify epistocracy or any other political system. Instead, it merely concludes that democracy is illegitimate and that we should demand that the incompetent be excluded from holding political power.

Notice where this leaves us. In light of reasonable objections to democratic rule, the commitment to liberal legitimacy requires us to hold that government should be competent. Public reason liberalism requires us to heed the reasonable demand for competent government. Yet there is no concrete theory of competence we must all accept. This means we have a case where an abstract principle can be conclusively justified, but no concrete interpretation of that principle has been conclusively justified. Everyone has conclusive grounds to accept the *abstract* claim that political competence should be a pre-condition for holding political power, at least provided we can adjudicate our disputes about what counts as political competence. If we reasonably disagree about what the exact nature of competence is, then we should look for a good umpire to adjudicate our disputes. If we can find such an umpire, and if that umpire selects a conception of competence, then we should accept that view of competence.

14.6 Democratic Methods of Adjudicating Competence

Epistocracy is at least in principle compatible with public reason liberalism. At this point, all it takes to justify epistocracy within public reason is for someone to describe a good umpire for adjudicating disputes about competence. I will discuss one possible umpire below, though there are others.

The competence principle is decision-specific. The competence principle requires that every decision be made competently, by a body generally competent to make that kind of decision. Perhaps democracy is incompetent to decide a large range of issues. However, democracy may be competent to decide some issues, if not all issues.

Even ardent democrats accept this claim. Christiano agrees that the electorate is incompetent to choose among rival political policies, and so should not be entrusted to do so. However, he argues that the electorate is competent to choose among the different possible aims of government policy (Christiano 2006, 2008, 104–110, 257–258).

Perhaps democracies are competent to adjudicate the nature of political competence. Perhaps citizens have sufficient knowledge and rationality to choose among competing conceptions of political competence. Perhaps democratic decision-making would itself be a fair and reliable way of adjudicating what counts as competence.

If so, then it would be consistent with the liberal principle of legitimacy to use a democratic decision-method to choose a legal conception of political competence, and then use that conception to decide who is allowed to vote. From the point of view of most democrats, this will seem like an insidious result. If the facts turn out the right way, democracies will be permitted, or even required, to use democratic procedures to establish a kind of epistocracy.

Perhaps—as Estlund argues—no one can prove any one concrete conception of political competence is superior to all other competing conceptions. So, it may be impossible to eliminate reasonable philosophical controversy over different concrete views of political competence.

Yet, the average citizen could produce a *reasonable* concrete theory of competence. Most citizens have good and reasonable intuitions about political competence.

The average citizen could give a reasonable account of the difference between a good and bad juror, between a well-informed and ignorant voter, between and incompetent and competent member of parliament, or between a competent and incompetent district attorney. If we asked democracy to try to operationalize the competence principle by delivering a legal definition of political competence, it would probably deliver a reasonable answer, that is, an answer within the range of reasonable competing views.

It is probably easier for citizens to articulate a concrete view of political competence than to identify and vote for competent candidates. The average citizen may be able to produce a good theory of political competence, even though she may be incompetent at applying her theory.[3] Even heavily biased and ideological voters can describe what makes a candidate competent. According to the empirical literature on voter irrationality, voters do not have bad standards, but they *misapply* their reasonable views.[4] There is nothing strange about this. Consider that almost anyone can give an excellent concrete account of what would make someone a good romantic partner. However, many us continue to have bad relationships. We have bad relationships not because we have false beliefs about what makes someone a good partner, but because we are bad at applying our standards to real people.

So, for instance, voters know senators should not be blamed for weather. Yet, when voters actually vote, they tend to punish incumbents for bad weather, even though they know senators are not to blame (Healy and Mahotra 2010). Voters know that politicians are not to blame for international events beyond their control. Yet, when voters actually vote, they actually do punish incumbents for international events beyond their control (Leigh 2009). Voters also know that corrupt liars should not be made president, but they often have difficulty determining which candidates are corrupt liars. Voters are more trustworthy and reliable in being asked what makes someone a good candidate than being asked to identify actual good candidates.

Questions about competence are easy. Questions about economic policy or about foreign policy are much harder. They require specialized knowledge, and sometimes require academic training. Also, we have positive evidence that citizens make systematic mistakes on these kinds of issues (Brennan 2012; Caplan 2007; Caplan et al. 2013). So, there is good reason to hold that democracy is incompetent to decide certain economic and political policies and yet competent to decide what counts as competence.

There are many different democratic methods for choosing a conception of political competence. The legislature could submit a range of candidate legal conceptions of competence to a public referendum. Or, citizens could elect a Competence Czar or

[3] David Dunning and Justin Kruger have famously shown that incompetent people are unable to identify who the most competent people are. Instead, the incompetent view themselves as competent, and when asked to select more competent people, they tend to select those who are just slightly more competent than themselves. See Ehrlinger et al. 2008; Dunning et al. 2003; Kruger and Dunning 1999, 2002.

[4] Caplan (2007) claims that voters tend to vote for candidates whom they believe will promote the national common good and increase national prosperity. However, voters are irrational in how they evaluate candidates by this standard. Voters have the right standards for selecting candidates, but at terrible at applying these standards. See also the previous note.

Competence Council, who would in turn produce a legal definition of competence. Or the government might employ deliberative polling. That is, it could randomly select a few hundred citizens, ask them to deliberate on the nature of competence, and then produce a concrete account of political competence (Ackerman and Fishkin 2005). Alternatively, a democracy might imitate the medieval Venetian system for selecting the *Doge* (Venice's lifetime leader). The Venetian system alternated between sortition (selection by lottery) and voting.[5]

In any of these cases, questions about political competence are decided democratically. Since—as I have argued—all citizens have grounds to submit to a fair and reliable procedure for determining the nature of competence, all citizens would then have grounds for accepting a democratically selected theory of competence. This would in turn legitimate epistocratic rule over *other* political decisions, decisions which democracies are incompetent to make. Questions about political competence are decided democratically, but other questions are decided epistocratically. Democracies may authorize an epistocracy, provided they retain democratic control over the legal interpretation of political competence.

I have provided some grounds to think that democracies are fair and reliable judges for deciding what counts as political competence. However, whether democracies are competent to decide questions of competence is partly an empirical matter. I cannot definitively demonstrate here that the facts come out the way my argument requires. Doing so would require much more of an empirical assessment than I have space to provide. However, Estlund's and Gaus's defenses of democracy also rely upon certain empirical facts about democratic competence, facts that they have not definitively established either.

Even without definitively settling the empirical issues, this is a troubling result for contemporary democratic theory. The main objection to epistocracy has been undermined. At this point in the dialectic, the permissibility of epistocracy depends on facts about what democratic methods are competent to decide, or whether there is an alternative fair and reliable umpire to adjudicate reasonable disputes about competence.

---

[5] See Dahl (1994, 14–16). Using a variation on the Venetian system, here is one way a democracy might reliably and fairly select a legal doctrine of competence. The process begins by randomly selecting 500 citizens from all adult citizens. A second lottery further cuts this 500 down to 100. These 100 randomly-chosen citizens would then produce a list of 100 other citizens from the original 500, whom they wish to serve as potential electors. To make it on the list of potential electors, each elector must receive 66 approving votes from the 100 previously selected citizens. The list of 50 potential electors would then be cut by lottery down to 25 electors. The 25 electors would then put produce a list of 100 citizens from the original 500, whom them wish to serve on a council that will be charged with determining a legal doctrine of political competence. Each of these 50 citizens would need to receive, say, 18 out of 25 votes. Finally, the 50 selected potential council members would be randomly cut to 21 actual council members. These 21 council members would then deliberate and select a formal, legal conception of competence. This conception would then becomes the legal definition of competence (for some period of time), and would be used to create an epistocracy of the competent. The Venetian system was convoluted by design. Sortition reduced bribery, corrupt campaigning, demagoguery, and special-interest rent-seeking. Voting (in this case) introduced an epistemic element.

References

Ackerman, B., and J.S. Fishkin. 2005. *Deliberation day*. New Haven: Yale University Press.
Althaus, S. 2003. *Collective preferences in democratic politics*. New York: Cambridge University Press.
Brennan, J. 2011. The right to a competent electorate. *Philosophical Quarterly* 61: 700–724.
Brennan, J. 2012. *The ethics of voting*. Princeton: Princeton University Press.
Brettschneider, C. 2007. *Democratic rights: The substance of self-government*. Princeton: Princeton University Press.
Caplan, B. 2007. *The myth of the rational voter*. Princeton: Princeton University Press.
Caplan, B. 2008. Reply to my critics. *Critical Review* 20: 377–413.
Caplan, B., E. Crampton, E. Grove, and I. Somin. 2013. Systematically biased beliefs about political influence: Evidence from the perceptions of political influence on policy outcomes survey. *PS: Political Science and Politics*.
Christiano, T. 2006. Democracy. In *The Stanford encyclopedia of philosophy*. http://plato.stanford.edu/entries/democracy. Accessed 10 May 2013.
Christiano, T. 2008. *The constitution of authority*. New York: Oxford University Press.
Dahl, B. 1994. *Venezia, et kulterhistorisk eventyr*. Oslo: Tell Forlag.
Dunning, D., K. Johnson, J. Ehrlinger, and J. Kruger. 2003. Why people fail to recognize their own incompetence. *Current Directions in Psychological Science* 12: 83–86.
Ehrlinger, J., K. Johnson, M. Banner, D. Dunning, and J. Kruger. 2008. Why the unskilled are unaware: Further explorations of (absent) self-insight among the incompetent. *Organizational Behavior and Human Decision Processes* 105: 98–121.
Estlund, D. 2008. *Democratic authority*. Princeton: Princeton University Press.
Gaus, G. 1996. *Justificatory liberalism*. New York: Oxford University Press.
Gaus, G. 2003. *Contemporary theories of liberalism*. Thousand Oaks: Sage.
Gaus, G. 2008. Is the public incompetent? Compared to whom? About what? *Critical Review* 20: 291–311.
Healy, A., and N. Mahotra. 2010. Random events, economic losses, and retrospective voting: Implications for democratic competence. *Quarterly Journal of Political Science* 5: 193–208.
Kelly, T. 2012. *Framing democracy*. Princeton: Princeton University Press.
Kruger, J., and D. Dunning. 1999. Unskilled and unaware of it: How difficulties in recognizing one's own incompetence lead to inflated self-assessments. *Journal of Personality and Social Psychology* 77: 1121–1134.
Kruger, J., and D. Dunning. 2002. Unskilled and unaware—But why? A reply to Krueger & Mueller. *Journal of Personality and Social Psychology* 82: 189–192.
Leigh, A.K. 2009. Does the world economy swing national elections? *Oxford Bulletin of Economics and Statistics* 71: 163–181.
Rawls, J. 1971. *A theory of justice*. Cambridge: Harvard University Press.
Rawls, J. 1996. *Political liberalism*. New York: Columbia University Press.

Chapter 15
Journalists as Purveyors of Partial Truths

Russell W. Waltz

Abstract Ideally, democratic citizens enjoy equal opportunity to deliberate, vote, and express feedback, as well as equal voice enabling them to civically participate in order to further their interests and concerns. To take full advantage of these equalities, journalism must serve as an effective mechanism to ensure that citizens are able to participate. Many news stories feature personal and dramatic elements of events exclusively (narrow-context information), but those hoping to become informed and motivated require socially contextualized (broad-context) information as well. In this chapter, I argue that the journalistic presentation of hybrid accounts consisting of narrow- and broad-context information best enables citizens to become informed about, and motivated to resolve, societal problems.

15.1 Introduction

Democratic deliberation and voting function politically and epistemically to legitimize government. The political function of democracy legitimizes the use of force and coercion (e.g., judicial rulings, legislative creation and enforcement, etc.) over citizens. To legitimate such force and coercion, citizens require equal opportunity under the law to deliberate, vote, and express feedback. Policies enacted must preserve and enhance citizens' opportunities to achieve such equality. The epistemic function of democracy best enables citizens to vote "correctly"[1] in hope of selecting successful solutions to societal problems. Doing so requires that individuals enjoy equal voice so that they can make full use of the opportunity to deliberate, vote, and

[1] Voting "correctly" means that citizens would select "the choice which would have been made under conditions of full information" (Lau and Redlawsk 1997, 586).

R.W. Waltz (✉)
Humanities and Social Sciences, Miami Dade College – Homestead Campus,
500 College Terrace, 33030 Homestead, FL, USA
e-mail: rwaltz@mdc.edu

A.E. Cudd and S.J. Scholz (eds.), *Philosophical Perspectives on Democracy in the 21st Century*, AMINTAPHIL: The Philosophical Foundations of Law and Justice 5,
DOI 10.1007/978-3-319-02312-0_15,

express feedback in order to further their interests and concerns. To take advantage of these equalities, citizens must be informed about social issues in ways that enable them to reasonably understand problems and possible solutions, their consequences, and their costs. Remaining uninformed makes it likely that citizens will fail to make full use of the equal opportunity and equal voice they share, as doing so requires that citizens be well informed.

In modern democratic states, journalism can serve as an effective mechanism to ensure that citizens are able to deliberate, vote, and express feedback after becoming informed, rather than leaving them without one of the most important mechanisms for obtaining information to make such decisions while uninformed. To accomplish this, journalists must be free to disseminate whatever information they deem pertinent to their audience. While a free press that presents contextually rich information to democratic citizens is required for the latter to make full use of the equal opportunity and equal voice they enjoy, only some journalistic methods are reliable generators of the type of narratives citizens require. Unreliable methods serve as sources of bias that negatively influence citizens' comprehension of events, inhibiting their ability to become informed about, as well as disposed to resolve, social issues. Journalists must avoid methods that exacerbate the presentation of partial truths that lead citizens to make false inferences, remaining mindful that no report, however framed, can present the whole truth. This is so, because framing requires that framers (e.g., journalists) give some experiential elements salience while omitting or downplaying the importance of other bits of information. Equally, news consumers inevitably filter the information they receive in ways that can be predicted based on perceptual psychology. The epistemological problem journalists face concerns how to avoid presenting news in ways that are liable to cause false inferences from the inevitably partial presentation of information. As a remedy, journalists should present hybrid accounts that relay the subjective experiences of individuals, as well as contextually rich information about the causal foundation and future significance of events.

15.2 Equal Opportunity and Equal Voice

Ideally, citizens enjoy equal opportunity and equal voice, which enables them to deliberate, vote, and express feedback to further their projects and interests. Deliberation is a key element in democratic decision-making. In "The Epistemology of Democracy," Elizabeth Anderson (2006) explains that John Dewey envisions the role of deliberation as

> a kind of thought experiment, in which we rehearse proposed solutions to problems in imagination, trying to foresee the consequences of implementing them, including our favorable or unfavorable reactions to them. We then put the policies we decide upon to an actual test by acting in accordance with them and evaluating the results. Unfavorable results—failures to solve the problem for which the policy was adopted, or solving the problem but at the cost of generating worse problems—should be treated in a scientific spirit as disconfirmations of our policies. They give us reasons to revise our policies to make them do a better job solving our problems (24).

Dewey recommends that citizens seek out enough information to reasonably understand problems and possible solutions, their consequences, and their costs. After such information has been gathered, citizens form a hypothesis about which solution may be best via deliberation, which occurs through venues such as public houses, town hall meetings, social media platforms, etc. Citizens must then vote upon proposed solutions, and since information is asymmetrically distributed among voters, diversity is essential, as it enables citizens to collect as much data as possible. Lastly, citizens must reflect upon the consequences from the adopted means enacted to solve a particular problem and provide feedback concerning the selected solution's success or failure by way of polling, elections, protests, etc. (Anderson 2006, 25).

15.3 Framing

Deliberating, voting, and expressing feedback as a means of furthering citizens' projects and interests requires that they become informed about social issues in ways that enable them to reasonably understand problems and possible solutions, their consequences, and their costs. In addition, individuals must become disposed to resolve such problems. To encourage citizens to take advantage of the equalities they share, journalists must avoid employing unreliable methods that serve as sources of bias, which negatively influence citizens' comprehension of events, inhibiting their ability to become informed and motivated. To avoid introducing bias, journalists must understand how their framing of information will affect citizens' comprehension of events.

Presenting news requires that journalists first determine which elements are most important for citizens to consume, a process called framing. After selecting particular aspects and ranking them in terms of most important to least, journalists proceed to organize that information in various ways and present it via narrative. Fortunately, citizens' projects and interests can serve as guides that journalists can use to emphasize the most significant elements relative to such concerns. As Matthew J. Brown states, "most truth is banal and insignificant … [therefore,] we need to understand how our questions and interests, both practical and theoretical, work to pick out certain things as significant" (Brown 2010, 9). What journalists must uncover is the importance information holds to the projects and interests of citizens.

The mere identification of salience, however, is only half of the story. Next, journalists must organize information into narratives consumable by citizens. Journalists use framing to organize information disseminated through news stories (Bennett 2008; Coleman and Thorson 2002; Entman 1993; Iyengar 1994). In general, framing is the act of "choosing a broad organizing theme for selecting, emphasizing, and linking the elements of a story" (Bennett 2008, 37). Frames provide meaning to stories and convey information to citizens by connecting news content together thematically (Bennett 2008, 37–38). In some cases, journalists use framing to provide stories with personal and dramatic elements, while at other times they use it to describe an event's contextual surroundings. Robert Entman claims that

> [f]raming essentially involves *selection* and *salience*. To frame is to *select some aspects of a perceived reality and make them more salient in a communicating text, in such a way as to promote a particular problem definition, causal interpretation, moral evaluation, and/or treatment recommendation* for the item described [emphasis in original] (Entman 1993, 52).

To accomplish this, journalists frame narratives in ways that make the significance of elements that comprise events perspicuous. Mirroring Entman's view, W. Lance Bennett claims that through framing, journalists communicate the significance of events, as they perceive them, to citizens (Entman 1993; Bennett 2008). Entman continues, claiming that framing provides salience by "making a piece of information more noticeable, meaningful, or memorable to audiences ... by highlight[ing] some bits of information about an item ... thereby elevating them in salience" (Entman 1993, 53). In some narratives, journalists feature exclusively (or almost so), personal and dramatic elements that provide information about the subjective experiences of individuals. These elements are known as narrow-context information (Bennett 2008, 40–52). When this is the case, abstract, contextually rich information concerning an event's socio-economic and political causal foundation, as well as any significance for future events, is absent. Information of this latter type is known as broad-context information (Bennett 2008, 40–52).

For example, take the case of a story published on *CNN.com* about the shooting that occurred in April 2007 on the campus of the Virginia Polytechnic Institute in Blacksburg, Virginia.

> Students describe panic and confusion after shooting
>
> POSTED: 8:29 p.m. EDT, April 16, 2007
>
> (CNN) -- A gunman shot and killed himself after opening fire in a dorm and classroom at Virginia Tech on Monday, killing at least 32 others in the deadliest shooting spree in U.S. history.
>
> Students in Blacksburg, Virginia, described a chaotic scene as word of the shootings spread by e-mail, word-of-mouth and the school's emergency loudspeakers:
>
> Tiffany Otey, Virginia Tech student: At first we really weren't sure what was going on. It sounded like construction. There's a lot of construction going on always during our classes at that time. Then it was like a continuous gunfire going off like every second or so there would be another shot. There was approximately probably 50 shots total. ... The police came up. They all had bulletproof vests on, machine guns. They were telling us to put our hands above our head and if we didn't cooperate and put our hands above our heads they would shoot[2] ("Students Describe Panic" 2007).

Much of the data presented in this narrative comes via an eyewitness account that reports the subjective experiences of the victims. The story begins by providing minimal contextually rich information by stating that the incident was "the deadliest shooting spree in U.S. history" ("Students Describe Panic" 2007), and the remainder of the piece offers a personal and dramatic account of the shooting. This narrative fails to present anything more than a shallow awareness of the incident and its immediate aftermath. Consuming this story leaves citizens unable to assemble anything more than an anecdotal account of the gunshots, screams, and confusion surrounding

[2] The segments cut from this story were additional eyewitness accounts that offered no broad-context information and their omission was intended to save space.

what transpired. Given this framing, it would be difficult for citizens to detect similarities with other events or link the event to societal problems that served as catalysts for the shooting. Further, citizens would be hard pressed to understand how it may influence future events. Because of this, the shooting's contextual significance may escape readers and instead, any intersubjective appreciation of it may be limited to how dangerous college campuses appear to be at present.

The type of framing exemplified in the above example is episodic framing. Narratives of this type negatively influence citizens' comprehension of events. Describing episodic framing, Shanto Iyengar states:

> episodic news fram[ing] takes the form of a case study or event-oriented report and depicts public issues in terms of concrete instances (for example, the plight of a homeless person or a teenage drug user, the bombing of an airline, or an attempted murder) (Iyengar 1994, 14).

Episodic news frames make events appear as isolated incidents, occurring at random, and since episodic framing does not provide citizens with any broad-context information, they have difficulty understanding how the phenomena presented connects to other issues or events. For instance, an episodically framed narrative may provide an eyewitness account of a gang-related murder, and fail to provide more contextually rich information such as current crime trends within the neighborhood in which the event occurred, or any citizen or governmental action plans to curb violence. The problem with episodic framing in cases like this would be that community residents may come to believe that the incident in question was an isolated event and would most likely not influence future events. Iyengar recognizes this problem and refers to episodic framing as the dissemination of information morsels that encourage audience members to view events as random happenings (Iyengar 1994, 136). Commenting further on this idea, Kimberly Gross states: "citizens exposed to a steady stream of episodic frames fail to see the connections between problems such as poverty, racial discrimination, and crime when they are presented as discrete and unconnected" (Gross 2008, 171). This is unfortunate, as such problems are often interconnected, and achieving resolution concerning one problem requires an understanding of other issues.

In addition, since episodic framing features a "just the facts" news style, citizens are led to assume that the journalist responsible for the story did not have an opportunity to introduce bias into the narrative. Not only is this assumption false, it is also problematic because it leaves citizens unwittingly exposed to the negative effects of *framing bias*. Picking out significant features of an event to present inevitably introduces bias. This is the case because value-laden assessments ground the selection of certain features and the suppression of others. Depending upon the ideological commitments one holds, the features deemed the most salient change. If biases are detectable and owned up to, they are not pernicious. Framing bias is detrimental when it is hidden. Episodic framing appears to give citizens an eyewitness account where the only bias is the viewer's own, but in fact it introduces a second perspective or bias—that of the journalist.

For instance, if a person without any knowledge of the Virginia Tech shooting asks me to describe the incident, I may provide the following account. "On

April 16, 2007 a mentally disturbed student with a documented history of displaying questionable behavior, who had managed to legally procure firearms due to restrictions in the state of Virginia's healthcare privacy laws, engaged in a killing spree on the campus of a rural Virginia state university that left 33 dead and another 23 injured." Surely there are other elements that someone else may deem important that I chose not to feature in the account I offered. Perhaps another person may deem it salient to note that the killer believed himself to be righting the wrongs of an unjust society. The point here is that whenever one attempts to describe an event, one must select out certain elements as more salient than others to provide an account of the incident being described. To accomplish this, one must rely upon value-laden appraisals during the act of description—as my decision to frame the account as a mental health issue, rather than a revenge plot—demonstrates that I assessed the killer's mental state as having more causal significance for the event than the issue of revenge. I grounded my decision upon a normative, value-laden assessment of the causal significance of the phenomena described. In particular, I value citizens' ability to become informed by developing contextually rich views of events. To that end, I framed the above account in a way that stressed the interconnection between the 2007 shooting and mental health, state legislation, and gun ownership. I deemed it necessary for citizens to understand that each of these topics is important to the story, and more so, that these topics are interrelated in various ways, making this is highly complex issue.

As noted above, framing bias proves harmful in some instances. In cases where journalists frame mere narrow-context information as salient while ignoring broad-context information, audience members find it difficult to appreciate what led to the event and how it may influence future events. If I had framed my narrative to include information pertaining merely to the victims' suffering, the killer's blood lust, or the parents' terror in my description of the shooting, one would be hard pressed to figure out what caused this incident to happen and how its occurrence may influence future events because of two problems. One, hidden framing bias disguised by a "just the facts" style causes citizens to ignore contextually rich information as evidenced in this example by its omission. Two, the framing in this case is shallow as no broad-context to put the event into perspective is provided. Only by discovering the event's interconnection with notions like healthcare privacy legislation, gun laws, early warning signs of mental illness, etc. can one understand the socio-economic and political context surrounding the shooting and how citizens could work toward preventing future incidents of this type.

In addition, if journalists provide more salience to broad-context information than narrow-context data, citizens would have the ability to make use of the former to help them judge for themselves whether journalists have provided the right information. With this judgment in hand, individuals could speak out whenever they believe that journalists are failing to present accounts that best enhance citizens' ability to hold deliberation, vote, and express feedback. Without journalists providing contextually rich information, citizens most likely would not even be aware that important elements were missing.

By providing information in a "just the facts" news style, journalists demonstrate that they assume that they are presenting facts without any normative, value-laden assessment of which facts are more important than others, while allowing those facts to solely represent the case under description. This is not the case, as framing bias is inevitable, and at times harmful. Without broad-context information, citizens are unable to appreciate why particular facts have been (or should have been) provided more salience than others.

Another concern related to episodic framing is the fact that upon consuming narratives framed episodically, citizens often encounter problems attributing responsibility. Commenting on how framing can influence citizens' claims of blame attribution, Renita Coleman and Esther Thorson assert: "how a message is framed can have an effect on how people attribute responsibility or place blame" (Coleman and Thorson 2002, 406). Shanto Iyengar has conducted numerous studies concerning the effects of framing to address the following question: Do citizens' attributions of blame change depending upon the type of media frame they are presented? His work suggests a resounding "yes" and shows that episodic framing directs claims of blame attribution toward individuals instead of complex social issues, governmental institutions, and policies (Iyengar 1994). Further compounding this problem is Iyengar's acknowledgment that "people typically exaggerate the role of individuals' motives and intentions and simultaneously discount the role of contextual factors when attributing responsibility for individuals' actions" (Iyengar 1994, 32–33).

People typically lack knowledge about many of the contextual, societal factors that are often at work behind individuals' actions, while people are already familiar with common, less complex reasons for why individuals act the way they do (Iyengar 1994, 32–33).

In his research, Iyengar found that when confronted with information focused solely upon the subjective experiences of a small number of individuals (which is indicative of episodic framing), citizens were more likely to blame the individuals featured in the story, rather than attribute responsibility to much more complex issues like unemployment, lack of healthcare, poorly managed governmental assistance programs, etc. (Iyengar 1994). Presenting news stories with an "unswerving focus on specific episodes, individual perpetrators, victims, or other actors at the expense of more general, thematic information inhibits the attribution of political responsibility to societal factors" (Iyengar 1994, 5). He also notes that "following exposure to episodic framing, Americans describe chronic problems such as poverty and crime not in terms of deep-seated social or economic conditions, but as mere idiosyncratic outcomes" (Iyengar 1994, 137). Iyengar's findings are troubling when citizens' ability to deliberate, vote, and express feedback is considered, since these functions are geared toward addressing problems at the societal level, rather than the individual one. It would be naïve, for instance, to posit that violence is simply an individualistic phenomenon, with no bearing on society at all. The same could be said for poverty and unemployment. One ramification concerning the shift in blame attribution is that audience members call the wrong entities into question and this means that citizens' deliberation, voting, and feedback would involve the wrong targets. For instance, if it is true that the most significant factor motivating violence is communal in nature and not individualistic, then to have citizens discussing, voting upon, and expressing feedback about a cause that is not to blame (or at least not so much) is counterproductive. Consider further the recent growth in both NRA membership and gun ownership. It is plausible to suggest that many who have joined the ranks of these groups have done so in the spirit of libertarianism. If so, this might indicate that these persons have adopted an individualistic attitude toward social issues. This is no surprise considering what Iyengar's work demonstrates. Episodic framing causes news consumers to lose sight of ways collective efforts can effectively solve societal problems. It is no wonder that many come to believe that solving such problems can only be accomplished individualistically, which drives them toward means that can literally put power in their own hands (i.e., guns). The problem remains, however, that more often than not the most effective solutions to societal problems comes through community-based or governmental initiatives and programs. For citizens to compartmentalize societal problems into individualistic issues constitutes a real concern, as successful solutions will most likely frequently be overlooked.

15.4 Selective Attention

Compounding the problem that citizens face when presented with episodically-framed information is the process of selective attention. Examining this process could help journalists better understand the danger that episodic framing poses, as it shows that framing itself, like selective attention, renders citizens unaware of certain elements in any given instance. William James claims that our senses, based upon delineations of space and time, combine, separate, emphasize, and ignore certain aspects of experience (James 1967, 21–74). He posits that

> [t]he phenomen[on] of selective attention [is an] … example … of this choosing activity … Accentuation and Emphasis are present in every perception we have[,] … [b]ut we do far more than emphasize things, and unite some, and keep others apart. We actually *ignore* most of the things before us [italics and capitalization in original] (James 1967, 70).

Through the process of selective attention, we focus our perceptual awareness upon certain elements while ignoring others. Until the point of selection, our world appears as "an indistinguishable, swarming *continuum*, devoid of distinction or emphasis" [italics in original] (James 1967, 70). Even though selective attention is a naturally occurring phenomenon, there is no guarantee that we will utilize this capacity effectively. Humans (journalists included) have the tendency to fail to emphasize elements of experience that should not be ignored. Quite frequently, individuals concentrate upon certain elements so exclusively that they fail to acknowledge other aspects of experience that may also prove valuable to furthering their projects and interests.

Like all observers, journalists must sort through information and organize it on a continual basis—and this requires them to prioritize some elements while ignoring others. Since framing is a process that involves the organization of information by way of placing emphasis upon certain elements while disregarding others, I argue that it mimics selective attention.[3] Journalists operate within the same pluralistic universe that James describes. To develop narratives out of a world comprised of a vast entanglement of elements, journalists must select a very limited number of those elements, which they organize in a manner they deem digestible by citizens.

Since framing, like selective attention, acts as a filter whereby certain elements of experience are emphasized at the expense of others, information contained within news stories is shaped via a double filtration process. Journalists should keep an awareness of this fact ready-at-hand, as this implies that framing doubles the chance that information about our environment will be fragmented and difficult to assemble into a coherent structure upon reflection. This is problematic, since citizens hoping to gain a contextually rich understanding of events from news stories are often inhibited from doing so when journalists frame narratives episodically.

15.5 Inattentional Blindness

Exercising selective attention causes humans to remain unaware of elements of experience outside of our focal point of attention. On selective attention's role in the creation of inattentional blindness, James states, "attention … out of all the sensations [in our perceptual space] … picks out certain ones worthy of its notice and suppresses all the rest" (James 1967, 70). Which elements enter and which exit our attentional locus varies in different instances. However, at any one time, there are always elements lying outside of our center of attention. Inattentional blindness is not problematic in and of itself, though it can become problematic. This is so if the aspects we fail to become aware of prove valuable to our attempts to deliberate, vote, and express feedback, since making full use of these capacities requires that citizens be informed, as well as disposed to resolve social issues.

15.6 Hybrid Narrow- and Broad-Context Accounts

To best enable citizens to become informed and motivated to select successful solutions to societal problems through deliberation, voting, and feedback, journalists must present hybrid accounts featuring narrow- and broad-context information. First, citizens must be presented information that is personal and dramatic so that it encourages them to become aware of, and disposed to act responsively toward the

[3] Selective attention concerns internally situated processing that is automatic and unconscious. Framing concerns externally situated processing that involves the conscious choosing of information and emphasis performed by journalists. Due to this difference, selective attention and framing are not identical.

projects and interests of others, as well as to attain the ability to cooperate with one another successfully (Anderson 2007, 596). Second, attaining contextually rich knowledge of societal problems requires abstract, impersonal information about the causal foundation and future significance of events (Anderson 2007, 596).

The following excerpt from a story featured at *Reuters.com* demonstrates how journalists can present information in ways that encourage citizens to become informed, as well as disposed to resolve societal problems.

> English major blamed for Virginia Tech shooting
>
> BLACKSBURG, Virginia (Reuters) – The gunman who massacred 32 people at Virginia Tech University was identified on Tuesday as a student from South Korea and a troubled loner whose behavior had sometimes alarmed those around him. As students and teachers grieved at a tearful memorial service led by President George W. Bush, police said Cho Seung-Hui, 23, acted alone on Monday in carrying out the deadliest shooting rampage in modern U.S. history. …
>
> The shooting spree on a sprawling rural campus in southwestern Virginia renewed heated debate over gun control in the United States. It prompted foreign critics to rail against a “gun culture” protected by the Western world’s most lenient gun-control laws. …
>
> Cho, who immigrated to the United States 15 years ago and was raised in suburban Washington, D.C., killed himself after opening fire in classrooms where he apparently chained doors to prevent escape before cutting down his victims one by one. He used two guns and stopped only to reload. …
>
> Lucinda Roy, an English professor, told CNN she became concerned after Cho’s creative writing instructor came to her about disturbing passages he had written.
>
> She said she took his writings to University officials, who said nothing could be done, and referred him to the University’s counseling services.
>
> Neighbors and roommates described Cho as quiet and withdrawn, but one former classmate said he was not surprised when he found out the shooter’s identity.
>
> “Looking back, he fit the exact stereotype of what one would typically think of as a ‘school shooter’ – a loner, obsessed with violence, and serious personal problems,” former classmate Ian MacFarlane wrote on an AOL blog site.
>
> Cho who was studying English literature, wrote profanity-laced plays and had characters talk of pedophilia and attack each other with chainsaws, said MacFarlane, now an AOL employee. …
>
> The campus, where there are more than 25,000 full-time students, reeled with shock and grief.
>
> For Tuesday’s memorial ceremony, an overflow crowd of several thousand filled most of the field in the neighboring football arena on a sunny spring day.
>
> Many students said they felt exhausted and numb. Some shook with sobs as the hymn “Amazing Grace” played.
>
> “We’re just trying to cope with everything,” said Jack Nicholson, 21, of Leonardtown, Maryland. “It’s just been crazy.” …
>
> White House spokeswoman Dana Perino acknowledged that “there is going to be and there has been an ongoing national discussion and debate about gun control policy,” but said the focus for now was on grieving families and the school.
>
> More than 30,000 people die from gunshot wounds every year in the United States and there are more guns in private hands than in any other country. A powerful gun lobby and grass roots support for gun ownership rights have largely thwarted attempts to tighten controls[4]. (Hopkins and Zengerle 2007)

---

[4] The segments cut from this story were mere filler and their omission was intended to save space.

The story above provides broad-context information alongside narrow-context data. Such testimony opens readers to the subjective experiences of others, and at the same time provides information about the causal foundation and future significance of the shooting. Concerning the latter, the narrative features information that provides citizens with knowledge about the severity of the attack in comparison to other school shootings; the debate over gun control in the United States; warning signs exhibited by troubled students; rates of incidence of gun deaths; gun ownership per capita in comparison to other countries; as well as failures to enact stricter gun controls domestically. This story serves as an example of how journalists can present information in ways that encourage citizens to develop an awareness of the problem at hand, a disposition to become responsive, a contextually rich understanding of how such a problem may be resolved, and the ability to successfully interact and cooperate with others. Presenting hybrid accounts framed in like manner best facilitates citizens' efforts to deliberate, vote, and express feedback as such accounts best enable citizens to become informed, as well as disposed to resolve social issues.

15.7 Possible Objections

Perhaps one might claim that hybrid accounts are susceptible to political bias. In other words, a journalist could present a hybrid account of a particular event with a marked liberal or conservative slant, while still relaying the subjective experiences of individuals to citizens, as well as contextually rich information about the causal foundation and future significance of events. To accommodate this concern, modern journalism should take a note from its early history. The early American press (late-1700s – mid-1800s) presented coverage that was markedly politically biased, churning out content that was largely geared toward particular political parties and ideologies. During this period, "reporting", meant providing a political analysis of events. Many journalists and intellectuals alike believed that encouraging citizens to consume information fueled by opposing political biases would enable them to debate differing viewpoints, which was deemed good for democracy. In fact, Thomas Jefferson favored this practice especially. So much so, that Jefferson collaborated with James Madison to urge the foundation of one such newspaper: *The National Gazette*. Their aim was to counter the Federalist sentiment furthered by a rival paper: *The Gazette of the United States*, which served as a mouthpiece for pro-Federalist ideology and hub for the writings of Alexander Hamilton and John Adams. Theoretically, I see no reason why it would be problematic for outlets to adopt a similar approach today. In fact, outlets like MSNBC and Fox News have already done so. In this model, the responsibility to seek information from a variety of news outlets lies with citizens. This is not controversial considering Dewey's recommendation that citizens seek out enough information to reasonably understand problems and possible solutions, their consequences, and their costs. In this case, seeking out information requires that citizens consume news crafted by journalists espousing a variety of political ideologies.

Related to the above concern is the worry that citizens will self-select which stories they consume based upon the ideological perspectives audience members hold. For instance, a conservative-minded citizen might choose to rely upon Fox News or the Wall Street Journal exclusively to receive information about social issues and events. This happens frequently. Since citizens self-select which narratives they consume, individuals may fail to develop contextually rich views of societal problems framed from a variety of ideological perspectives. My response to this objection is the same as the reply I offered to the first objection I entertained. To effectively solve problems via civic participation, citizens must seek out numerous sources of information from a diverse variety of ideological perspectives if individuals hope to reasonably understand problems and the possible solutions, their consequences, and their costs. Consuming hybrid accounts framed from a mere politically conservative ideological perspective would fail to satisfy Dewey's experimentalist model of effective problem solving.

Another worry worth considering concerns my prescription for journalists to avoid framing narratives episodically, as this causes consumers to seek individualistic solutions to problems, rather than appreciate how citizens can collectively work toward resolving social issues. Perhaps one might claim that social problems are best resolved individualistically, one person at a time. Sally Struthers's work for the Christian Children's Fund furthers this view, since it presupposes that citizens can save the lives of children living in poverty through individual personal donations rather than collective efforts such as governmental aid programs. Her infomercials, and others like them, indicate that only by developing a personal relationship with a child can real progress be made. This demonstrates that the solution to child poverty she favors is individualistic, in that both the giver and receiver of aid are bonded together particularistically, rather than through a broader social arrangement. This strategy is wrongheaded. This is the case because issues such as poverty, the obesity epidemic, violence, etc., are complex social concerns and cannot be treated individualistically, as that type of thinking is too simplistic. To reasonably understand social issues and their possible solutions, consequences, and costs requires a comprehension of their contextual environment that lies beyond mere 1:1 relations between victim and savior.

15.8 Concluding Remarks

Democracy ideally affords citizens equal opportunity and equal voice to deliberate, vote, and express feedback to further their projects and interests. To make full use of these equalities, citizens must become informed about social issues in ways that enable them to understand problems and possible solutions, their consequences, and their costs. Further, while journalism can serve as an effective mechanism to ensure that citizens become informed and motivated, only some journalistic methods are reliable generators of the type of narratives citizens require. Unreliable methods serve as sources of bias that negatively influence citizens' comprehension of events, inhibiting their ability to become informed, as well as disposed to resolve social issues. In particular, journalists must avoid framing narratives episodically due to the negative effects of framing bias, as well as problems concerning blame attribution. Further, since consumers inevitably filter the information they receive due to selective attention, episodic framing provides a second layer of filtration. This compounds the chance that citizens will remain inattentionally unaware of elements necessary to becoming informed and motivated. As a remedy, journalists should present hybrid accounts that relay the subjective experiences of individuals to citizens, as well as contextually rich information about the causal foundation and future significance of events.

References

Anderson, E. 2006. The epistemology of democracy. *Episteme* 3(1–2): 8–22.

Anderson, E. 2007. Fair opportunity in education: A democratic equality perspective. *Ethics* 117(4): 595–622.

Bennett, W.L. 2008. *News: The politics of illusion*, 8th ed. New York: Pearson/Longman.

Brown, M.J. 2010. Genuine problems and the significance of science. *Contemporary Pragmatism* 7(2): 131–153.

Coleman, R., and E. Thorson. 2002. The effects of news stories that put crime and violence into context: Testing the public health model of reporting. *Journal of Health Communication* 7(5): 401–425. doi:10.1080/10810730290001783.

Entman, R.M. 1993. Framing: Toward clarification of a fractured paradigm. *Journal of Communication* 43(4): 51–58. doi:10.1111/j.1460-2466.1993.tb01304.x.

Gross, K. 2008. Framing persuasive appeals: Episodic and thematic framing, emotional response, and policy opinion. *Political Psychology* 29(2): 169–192. doi:10.1111/j.1467-9221.2008.00622.x.

Hopkins, A., and P. Zengerle. 2007. English major blamed for Virginia Tech shooting. *Reuters*. http://www.reuters.com/article/2007/04/17/us-usa-crime-shooting-idUSN1631133620070417. Accessed 26 Aug 2012.

Iyengar, S. 1994. *Is anyone responsible? How television frames political issues*. Chicago: University of Chicago Press.

James, W. 1967. The stream of thought. In *The writings of William James: A comprehensive edition*, ed. J.J. McDermott, 21–74. New York: Random House.

Lau, R., and D. Redlawsk. 1997. Voting correctly. *American Political Science Review* 91(3): 585–598.

Chapter 16
Motivated Reasoning, Group Identification, and Representative Democracy

Kenneth Henley

Abstract Research in moral, social and cognitive psychology undermines confidence in reasoning in representative democracies. Research seems to show that reasoning, especially in the political sphere, is not exploratory, but rather confirmatory, and that group identification bolsters such motivated reasoning. I argue that there are resources available in representative democracy that can be used to diminish the tendency to engage in confirmatory reasoning and group motivated thought, and so open a limited sphere where a significant degree of exploratory reasoning can occur.

Recent research in moral, social and cognitive psychology undermines confidence in reasoning in representative democracies. The research is detailed in Jonathan Haidt, *The Righteous Mind: Why Good People Are Divided by Politics and Religion* (Haidt 2012). There are two interacting features of the human mind that block genuine dialogue and perhaps reaching reasoned agreement about public policy (or, a rather different matter, the constitutional limits of government in a particular polity): motivated reasoning and group identification.

First, research seems to show that reasoning, especially in the political sphere, is not exploratory reasoning, but rather motivated reasoning (Haidt 2012, 72–92). Exploratory reasoning, as will be explained in more detail below, seeks to survey the relevant evidence concerning an issue to discover the best supported conclusion.

Motivated reasoning encompasses all forms of seeking to justify prior beliefs or desired actions by selective use of evidence or arguments biased in favor of the sought outcome, while ignoring or discounting factors that point in a different direction (Mercier and Sperber 2011, 66–68). Confirmatory reasoning (a form of motivated

K. Henley (✉)
Department of Philosophy, Florida International University,
11200 SW 8th St., 33199 Miami, FL, USA
e-mail: henleyk@fiu.edu

A.E. Cudd and S.J. Scholz (eds.), *Philosophical Perspectives on Democracy in the 21st Century*, AMINTAPHIL: The Philosophical Foundations of Law and Justice 5,
DOI 10.1007/978-3-319-02312-0_16,

reasoning) seeks to bolster a conclusion already believed. Confirmation bias is the tendency to cherry-pick evidence or argumentative points that favor the prior belief. Disconfirmation bias leads to dismissing the relevance or importance of factors that undermine the prior belief. Confirmation bias dominates us. When motivated to believe something or to do something, we garner arguments for that belief or to justify that action, and form interpretations of evidence to reach the motivated conclusion. As Haidt puts it, when intent upon believing something, we ask: "Can I believe it?" When intent upon not believing, we ask: "Must I believe it?" (Haidt 2012, 83–88).

A particularly significant form of motivated reasoning is found when there is a strong motivation to abandon prior beliefs or switch course, leading to a reversal of confirmation and disconfirmation bias. This switching is found in both political and religious spheres: after calling for the abolition of the United States Department of Education and proclaiming that there is no Federal role in education, the Republican Party reverses course under George W. Bush ("The Education President"); after his conversion on the road to Damascus, Saul switches from opponent of the followers of Jesus to their leader, the Apostle Paul.

We can struggle against motivated reasoning in all of its forms, but we cannot eliminate the natural tendency. The first step is awareness of the strong tendency toward motivated reasoning. Usually there is no need to fight confirmation bias in everyday life, for most of our background beliefs about ordinary things do not require revision. We are guided by innumerable beliefs as we negotiate the world through space and time, and skeptical philosophical arguments do not (and need not) get much of a hearing. The distinction between such beliefs and beliefs in need of critical reflection is hard to articulate. Beliefs wholly based on group norms are candidates for reflection, though it must not be assumed that they should be revised or abandoned. Beliefs about complex matters, physical or social, are clear candidates for reflection. Consider the rising and setting of the sun. From the viewpoint of ordinary human experience there is no need to resist our confirmation bias supporting the belief that the sun rises in the east and sets in the west, to rise again the next morning. But the belief that this phenomenon is caused by the sun's movement was eventually subjected to reflection and abandoned. The shared belief that women could not be full and equal participants in all levels of society, holding political offices such as Supreme Court justice or President, was challenged and shown to be untenable.

Reflection about a problem or issue requires exploring various possible accounts or explanations. Exploratory reasoning (the opposite of motivated reasoning) must not be confused with the notion of setting aside all prior beliefs, which is both psychologically and epistemologically impossible. We always think and act with a background of prior beliefs. Exploratory reasoning allows those priors to be impacted by new evidence and arguments. When we engage in exploratory reasoning we attempt to evaluate the reliability and strength of new evidence and the force of new arguments independently of our prior beliefs, and then assess the resulting combination. It is reasonable, even in the light of new evidence, to give significant (though not insurmountably great) weight to prior beliefs, but that weight needs to reflect a sense of the basis upon which the prior belief was formed.

As indicated in the introduction, in addition to motivated reasoning and interacting with it, there is a second barrier to productive dialogue: we identify with groups (for instance, political parties, religions, ethnicities, clubs, fraternities, or fellow fans of a sports team) and "groupish" identification bolsters motivated reasoning to reach a view shared within the group and in clear opposition to other groups (Haidt 2012, 189–220). Haidt argues extensively in favor of group selection (as part of multi-level selection) in our evolution: "Once human groups had some minimal ability to band together and compete with other groups, then group-level selection came into play and the most groupish groups had an advantage over groups of selfish individualists" (2012, 193–194). Whether or not there was group selection, human groupishness is attested by anthropology, history, literature, and experience of the human societies we know.

Group identification leads to the formation of stereotypes of excluded groups. Groupish biases are often not conscious, yet still influence interpretations of evidence and events. Such implicit biases are found regarding race and gender (Greenwald and Krieger 2006, 945–967). It seems likely that there are implicit biases regarding other groups, perhaps even political groups such as Southern Conservatives or Northern Liberals. Motivated reasoning may be triggered not only by conscious beliefs and consciously desired outcomes, but also by implicit biases.

Both motivated reasoning and groupishness are deep features of our evolved mental structures, according to the research—reason itself serving as an adaptation for persuasion rather than discovery of truth. I shall argue that there are resources available in representative democracy that can be used to diminish the tendency to engage in confirmatory and motivated reasoning and groupish thought, and so open a limited sphere where a significant degree of exploratory reasoning can occur.

I mean by "representative democracy" a constitutional polity that structures the expression of popular sovereignty through assemblies of elected representatives whose role is classically explained by Edmund Burke in the "Speech to the Electors of Bristol." Burke distinguishes between two very different kinds of representation: the instructed delegate, whose role is to represent the will of constituents, and the representative who respectfully attends to the will of the constituents, but, as a trustee, in the end follows his own reasoning and conscience. Burke rejects instructed delegation: "Your Representative owes you, not his industry only, but his judgement; and he betrays, instead of serving you, if he sacrifices it to your opinion" (Burke 1999, 11). The distinction is important for my argument, for instructed delegation provides no resources for diminishing motivated reasoning in legislating and governing. The instructed delegate is committed to refuse to engage in exploratory reasoning regarding any issue upon which his constituents have a clear will. The Burkean ideal, however, rests upon a confidence in reasoning that now seems quaint. Even though not instructed by their constituents, representatives are instructed by their own commitments and group identifications to use reason to support prior positions, finding evidence and arguments in one direction, and ignoring anything that leads away from the instructed conclusion.

John Rawls's insistence upon the need for public reason is also undermined by the dominant role of motivated reasoning and group identification in human nature. Public reason requires setting aside appeals to the truth of religious, philosophical, or moral comprehensive doctrines (Rawls 1996, 62–63). Perhaps open and acknowledged appeals to comprehensive doctrines by legislators and other officials could be minimized in a liberal representative democracy (though even this has yet to occur), but given human nature that will often mean only that the driving force of motivated reasoning goes unacknowledged, while still dominating the use of reason in support of the doctrine and group. Rawls seems to depend upon reasoning to probe issues in an exploratory manner, once comprehensive doctrines are set aside, without the need of contrivances that will diminish the evolved, innate propensity of reasoning to evince motivated reasoning. Although religious and philosophical comprehensive doctrines are an important source of motivated reasoning, there are many other sources, such as economic interests.

Jurgen Habermas's account fares no better: "Discourse theory works…with the *higher-level intersubjectivity* of communication processes that unfold in the institutionalized deliberations in parliamentary bodies, on the one hand, and in the informal networks of the public sphere, on the other….these subjectless modes of communication form arenas in which a more or less rational opinion- and will-formation…can take place" (Habermas 2011, 769). There is here no recognition of the barriers *within human rationality itself* to opening such arenas of higher-level intersubjectivity. Habermas asserts that the resources needed for deliberative communication "emerge and regenerate themselves spontaneously for the most part…" (2011, 771). Motivated reasoning and group identification, deeply embedded in human nature, make such optimism untenable in all aspects of life, but political arguments trigger especially strong motivated reasoning (Taber et al. 2009, 137–155). Artificial means are needed to remedy, even partially, the very nature of human reasoning.

We naively rely upon reason to correct the defects caused by our emotions and our social conditioning. Ever since Plato, a major philosophical viewpoint has focused on the capacity to use reasoning to clear away the fog of the passions and see reality as it is. Passions and emotions have been seen as impediments to what is distinctively human. In this view, increased exposure to new evidence and new reasoned arguments should have a tendency to lead to an increasingly dispassionate grasp of the dispute, leading to a convergence on the part of disputants. The convergence might not be to a full agreement, but at least to a recognition on the part of the disputants that there are points on both sides and that the issue is difficult.

It is this picture of the capacity to engage in reasoning that the research on motivated reasoning undermines. Exploratory reasoning is not natural to us—it requires special artifices and effort. Our natural capacity for reasoning, exercised without special guards, supports what we are motivated to believe or to do. Thus, increased exposure to new evidence and arguments does not lead to convergence, but to even more intense polarization. And this is a more marked tendency the more sophisticated and the more initially committed the person is (Taber and Lodge 2006, 755–769).

Although there is a great deal of recent research that elaborates the limited role of exploratory reasoning and the centrality of motivated reasoning and groupishness in human nature, the basic ideas are not new. Jonathan Haidt's philosophical hero is David Hume, for his emphasis on the sentiments and passions that drive reasoning. Haidt uses evolutionary psychology throughout his account of the human mind's lack of innate capacity for exploratory reasoning when group commitments or an individual's prior beliefs are at stake. Without knowledge of Darwinian evolution,[1] from history, literature, and his experience of the political realities of the society he lived in, Hume perceived the way motivated reasoning and group identification impacts political life and discourse. Haidt does not discuss Hume's more specifically political writings—all 17 references to Hume are to Hume's *Treatise of Human Nature* or *Enquiry Concerning the Principles of Morals*. Yet Hume's focused political writings include rich accounts of the roles of groupishness and motivated reasoning. For these issues, the most important of Hume's works are "Of Parties in General", "That Politics may be reduced to a Science," and "Of the First Principles of Government" (Hume 1987, 54–63, 14–31, 32–42). These essays influenced the thought of James Madison, as especially evinced in *Federalist* 10 (Adair 1957, 343–360). Hume gives an account of political strife that focuses upon group identification, whether or not connected to the actual interests of groups. Hume's classification of factions or parties (in a broad sense, including but not limited to political parties) carries through his broader view that demotes reason to an instrument of non-rational passions.

Even trivial differences can lead to group identification and faction. Hume instances cases from ancient Greece and Rome, and from more recent European history (e.g., the Guelf and Ghibbelline factions persisted long after any real difference between the groups). Hume is particularly harsh about the group differences in the European religious wars: "…the controversy about an article of faith, which is utterly absurd and unintelligible, is not a difference in sentiment, but in a few phrases and expressions, which one party accepts of, without understanding them; and the other refuses in the same manner" (Hume 1987, 59). The sometimes deadly differences in religion express group identifications that have arisen through complex and contingent historical developments. In Hume's view there is nothing substantive under the elaborate theological reasoning of the competing sects. Reasoning masks the partisan oppositions.

Abstracting from much rich detail, the differing kinds of party (faction) relevant to our current issue are parties of interest and parties of principle. Parties of interest connect people who believe that they can gain from acting together, promoting individual self-interest. For instance, the landed gentry would form a different party from those in commerce. Parties of principle are formed by those committed to philosophical, moral, or religious doctrines. For instance, those committed to a contract theory of legitimate government would form a different party from those believing in the divine right of kings. Hume considers parties of interest "the most reasonable, and the most excusable….considering that degree of selfishness implanted in human nature" (1987, 59). Most troublesome and disruptive are parties of principle. Both religious and philosophical principles can lead to fanaticism.

[1] F.A. Hayek argued that the social evolutionary views of Hume both pre-dated and influenced the development of theories of biological evolution. See F.A. Hayek, "The Legal and Political Philosophy of David Hume," in *Hume: A Collection of Critical Essays*, ed. V. C. Chappell (Garden City, New York: Anchor Books, 1966), 356.

Parties of interest can disguise themselves as parties of principle. There are often also parties that have a mixture of followers, some out of interest some out of principle. Parties of principle are a danger to stable rule-of-law government in a way that parties of interest are not. Parties of interest can enter into exploratory reasoning to find a compromise that furthers their goal, even if less robustly than they wish. Unwavering principle leads to refusal to compromise, even if self-interest would be furthered. Hume understood that self-interest is not the whole game in politics: "…though men be much governed by interest; yet even interest itself, and all human affairs, are entirely governed by *opinion*" (1987, 51). Current research supports this view: "…self-interest does a remarkably poor job of predicting political attitudes" (Haidt 2012, 277).

Groupish behavior in partisan political life is part of Hume's argument for "checks and controuls" in governmental structure. Hume writes,

> It is, therefore, a just political maxim, that every man must be supposed a knave: Though at the same time, it appears somewhat strange, that a maxim should be true in politics, which is false in fact....men are generally more honest in their private than in their public capacity....Honour is a great check upon mankind: But where a considerable body of men act together, this check is, in a great measure, removed; since a man is sure to be approved of by his own party …and he soon learns to despise the clamours of adversaries (1987, 42–43).

For instance, during 2009–2010 in the United States, the extreme partisan debates triggered by the Patient Protection and Affordable Care Act (U.S. Public Law 111–148 2010) vividly illustrate the strength of motivated reasoning. Partisan group identification motivated reasoning to a shared viewpoint—one that must be in opposition to the rival group's view – even when that required rejection of a previously much confirmed view. The mandate that individuals purchase health insurance[2] originated in conservative and Republican quarters, but once it became part of Barack Obama's and the Congressional Democrats' legislation, fierce opposition solidified among those partisans who had originally seen such mandates as enforcing individual responsibility, a core value for conservatives.[3] There was intense motivation to reverse course, and reason busied itself to justify the about-face. (My point has nothing to do with whether the individual mandate is good policy or constitutional.)

Hume argued that justice (honesty concerning property) depends upon the use of long-term self-interest to confine the troublesome graspingness of self-interest in the short term (1888, 492). In similar fashion, I propose that groupish motivated reasoning be used to confine groupish motivated reasoning. Once campaigns for office end and holding office begins, identification with the partisan group will

[2]The mandate is enforced by a penalty to be collected by the Internal Revenue Service when the individual files his tax return: 26 U. S. C. 5000A. The U. S. Supreme Court upheld the mandate as constitutional under the Taxing Clause, although rejecting the view that it was constitutional under the Commerce Clause: *National Federation of Independent Business v. Sebelius,* 567 U.S. ___ (2012).

[3]A clear account is provided in Ezra Klein, "Unpopular Mandate: Why do politicians reverse their positions?" *The New Yorker*, June 25, 2012, 30–33. Klein recounts work by Jonathan Haidt and others regarding motivated reasoning and groups.

certainly continue (just as short-term self-interest continues within the framework of justice), but now the lip-service given to the larger group during the campaign needs to be replaced with a genuine commitment to the people as a whole. If this can be done to a significant degree, the partisan groupish motivated reasoning will be supplemented with civic groupish motivated reasoning. And perhaps civic motivated reasoning can, on at least some kinds if issue, morph into exploratory reasoning concerning the common good.

How can this transition from the almost entirely partisan groupishness of campaigns to the dual groupishness (the people/nation first, party second) of governing be engineered? In Humean fashion, we need to find artificial means to supplement the limited perspective natural to us. I think that four mechanisms are available: (1) holding politicians and their parties responsible at subsequent elections for failure to engage in exploratory reasoning to promote the common good, (2) education of both the political elites and the general public concerning the way motivated reasoning, confirmation bias, and groupish thinking impact our lives (public and private), (3) sacralizing (literally or metaphorically) the oath of office as marking a bright line between seeking office and holding office, and (4) invoking the "moral equivalent of war" (James 1968, 660–671). when confronting vital interests of the nation.

I put the electoral remedy first because it is the dominant remedy in representative democracies, supposedly effective when the faction blocking or misusing the legislative process is composed of less than a majority. However, groupishness and motivated reasoning are barriers to the electoral remedy, for they are fueled by the very nature of political campaigning. Steps must be taken if the electoral remedy is to have a chance at even a partial success. The electoral remedy requires that opposing candidates focus on the issue of excessive partisanship and refusal to engage in exploratory reasoning. So this remedy must be combined with the second—education of elites and the general public about motivated reasoning. Even combining these, committed partisan voters and voters of unwavering principle are unlikely to punish representatives sharing their own motivated reasoning and its underlying basis—they will use confirmatory and motivated reasoning to find evidence that the opposing candidate does not have a point when making the criticism. But a concerted effort over time might make inroads among the committed, and many of those without such strong unwavering principles or party groupishness would be open to taking the point that the incumbent has refused to explore ways to reach agreement in order to legislate and govern.

Erecting a bright-line between campaigning for office and holding office would contribute to diminishing the impact of motivated reasoning and groupishness, especially when the campaign was waged wholly or partially on unwavering principles. As mentioned previously, there is usually lip-service to the transition, with fine words about serving all the people. But greater emphasis needs to be given to the difference between campaigning and governing. As with the electoral remedy, there must be education of both elites and the public about the difference and its relationship to motivated reasoning and groupishness.

One vehicle for creating the bright-line is the oath of office, which needs greater attention in political culture and public opinion. Whether the oath is literally an invocation of God, or a simple affirmation of the duties of office, the moment should be treated as similar to the kind of change of status found in ordinations. This does not require that the person swearing or affirming have any religious beliefs, although if she does, those beliefs should reinforce the commitment to serve faithfully, putting into second place the partisan or other commitments that played a role in getting elected.

There is an important distinction between oath-taking officials (including both governmental officials and, for instance, those taking the office of juror) and citizens without such legally defined roles. (Henley 2010, 166–170). Although they arguably have moral obligations to treat everyone fairly and set aside bias and prejudice, outside of the context of official roles ordinary citizens are legally free to voice their unrefined (even biased) beliefs as they wish in the political process. Thus in *Romer v. Evans* (517 U.S. 620, 1996) the U.S. Supreme Court nullified a state constitutional amendment, passed by popular vote, that prohibited anti-discrimination legislation or ordinances protecting those with homosexual orientation. The Court held that there was no legitimate state interest that the amendment furthered, and that its passage seemed to have only a discriminatory basis. On my view, since the voters were under no duty of office to resist their discriminatory feelings, they were legally free to ignore the command of the 14th Amendment Equal Protection Clause, if they knew of its existence. The rationale of this decision supports the view that plebiscites and referendums concerning fundamental rights are inimical to constitutional representative democracy. The role of plebiscites is arising again regarding state constitutional amendments (such as California's Proposition 8) denying same-sex couples the right to marry—here again there is the problem that unrefined beliefs and biases have free reign (Perry v. Brown 2012).

So voters, not taking an oath of office, are under no formal legal requirement to treat all with equal respect, seek the common good, or promote the public interest—each is free to vote in furtherance of private interest, or in groupish support of party, or to express religious, philosophical, or moral comprehensive doctrines, or even to express invidious discrimination and hatred. Constitutional representative democracy, generally opposed to the use of referendums and plebiscites, places barriers upon such unlimited license. For elected officials (and, even more, judges) formally give up such unrestrained believing and behaving when within their official role. Not only Presidential oaths, but also the oaths of legislative representatives (and judges) should be a focus of mass media. Media attention might even include education about the difference between campaigning and holding office, with some account of the need of office-holders to use exploratory reasoning in the pursuit of the common good.

To use group identification to restrain group identification, loyalty to the larger group—the people as a whole or the nation—must be made paramount on matters of vital national interest and at times on serious but not vital matters. In war or when under threat, there is a strong tendency for national cohesiveness and putting away the usually intense loyalties to partisan and other less inclusive groups. Anticipating much research in evolutionary psychology, William James even delineated the basics of the evolution of such cohesiveness in war and group rivalry: "Such was the gory nurse that trained societies to cohesiveness. We inherit the warlike type; and for most of the capacities of heroism that the human race is full of we have to thank this cruel history. Dead men tell no tales, and if there were any tribes of other type than this they have left no survivors. Our ancestors have bred pugnacity into our bone and marrow…" (1968, 662). I consider, as did James, this innate tendency an unfortunate barrier to exploratory reasoning when we confront the question of war in the literal sense or in application to such threats as terrorists pose—here the groupish identification with the nation leads to the most dangerous kind of motivated and confirmatory reasoning. But on vital or serious issues within the polity, not regarding military force projecting national might abroad, invoking loyalty to the people and the nation can help create a sphere for exploratory reasoning. The pugnacity that fuels partisan (or religious, or philosophical) oppositions can be redirected to promote exploratory reasoning to respond to the crisis that evokes the cohesiveness like that found in war.

There are at least two general lines of objection to my argument: denying the need to diminish motivated reasoning and groupishness in the political sphere, or rejecting my four mechanisms as inadequate to the task. The second line of objection makes a good point. The strength of motivated reasoning and groupishness is so great that no efforts can reliably ensure opening a space for exploratory reasoning and genuine dialogue. We must always remind ourselves of the need in the political sphere to struggle against the natural human tendencies that block mutual understanding as we search for agreement. But I think that the four mechanisms would help.

The rejection of the need to diminish the barriers to exploratory reasoning and genuine dialogue is a different matter. There are views of the political sphere that endorse unrestrained conflict and see dialogue as weakness (unless used as a temporary strategy). Groups of any kind are to be left to battle with other groups, and to the victor belong the spoils, including unrestrained political power as long as it can be maintained. In contrast, my argument depends upon a framework of representative democracy with constitutional constraints including fundamental human rights to equality of respect. Within such constitutional polities, there is clearly a need for genuine dialogue and exploratory reasoning.

References

Adair, D. 1957. 'That politics may be reduced to a science': David Hume, James Madison, and the Tenth Federalist. *Huntington Library Quarterly* 20: 343–360.

Burke, E. 1999. *Select works of Edmund Burke*, vol. 4. Indianapolis: Liberty Fund.

Greenwald, A., and Linda Hamilton Krieger. 2006. Implicit bias: Scientific foundations. *California Law Review* 94: 945–967.

Habermas, J. 2011. Three normative models of democracy. In *Political philosophy: The essential texts*, ed. Steven M. Cahn. New York: Oxford University Press.

Haidt, J. 2012. *The righteous mind: Why good people are divided by politics and religion*. New York: Pantheon Books.

Hayek, F.A. 1966. The legal and political philosophy of David Hume. In *Hume: A collection of critical essays*, ed. V.C. Chappell. Garden City: Anchor Books.

Henley, K. 2010. Oaths and the pledge of allegiance: Freedom of expression and the right to be silent. In *Freedom of expression in a diverse world*, ed. Deirdre Golash. Dordrecht: Springer.
Hume, D. 1888. *A Treatise of human nature*, ed. L.A. Selby-Bigge. Oxford: Clarendon Press.
Hume, D. 1987. *Essays moral, political, and literary*, ed. E.F. Miller. Indianapolis: Liberty Fund.
James, W. 1968. The moral equivalent of war. In *The writings of William James*, ed. John J. McDermott. New York: Modern Library.
Klein, E. 2012. Unpopular mandate: Why do politicians reverse their positions? *The New Yorker*, June 25.
Mercier, H., and Dan Sperber. 2011. Why do humans reason? Arguments for an argumentative theory. *Behavioral and Brain Science* 34: 57–74.
Perry v. Brown, 671 F.3d 1052 (9th Cir. 2012), now (May 2013) on appeal to the Supreme Court as *Hollingsworth v. Perry*.
Rawls, J. 1996. *Political liberalism*. New York: Columbia University Press.
Taber, C.S., and Milton Lodge. 2006. Motivated skepticism in the evaluation of political beliefs. *American Journal of Political Science* 50: 755–769.
Taber, C., D. Cann, and Simona Kucsova. 2009. The motivated processing of political arguments. *Political Behavior* 31: 137–155.
U.S. Public Law 111–148 (Mar. 23, 2010).

Chapter 17
Republics, Passions and Protests

Wade L. Robison

Abstract David Hume and James Madison argued that large republics are more likely to survive than small republics because they are too large for factions to form and grow to a critical mass. But new forms of communication have undercut their argument and fundamentally altered the geography of relations between citizens and states.

New forms of communication have fundamentally altered the relation of citizens and governments. Citizens can now determine if others are of a like mind and use the new forms of communication to "act in unison with each other," to quote James Madison (Carey and McCellan 2001, 48). In a city-state, passions can sweep through the populace and allow factions to reach critical mass, potentially producing unrest and instability. As David Hume puts it, "The passions are so contagious, that they pass with the greatest facility from one person to another, and produce correspondent movements in all human breasts" (Hume 2007, 386). Madison and Hume argue that in an extensive republic, the contagion is contained.

This argument was "controlled by the absolute certainty that distance delayed the delivery of information" (Wheeler 2006, xvi). But with new forms of communication, a passion can go viral and sweep through a large country's population. We see this happening now whenever there is some kind of disaster. A rumor starts and spreads quickly through Twitter and Facebook. In the immediate aftermath of the bombings at the Boston marathon, for instance, a Brown University student was misidentified as a suspect. The misidentification went viral as more and more people passed on the mistake. The student had been missing since March 16th, and the family had been sick with worry. The misidentification added to their misery as they

W.L. Robison (✉)
Department of Philosophy, Rochester Institute of Technology,
23 Lomb Memorial Drive, 14623 Rochester, NY, USA
e-mail: wade.robison@gmail.com

A.E. Cudd and S.J. Scholz (eds.), *Philosophical Perspectives on Democracy in the 21st Century*, AMINTAPHIL: The Philosophical Foundations of Law and Justice 5,
DOI 10.1007/978-3-319-02312-0_17,

were besieged by news media eager to get a story, and because the student was of Indian descent, the rumor spread that somehow, someone from India was involved (Mistaken identity 2013).

We shall first examine the arguments Hume and Madison give and then look at an argument from Hamilton regarding *habeas corpus* about why publicity is the enemy of tyranny. In Sect. 17.2, we shall examine Madison's argument in more detail and see how his concerns played out in Monrovia and Iran as a passion went public. In Sect. 17.3, we will see just how public that passion became, and in the final section, we turn to the Arab Spring to show how these new forms of communication have altered the relation between citizens and their states.

17.1 A Republican Government in an Extensive Country

David Hume argues that in a city, "however the people may be separated or divided into small parties,…their near habitation…will always make the force of popular tides and currents very sensible" (1987, 528). But, he adds, although "it is more difficult to form a republican government in an extensive country than in a city; there is more facility, when once it is formed, of preserving it steady and uniform, without tumult and faction" (Hume 1987, 527). Distances sap passion and slow intrigue.

He could well have been observing the coming United States. It was difficult to form a United States merely because of the distances involved. In 1800 a half million settlers lived west of the Alleghenies, separated from the population along the coast, but, as Henry Adams put it, "Nowhere did eastern settlements touch the western. At least one hundred miles of mountainous country held the two regions everywhere apart." Some thought that settlement and separation "the germ of an independent empire" (Adams 1889, 3).We can understand the problem of forging a unified republic in such circumstances.

Even by the time Washington died, it took 7 days for the news to reach New York City —a "sluggish pace" indeed, and it had not improved by the end of the War of 1812. It took 27 days for news of the battle of New Orleans to reach New York City, for instance (Pred 1973, 13). What could travel throughout Philadelphia within a day or two of gossip would take more than a month in 1790 to reach Pittsburgh, and news from Portland, Maine took 40 days to reach Savannah (Wood 2009, 479). "[T]he parts are so distant and remote," Hume argued, "that it is very difficult, either by intrigue, prejudice, or passion, to hurry [the people] into any measures against the public interest" (1987, 528).

James Madison makes a similar point in *Federalist Paper No. 10*:

> Extend the sphere, and you take in a greater variety of parties and interests; you make it less probable that a majority of the whole will have a common motive to invade the rights of other citizens; or if such a common motive exists, it will be more difficult for all who feel it to discover their own strength, and to act in unison with each other (Carey and McCellan 2001, 48).

Madison adds to Hume's observations that an increase in size increases the "variety of parties and interests." No common motive is then likely to find a majority in support, and even if it did, he adds, making explicit what is arguably implicit in Hume: (1) those so motivated would be unable to determine if they have widespread support, and (2) even if they did, they would be unable to coordinate their actions with supporters.

So an underlying problem in an extensive republic is epistemological. Factions pose a danger only if they reach a critical mass, but in an extensive country individuals cannot know whether others share their motive and, if they do, cannot let them know.

That problem began to disappear with the telegraph and the installation of enough lines to bind great parts of the nation, with over 50,000 miles of line by 1860 (Crofts 2011). "Prior to the telegraph, the distribution of news was regulated by the speed of the mail, but now news was potentially both instantaneous and simultaneous" (Schulten 2012). "The telegraph upended [the] truth" that distance impeded information (Wheeler 2006, xvi).

The news of the Confederates firing on Fort Sumter the morning of April 12th, 1861 made it to New York City that evening, with newsboys hawking their papers with cries of "Extry – a Herald! Got the Bombardment of Fort Sumter!!!" (The Diary 2011).[1] The response to Lincoln's call for 75,000 troops on April 15th was "instantaneous – northerners embraced it enthusiastically, and signed up in huge numbers" (Widmer 2011). Passion swept through the North, with enormous crowds cheering the volunteers and so many volunteering that governors "worried… about how they could deal with the onrush of eager patriots" (Goodheart 2011, 210).

So much for the assumption undergirding Hume's and Madison's arguments. Once citizens can obtain and send news almost instantaneously, passions can sweep through a large nation as they sweep through cities. A citizen can readily get a sense of how many are supportive of a particular view.

Hume thinks there are only two impediments to passions sweeping away a society and, in Madison's words, invading "the rights of other citizens." One is the distance within a large republic which will delay the flow of passion; the other is that the structure of a republican government can arrest the flow. With its powers divided, the flow of passion will be dissipated. The good news, and bad, is that little gets done—as we all know from how the passions of the Tea Party have spread and produced a Congressional quagmire. The Tea Party constitutes what Madison and Hume would call a faction, and that faction has gathered enough power in Congress to bring to a halt the legislature's business when it does not further the faction's agenda. The result has been to bring to a screeching halt the normal legislative process that requires the give-and-take of compromise. As Hume puts it, "We know not to what length enthusiasm, or other extraordinary movements of the human mind, may transport men, to the neglect of all order and public good" (1987, 528–529).

[1] "The Diary of George Templeton Strong: April 12, 1861," *Disunion, New York Times*, April 12, 2011. For a more extended discussion of how quickly the news spread, see Adam Goodheart, *1861: The Civil War Awakening* (New York: Vintage Books, 2011), 176–178.

17.2 Hamilton's Argument

Hume and Madison both assumed, it seems, that though citizens would be involved with local elections, they would leave their representatives to represent them, trusting that the representatives would share, and so vote, their interests and concerns since they were themselves locals. After all, citizens would not be in a position to know much, if anything, about what was going on. As one Connecticut constituent told his Congressman in 1791, he "used to hear what was going on in the Congress" when it met in New York, but once it moved to Philadelphia, "we scarce know you are in session" (Wood 2009, 479–481).

But once the telegraph telescoped communication, every citizen could know what was going on, and as the reaction to Lincoln's call for troops shows, they could act quickly on what they knew. Representatives could no longer assume that what they said and how they voted would come only sporadically to their constituents' attention.

We can find a more significant implication in an argument Hamilton gave in the *Federalist Papers.* The most important safeguard for civil liberty is the writ of *habeas corpus*, he argued, guaranteed within the body of the Constitution. That writ is meant to protect against the "confinement of [a] person, by secretly hurrying him to jail, where his sufferings are unknown or forgotten…" Such confinement "is a less public, a less striking, and therefore a more dangerous engine of arbitrary government" (Carey and McCellan 2001, 444). Secrecy is the enemy of freedom, Hamilton argues, and a weapon for despots.

But a writ of *habeas corpus* can be effective against an arbitrary government only if, among other things, citizens know that a person is in jail. For that freedom of the press is crucial but depends wholly, Hamilton says, "on public opinion, and on the general spirit of the people and of the government" (Carey and McCellan 2001, 444).

Hamilton was thinking of broadsheets and pamphlets, but technology has produced new ways of communicating that would beggar Hamilton's imagination. We get used to technological newbies so quickly that those reared with them can hardly imagine a world without them,[2] but, obviously, it is freedom of communication that should be our concern, not freedom of the press. New forms of communication give us the potential for far more informed citizens and, as the protests in Moldova best illustrate, the potential for new ways to mobilize and organize citizens.

Moldova had parliamentary elections on Sunday, April 5th, 2009. The Communists gained control, and the next day several hundred people gathered to protest peacefully. They agreed to meet Tuesday to protest again. "A crowd of more than 10,000 young Moldovans materialized seemingly out of nowhere … to protest against Moldova's Communist leadership, ransacking government buildings and clashing with the police." Some at Monday's protest "began spreading the word

[2] To illustrate this point, I tell students about my being stuck in the south of Portugal in 1990 unable to call out to find out why the NEH had not deposited a check in my account. After the story, one student asked, "Why didn't you use your cell phone?" Point made.

through Facebook and Twitter, inventing a searchable tag for the stream of comments: #pman, which stands for Piata Marii Adunari Nationale, Chisinau's central square" (Barry 2009). Everyone with a cell phone became an organizer—and so invested in the protest.

A small gathering, easily ignored, became a major event, not to be ignored. The crucial factor in turning a minor protest into a major political test of the new government was the number of individuals involved. As protesters discovered, a common passion existed among many citizens, and, contrary to Hume and Madison, new technologies made it easy "for all who feel it to discover their own strength."[3] They were also able to "act in unison with each other," as Madison puts it, determining when and where to meet via Facebook and Twitter.

One other effect of new technology was illustrated in the protests after the June 2009 election in Iran. Iranian authorities responded to the protests by shutting down internet servers, but Twitter "allowed younger protesters, particularly those affiliated with universities in Tehran, to organize and to follow updates by Mir Hossein Mousavi; by spreading the word about the location of government crackdowns and the threat of machine-gun-wielding soldiers, it probably saved the lives of any number of would-be revolutionaries" (Ambinder 2009). The new technologies not only allow those protesting to measure their strength and organize, but to respond on short notice, in the streets, to the counter-moves of the authorities.

17.3 Citizens of the World

The protests in Moldova did not lead to significant changes, and neither did the protests in Iran— although the government's willingness to kill protesters, and especially to kill them on "the holiday commemorating the death of Imam Hussein, Shi'ite Islam's holiest martyr," escalated the confrontation and served to legitimize the protest movement:

> The authorities' decision to use deadly force on the Ashura holiday infuriated many Iranians, and some said the violence appeared to galvanize more traditional religious people who had not been part of the protests until then. Historically, Iranian rulers have honored Ashura's prohibition of violence, even during wartime (Worth and Fathi 2009).

Iran's shooting of protestors on a holy day went viral. The world became a witness to the protest and the Iranian government's response. The shooting death of a young woman, Neda Agha-Soltan, was videotaped, uploaded to YouTube, and became headline news around the world, "the public face of an unknown number of Iranians who have died in the protests" (Fathi 2009). As one commentator, Ari Berman, put it,

[3] It is this point that undercuts Malcolm Gladwell's claim that revolutions "will not be tweeted" ("Annals of Change: Small Change," *New Yorker*, October 4, 2010).

> I'm not sure what the Iranian regime expected when they fixed the election, but the outpouring of texts, tweets and video from Tehran has sparked a worldwide solidarity movement. Whatever the outcome, there is no going back (Berman 2009).

Hamilton's concern was parochial in two different ways. First, the citizens of a nation must bc protected from a government that has a tendency to become arbitrary, and, second, they are to be protected by ensuring that the government is unable to imprison its citizens secretly. The new forms of technology have expanded Hamilton's vision. First, we have a world-wide community of citizens, a much wider public than Hamilton envisaged, who now can know what a government is doing, and, second, it is not just arbitrary imprisonment that becomes public, but any acts of the government that harm citizens—from photos and videos of police using undue force to arrest a citizen to photos and videos of a government arresting, beating, or killing innocent protesters.

As Berman put it,

> Some absolutely riveting and thrilling reporting has been done over Twitter by a university student in Tehran who goes by the moniker Tehran Bureau. The Iranian authorities shut his website down over the weekend and he was attacked by hard-line militias but he's been able to send short posts around the world over Twitter. (Berman 2009)

Just as the tweets from Tehran went viral, YouTube videos went viral as well, with hundreds of thousands seeing individuals being killed and beaten by Iranian militia.

What the Iranian regime did played out on an international stage. We only had bits and pieces of what happened, single photos and segments, grainy, blurred, jumpy, and so we must be cautious not to take rumor as truth. But I would suggest that what we had was enough to get a broad picture. The bits and pieces came through different modes of communication, at different times during a single protest and different locations within the areas of protest, from different individuals with different email, Twitter, and cellphone monikers, over a period of weeks and months. We cannot verify much of what we saw and read, and so we cannot easily sort out what is false or misleading.[4] As Roland Hedley in *Doonesbury* puts it, "Twitter is the first rough draft of gossip" (Trudeau 2009). But bits and pieces can readily be stitched together into a coherent narrative, confirmed by new bits and pieces from different sources at different times in different places—enough to justify a judgment about the Iranian state.

Some of the political consequences of the world's awareness of events within Iran are straightforward. It becomes easier for those who want to impose sanctions to make their case. It becomes far harder to argue that such a government should have atomic weapons. It ought to change the responses of the government and those protesting: they now must take into account how what they do will play out internationally. They cannot know who is videoing what they do or sending a tweet about something the world would consider criminal.

---

[4] For a helpful discussion of the origin of rumors and the difficulties of winnowing out whatever truths they may contain, see Nicholas DiFonzo, *The Watercooler Effect* (New York: Penguin, 2008).

Whether the government of Iran does a good job of taking those effects into account is another question. Firing on and killing protesters on the Ashura holiday suggests it does not, that act having gratuitously angered Muslims both within and without Iran. In any event, citizens of the world will come to have an opinion on what Iran does, whether Iran cares about that opinion or not.

17.4 The Arab Spring

Some argue that tweeting and other modes of the new forms of communication are not revolutionary for at least two different reasons. First, Malcolm Gladwell argues that networks do not provide the "discipline and strategy" necessary for a revolution because they are not hierarchical, and if you are "taking on a powerful and organized establishment you have to be a hierarchy." He adds, "Because networks don't have a centralized leadership structure and clear lines of authority, they have real difficulty reaching consensus and setting goals" (Gladwell 2010, 48).

Second, revolutions need what Gladwell calls "strong-ties" between the participants because revolutions are high-risk, but networks provide only loose ties between individuals who are not asked to do much more than "be a friend." The new forms of communication fail to create the sustained fervor and level of commitment necessary to power revolutions, he claims, because they cannot create strong ties between those who network (2010, 45).

It is difficult to know what to make of this position. Gladwell seems to be making a category mistake. "Of course," I want to say, "forms of communication fail to create fervor." People can have fervor; they can create fervor. But cell phones? Modes of communication, new or old, are not the sort of things that can have or create fervor. He also seems to be making unsupported assumptions about how "discipline and strategy" come about. It is not a necessary truth that only revolutions organized along hierarchical lines succeed, and, indeed, it is not an obvious contingent truth that only a "centralized leadership structure and clear lines of authority" provide the "discipline and strategy" necessary for a revolution. One of the striking features of the Arab Spring was the amazing discipline of those who participated: think here of how long Syrian protesters continued to gather, peacefully, after Friday afternoon prayers, despite being fired upon by government snipers and soldiers. And strategy? The choice of peaceful protest in the face of governmental force is a strategy, and it came from no other authority than individuals not responding in kind to force.

So it is difficult to take the grounds of Gladwell's argument seriously. It is even more difficult to take seriously his *dismissal* of the power that cellphones and the internet have given protesters. His dismissal misses the changes that new forms of communication have brought. We need to go back to Madison's concerns to understand how the new modes of communication have powered revolutions such as those of the Arab Spring.

Madison was right when he claimed in *Federalist Paper No. 10* that even if, in a large republic, "a common motive [i.e., fervor] exists, it will be more difficult for all who feel it to discover their own strength, and to act in unison with each other." With new forms of communication, those with a common motive can discover their own strength. The telegraph allowed for almost instantaneous communication from one part of a country to another, but now anyone with internet access or a cellphone can be a telegraph operator, as it were, sending and receiving, discovering quickly whether others share their motive, and mobilizing all who share the motive to act in unison. The new forms of communication do not create the fervor necessary to power a revolution; they allow those with the passion to act to tap into the common passion. In the right conditions, the discovery that many share a passion and are willing to act on it can lift it to a fever pitch, a fervor that will express itself in the kinds of actions that can bring change—like blacks sitting at segregated lunch counters in the south in the 1960s, to use Malcolm Gladwell's example (2010, 42).

When we look at the Egyptian revolution, we can see the role played by Facebook in particular and how Gladwell's concerns played out as well. The protests began with a call for a Silent Stand. That call to protest went out on Facebook and through emails and Twitter, and in a computer-literate generation, it reached more than enough citizens to create a critical mass who indicated online that they would be willing to gather in protest. And they did. Citizens stood silently in lines, a meter apart, and as Wael Ghonim puts it, "Each participant stood silently next to someone he or she probably did not know. They only knew they were both members of a page on the Internet and that they believed in the same cause … Feelings of solidarity overwhelmed the participants and turned the stand into a new social environment" (2012, 80). A common passion was tapped and turned into action: "The revolution successfully proved that a multifaceted society like Egypt's could easily unite when its members shared the same dream, and could do so with dignity" (Ghonim 2012, 225–226).

The strategy of having a silent protest was created via Facebook and email as those concerned to tap that passion worked through what might best rattle the government without endangering participants while allowing them to see that others shared their passion. They worked without even knowing each other, without meeting, without any one of them being in a position of authority and so, obviously, without any clear lines of authority. They worked together in a virtual world to create change in the real world, via "a means of communication that offers people in the physical world a method to organize, act, and promote ideas and awareness" (Ghonim 2012, 51).

Networks can survive with weak ties between participants, but, as in Moldova, participants in Egypt were asked to do more than befriend each other. "A call was put out," for instance, "to all professional graphic designers who were willing to help design logos and banners for the Silent Stand" (Ghonim 2012, 74). The supposed weak-tie connections of the internet can be overcome and strong ties created by asking participants to take part in various aspects of the protest. Everyone who retweets, for instance, becomes invested in the protest—and so invested in the outcome. The gap between using a cellphone to support a protest and protesting needs to be bridged, of course, but when others respond to tweets or a note on Facebook, we get a sense of how widespread the passion is. When enough telegraph their intentions to protest, they can pull along those who were hesitant—at a minimum a widening circle of friends who do not want to let other friends down by saying they are coming and then not coming.

All this happened without any clear lines of authority and without any overall pre-existing plan. What we might call a sketch of a plan was created via the internet and especially Ghonim's Facebook page. He asked for suggestions about how to proceed, and the idea for a silent wall of protest grew out of the response to his query. The plan was a cooperative enterprise that was subject to constant change in response to events on the ground and suggestions and comments via the Internet. The father of the Iditarod, Joe Redington Sr., is reported to have said when asked about his not having any overall plan for the event, "If you don't have a plan, that's one less thing that can go wrong" (Hegener 2011).[5] What matters are not plans, but contacts since something can—perhaps "will" is better—always go wrong with plans.

Of course, none of this could have happened without the internet and without someone with expertise in using it. As Ghonim puts it, "As an experienced Internet user, I knew that a Facebook page was much more effective in spreading information than a Facebook group." Once information is posted, "it appears on the walls of the page's fans." "This is how ideas can spread like viruses" (Ghonim 2012, 43). And, of course, they spread not just to those within Egypt, but across the world as Facebook pages, Twitter profiles, and emails proliferate and pass on events almost as they occur (Ghonim 2012, 235–236).

Madison was correct. Once those with a passion can tap the passions of others in a large country, they can determine the level of support and coordinate their actions with supporters. Egypt is a large country, with a diverse population with presumably different passions and interests, but the revolution in Egypt was organized on the internet. Because of the new forms of communication, protesters were able to determine their strength, communicate with one another to mobilize, thwart the governmental responses by those new forms of communication, and let the world see what they, and their government, were doing. As with many a pick-up game and other spontaneous group activities, order arose out of individual decisions, not through some hierarchical system. To paraphrase Hume, "Two men, who pull the oars of a boat in an orderly fashion, do it by an agreement or convention, though they have never agreed to follow orders and do not think of themselves as leader and follower" (2007, 315). They do not need a coxswain.

A cooperative enterprise can arise between individuals who share a common passion or a common goal, and they can work together and sustain their cooperation without the sort of hierarchy Gladwell thinks essential. Those pulling oars together in a boat have no "centralized leadership structure [or] clear lines of authority," and yet "they have [no] real difficulty reaching consensus and setting goals." When we empower individuals—by giving them an oar or a cellphone—they can create "the strong ties" they need to pursue their common end. They do not need someone to tell them what to do and then order them to do it. Individuals

[5] Helen Hegener, "New book chronicles life of Joe Redington, Sr.," *Alaska Dispatch*, August 4, 2011.

with a common purpose create the order and discipline they need to pursue and sustain a common end, and they can do it all the more easily, across far greater distances than we find in any rowboat, when they can send and receive communications almost instantaneously.

17.5 Changes in Political Geography

Just as the telegraph allowed Lincoln to tap into the latent patriotism of citizens of the North to save the Union when he called for 75,000 troops immediately after Fort Sumter, the newest forms of communication have made it far easier for citizens to tap into latent passions when there is a common purpose. The distance Hume and Madison assumed would limit the spread of passions has disappeared, and with the new forms of communication, citizens can not only receive information (and rumors) instantly, they can themselves each telegraph what they wish far and wide. Each citizen's effective reach can go far beyond the circle of acquaintances that, even with quidnuncs telling all and sundry, used to limit the spread of information and rumor.

It is thus far easier "to hurry [the people] into…measures against the public interest," but also far easier to marshal the people to a common purpose for the public good—as the Arab Spring shows. Citizens more easily became active participants in the political scene.

Yet with distance no longer an impediment, a passion can sweep through a country's population and, whether grounded in real grievances or not, come to dominate the political scene. As Hume argued, pressure then falls on the structure of a republican government to arrest the flow. Whether such pressure will so distort the normal flow of the people's business within that structure that little moves or will collapse the system is a nice question.

We do know that every structure has a tipping point where the norms about how to proceed within that structure are challenged and changed. How many drivers does it take to turn the norm of taking turns at a four-way stop into a free-for-all? How many need to stop buying genetically modified food for food companies to reverse course?[6] How many intransigent politicians does it take to clog up the movement of a government's business? These look to be empirical questions, and the most common answer seems to be "about 5 %."[7] How we might determine the truth or falsity of that number is unclear since once a tipping point is reached, things

[6] It has been claimed that "as little as 5 percent of consumers avoiding GM brands would start the non-GMO avalanche" (Jeffrey M. Smith, "GMOs: Is the End Near?", *Heirloom Gardener*, Summer 2012, 44).

[7] The 5 % figure refers to how many it takes to disrupt a social norm such as stopping at a four-way stop or voluntarily paying one's taxes. Legislative bodies may require more or less a percentage of members. The United States Senate allows "holds" by individual senators to stop a nomination, for instance. So one senator out of one hundred can bring the legislative business to a halt – 1 %, not 5 %.

move much too quickly for us to be sure we have captured the point itself. But we need not be sure about the figure to see the danger produced for a republic when distance no longer delays information. The new forms of communication have telescoped the distances that used to sap passions and slow intrigues and so put our large republic, and others, at the risk of the instability and dissolution Hume and Madison thought were endemic to republics in small city states.

The new forms of communication empower citizens—both for ill and for good. Although we have seen and can imagine the harms factions can produce for republics, we are also seeing how empowering citizens with new forms for communication has opened up societies which were closed to change and allowed citizens to swept out old forms of authoritarianism. Whatever the future of these evolving forms of communication, they have already produced a tectonic shift in the political geography of some countries and are likely to change the geography of others as well—in ways we cannot now predict.

References

Adams, H. 1889. *History of the United States*, vol. 1. New York: Charles Scribner's Sons.

Ambinder, M. 2009. The revolution will be twittered. *The Atlantic, Politics*, June 15.

Barry, E. 2009. Protests in Moldova explode, with help of Twitter. *New York Times*, April 8.

Berman, A. 2009. Iran's Twitter revolution. *The Nation*, June 15.

Carey, G.W., and J. McCellan (eds.). 2001. *The federalist: The Gideon edition*. Indianapolis: Liberty Fund.

Crofts, D. 2011. Communication breakdown. Disunion, *New York Times*, May 21.

Fathi, N. 2009. In a death seen around the world, a symbol of Iranian protests. *New York Times*, June 22.

Gary Trudeau, Doonesbury, December 14, 2009. Online at http://www.gocomics.com/doonesbury/2009/12/14. Accessed 18 Aug 2012.

Ghonim, W. 2012. *Revolution 2.0: The power of the people is greater than the people in power*. Boston: Houghton Mifflin Harcourt.

Gladwell, M. 2010. Annals of change: Small change. *New Yorker*, October 4.

Hegener, H. 2011. New book chronicles life of Joe Redington, Sr. *Alaska Dispatch*, August 4.

Hume, D. 1987. *Essays moral, political, and literary, revised edition*. Indianapolis: Liberty Classics.

Hume, D. 2007. *A treatise of human nature*. Ed. David Fate Norton and Mary Norton. Oxford: Oxford University Press.

Mistaken identity sparks social media rumours of Indian link in Boston bombing. *The Economic Times*, April 20, 2013. Accessible at http://articles.economictimes.indiatimes.com/2013-04-20/news/38693128_1_marathon-blasts-social-media-users-boston-police.

Pred, A.R. 1973. *Urban growth and the circulation of information: The United States system of cities, 1790–1840*. Cambridge, MA: Harvard University Press.

Schulten, S. 2012. News of the wired. Disunion, *New York Times*, January 13.

Smith, J.M. 2012. GMOs: Is the end near? *Heirloom Gardener*, July.

The Diary of George Templeton Strong: April 12, 1861, Disunion, *New York Times*, April 12, 2011.

Wheeler, T. 2006. *Mr. Lincoln's t-mails*. New York: Harper Collins.

Widmer, T. 2011. Lincoln declares war. Disunion, *New York Times*, April 14.

Wood, G.S. 2009. *Empire of liberty: A history of the early republic, 1789–1815*. Oxford: Oxford University Press.

Worth, R.F., and Nazila Fathi. 2009. Deaths and fury in Iran protests. *New York Times*, December 28.

Author Bios

Jason Brennan is an Assistant Professor of Economics, Ethics, and Public Policy at the McDonough School of Business, and Assistant Professor of Philosophy, at Georgetown University. His is the author of *Compulsory Voting: For and Against* (Cambridge University Press, 2013), with Lisa Hill, *Libertarianism* (Oxford University Press, 2012), *The Ethics of Voting* (Princeton University Press, 2011), and *A Brief History of Liberty* (Wiley-Blackwell, 2010), with David Schmidtz. His is currently writing *Why Not Capitalism?* and *Markets without Limits* for Routledge Press, and *Against Politics* for Princeton University Press. He specializes in democratic theory and issues in liberalism.

Ann E. Cudd is University Distinguished Professor of Philosophy and Vice Provost and Dean of Undergraduate Studies at the University of Kansas. She is the author of *Analyzing Oppression* (Oxford University Press, 2006), co-author with Nancy Holmstrom of *Capitalism, For and Against: A Feminist Debate* (Cambridge University Press, 2011), and over 50 articles in social and political philosophy, feminist theory, and philosophy of economics. She is currently working on a series of articles in contractarian political theory.

Richard T. De George is Distinguished Professor Emeritus at the University of Kansas. He received his Ph.D. from Yale University. He is the author or editor of 20 books and over 200 articles in political and social philosophy, business ethics, and contemporary Marxism. He is former President of the American Philosophical Association (Central Division), the International Society for Business, Economics and Ethics, and Amintaphil, among others. In 1994 he received an honorary doctorate from Nijenrode University, The Netherlands.

Imer B. Flores is a Professor-Researcher at the Legal Research Institute and Law School, UNAM (Mexico). He is author of several articles on jurisprudence, legal and political philosophy, and constitutional law and theory; co-editor of *Law, Liberty and the Rule of Law* (Springer, 2013); and co-founder of Problema. Anuario

A.E. Cudd and S.J. Scholz (eds.), *Philosophical Perspectives on Democracy in the 21st Century*, AMINTAPHIL: The Philosophical Foundations of Law and Justice 5,
DOI 10.1007/978-3-319-02312-0,

de Filosofía y Teoría del Derecho. He has been Visiting Scholar in several institutions and more recently Visiting Professor of Law at Georgetown University Law Center (2012–2013).

Emily R. Gill is Caterpillar Professor of Political Science at Bradley University. In addition to a number of articles and book chapters, she is the author of *Becoming Free: Autonomy and Diversity in the Liberal Polity* and *An Argument for Same-Sex Marriage: Religious Freedom, Sexual Freedom, and Public Expressions of Civic Equality*. Along with Gordon A. Babst and Jason Pierceson, she is co-editor of *Moral Argument, Religion, and Same-Sex Marriage: Advancing the Public Good.*

Kenneth Henley is Professor of Philosophy at Florida International University. He has published articles on ethics and political and legal philosophy in various books and journals. He has recently focused on the political and moral philosophy of David Hume, especially in relationship to the topic of the rule of law.

F. Patrick Hubbard is the Ronald Motley Distinguished Professor of Law at the University of South Carolina School of Law. His recent publications have focused on the intersection of law, politics, and culture in the context of diverse issues, such as: citizens' right to use deadly force, direct populist legislation through referendums, and legal personhood for intelligent artifacts.

Steven P. Lee teaches philosophy at Hobart and William Smith Colleges in Geneva, New York, where he is the Donald R. Harter '39 Professor in the Humanities. He writes and teaches on issues in social, moral, and political philosophy, especially on morality and war. He is the author most recently of Ethics and War (Cambridge University Press, 2012). He is past president of Amintaphil and of Concerned Philosophers for Peace.

Alistair M. Macleod teaches moral and political philosophy in the graduate program of the Department of Philosophy at Queen's University. In addition to a short book on Social Justice, Progressive Politics, and Taxes, his recent publications include papers on freedom of speech, coercion, economic justice, human rights, the free market ideal, invisible hand arguments, and G.A. Cohen's critique of John Rawls.

Rex Martin is Professor of Philosophy, Emeritus, at the University of Kansas and Honorary Professor in the School of European Languages and Politics at Cardiff University. Martin's fields of major interest are political and legal philosophy and history of political thought. His books include *A System of Rights* (Oxford 1993) and *Rawls's Law of Peoples: A Realistic Utopia?* co-editor (Blackwell, 2006).

Stephen Nathanson is Professor of Philosophy at Northeastern University. He has written numerous articles on subjects in ethics and political philosophy. He is the author of *Economic Justice* (1998) and edited the Hackett edition of J. S. Mill, *Principles of Political Economy* (2004). His other books include *Patriotism, Morality, and Peace* (1993), *Should We Consent to be Governed* (2nd ed., 2000), and *Terrorism* *and the Ethics of War* (2010), which was named the Best Book in Social Philosophy for 2010 by the North American Society for Social Philosophy.

Mark Navin is an Assistant Professor of Philosophy at Oakland University (Rochester, MI). His research is primarily in social and political philosophy, and it includes topics in global justice, human rights, and international and domestic inequality. He is currently writing a manuscript on ethical and epistemological issues surrounding the mass refusal of routine childhood vaccines. His work has appeared in journals including *Social Theory and Practice*, *Public Affairs Quarterly*, *Ethical Theory and Moral Practice*, and the *Journal of Military Ethics*.

Richard Nunan (Ph.D. University of North Carolina/Chapel Hill) is Professor of Philosophy at the College of Charleston (nunanr@cofc.edu). He writes chiefly in the areas of Philosophy of Law/Political Philosophy, Gender Studies, and Philosophy and Film. Recent work in legal and political philosophy includes three articles on Same Sex Marriage in legislative bodies and the courts (two before and one after the 2013 Supreme Court decisions in U.S. v Windsor and Hollingsworth v Perry), and "Social Institutions, Transgendered Lives, and the Scope of Free Expression," an article on recent judicial treatment of transgendered marriage, as it relates to gender identity and the constitutional right of free expression.

Richard Barron Parker is Professor Emeritus from Hiroshima Shudo University where he taught American law and politics from 1990 until 2008. He has a Ph.D. in philosophy from the University of Chicago and a J.D. from Harvard Law School. He enjoys an active retirement with his wife of 46 years in Falmouth, Maine, USA.

Wade L. Robison is the Ezra A. Hale Professor of Applied Ethics at the Rochester Institute of Technology. He has published extensively in philosophy of law, David Hume, and practical and professional ethics. His book *Decisions in Doubt: The Environment and Public Policy* won the Nelson A. Rockefeller Prize in Social Science and Public Policy.

Sally J. Scholz is Professor of Philosophy at Villanova University. Her research is in social and political philosophy and feminist theory. She is the author of *On de Beauvoir* (Wadsworth 2000), *On Rousseau* (Wadsworth 2001), *Political Solidarity* (Penn State Press 2008), and *Feminism: A Beginner's Guide* (One World 2010). Scholz has also published articles on violence against women, oppression, and just war theory among other topics. She is a former editor of the APA Newsletter on Feminism and Philosophy and is currently Editor of *Hypatia: A Journal of Feminist Philosophy*.

Jonathan Schonsheck is Professor of Philosophy at Le Moyne College in Syracuse, NY. He enjoys a joint appointment to the Division of Liberal Arts, and the Madden School of Business. His areas of specialization include Social and Political Philosophy, the Philosophy of Law, and Ethics/Applied Ethics. He is the author of *On Criminalization: An Essay in the Philosophy of the Criminal Law* (Kluwer), and more than 40 articles in refereed journals and collections. He is currently working on various components of a project entitled "Conscientious Capitalism." This includes analysis of the crises in financial markets, 2008ff, and preventing encore crises by constraining capitalism within a theory of justice.

Russell W. Waltz is an Assistant Professor of Philosophy at Miami Dade College in Miami, FL. His research interests are social and political philosophy, the philosophy of mass communication, applied ethics, and the philosophy of emotion.

Index

A.E. Cudd and S.J. Scholz (eds.), *Philosophical Perspectives on Democracy in the 21st Century*, AMINTAPHIL: The Philosophical Foundations of Law and Justice 5,
DOI 10.1007/978-3-319-02312-0,

MIX
Papier aus verantwortungsvollen Quellen
Paper from responsible sources
FSC® C105338

If you have any concerns about our products,
you can contact us on
ProductSafety@springernature.com

In case Publisher is established outside the EU,
the EU authorized representative is:
Springer Nature Customer Service Center GmbH
Europaplatz 3, 69115 Heidelberg, Germany

Printed by Libri Plureos GmbH
in Hamburg, Germany